SOCIAL SECURITY DISABILITY LAW AND THE AMERICAN LABOR MARKET

Social Security Disability Law and the American Labor Market

Jon C. Dubin

NEW YORK UNIVERSITY PRESS
New York

NEW YORK UNIVERSITY PRESS
New York
www.nyupress.org

Library of Congress Cataloging-in-Publication Data
Names: Dubin, Jon C., author.
Title: Social security disability law and the American labor market / Jon C. Dubin.
Description: New York : New York University, [2021] | Includes bibliographical references and index.
Identifiers: LCCN 2021001799 | ISBN 9781479811014 (hardback) | ISBN 9781479811021 (ebook) | ISBN 9781479811045 (ebook other)
Subjects: LCSH: Disability insurance—Law and legislation—United States. | Social security—Law and legislation—United States. | Labor market—United States. | Labor laws and legislation—United States.
Classification: LCC KF3650 .D83 2021 | DDC 344.7302/3—dc23
LC record available at https://lccn.loc.gov/2021001799

New York University Press books are printed on acid-free paper, and their binding materials are chosen for strength and durability. We strive to use environmentally responsible suppliers and materials to the greatest extent possible in publishing our books.

Manufactured in the United States of America

10 9 8 7 6 5 4 3 2 1

Also available as an ebook

CONTENTS

Introduction 1

PART ONE: THE HISTORY AND EVOLUTION OF LABOR MARKET CONSIDERATIONS IN THE SOCIAL SECURITY DISABILITY BENEFITS PROGRAMS

1. The Disability Category and the Congressional Ideal 9
2. The Judicial Gloss 18
3. The Congressional Response 22

PART TWO: LABOR MARKET WORK ADJUSTMENT ASSESSMENTS AND THE SOCIAL SECURITY ADMINISTRATION'S BASIC ADJUDICATIVE SYSTEM

4. The Official Notice/Administrative Notice Doctrine 31
5. Vocational Expert Evidence and the Vocational Expert Program 40

PART THREE: THE CONCEPTUAL AND ADJUDICATIVE STRUCTURE OF THE GRID REGULATIONS

6. "Gridding" the Labor Market Work Adjustment Assessment 61
7. Gaps in the Grid: The Grid's Adjudicative Framework and Occupational Base Erosion Approach for Work Adjustment Assessments in Grid Exception Cases 72
8. The Adjudicative Use of the Official Notice/Administrative Notice Doctrine in Grid Exception Cases 89

PART FOUR: THE EMPIRICAL AND TAXONOMIC FOUNDATION FOR LABOR MARKET WORK ADJUSTMENT ASSESSMENTS

9. The Dictionary of Occupational Titles in Work Adjustment Assessments 103

10. Progress Toward a New Occupational Taxonomy for Work Adjustment Assessments 107

PART FIVE: ALTERNATIVES TO THE CURRENT SSA DISABILITY SYSTEM, THE TWENTY-FIRST CENTURY LOW-SKILL LABOR MARKET, AND THE CONTEMPORARY CALL FOR DISABILITY BENEFITS REFORM

11. Introduction to the Debate Over Alternatives to the Current Disability Standard and Program 115

12. Amendments to Simplify Work Adjustment Assessments by Restricting Eligibility: The Elimination of Labor Market and Vocational Factors 118

13. The Twenty-First Century Labor Market for Low-Skill Work 124

14. The Disability Benefits Reform Debate 129

15. Amendments to Simplify Work Adjustment Assessments by Expanding Eligibility: A European-Style Occupational Standard 151

16. Proposals to Impose a "Welfare Reform" Mandatory Work Incentives Model 154

Conclusion 161

Acknowledgments 167

Notes 169

Index 257

About the Author 269

Introduction

Where Are the Jobs for Persons with Medical and Vocational Challenges?

Walk for a moment in Michael Biestek's shoes. As part of your application for disability benefits, you've proven that you suffer from serious health problems and can't return to your old construction job. Like many cases, yours turns on whether a significant number of other jobs remain that someone of your age, education, and experience, and with your physical limitations, could perform. When it comes to that question, the Social Security Administration bears the burden of proof. To meet its burden in your case, the agency chooses to rest on the testimony of a vocational expert the agency hired as an independent contractor. The expert asserts there are 120,000 "sorter" and 240,000 "bench assembler" jobs nationwide that you could perform even with your disabilities. Where did these numbers come from?
Biestek v. Berryhill, 139 S.Ct. 1148, 1154 (2019) (Opinion of Gorsuch, J., joined by Ginsburg, J., dissenting).

The Social Security programs are America's largest social benefit programs, and they affect nearly all of us.[1] These programs provide a lifeline for many Americans, especially those living on the margins.[2] Among the various forms of government benefit programs, Social Security, also known as Old Age, Survivors, and Disability Insurance

(OASDI), is a social insurance program. It is financed from separate trust funds for the Disability Insurance (DI) and the Old Age and Survivors' Insurance (OASI) programs supported by payroll taxes on earnings of insured workers. Premiums in the form of Federal Insurance Contribution Act (FICA) taxes are automatically withheld from workers' paychecks, enabling covered workers, and sometimes their families, to receive monthly benefits if the worker retires, dies, or becomes disabled.[3] The Social Security Administration (SSA) also operates a means-tested income support program for low-income disabled and elderly persons entitled under the Supplemental Security Income (SSI) program, mostly for those lacking insurance coverage for OASDI.[4] The disability definition and the Social Security Administration's system for processing and adjudicating disability claims under the Social Security Disability Insurance (SSDI) and SSI disability benefits programs are the same.

The SSA's disability adjudication system has been characterized as the "Mt. Everest of bureaucratic structures"[5] in the "largest adjudicative agency in the western world."[6] There are more SSA administrative law judges (ALJs) adjudicating social security disability administrative hearings than there are federal judges deciding and presiding over civil and criminal cases in all of the federal courts of the United States.[7] Moreover, there are three additional administrative stages (initial application, reconsideration, and posthearing administrative appeal), beside the hearing level, in the adjudication of disability program cases in the SSA's four-stage administrative structure.[8] The SSA processes over two million new claims and issues over 3.4 million decisions at various stages each year.[9] Approximately 20,000 final agency disability program decisions are then appealed to the federal district courts in actions for judicial review each year.[10]

The considerable quantitative "mass justice" challenges of SSA disability program adjudication are compounded by the elasticity and imprecision of a socially constructed substantive disability legal standard. The social security disability standard is commonly misperceived as a solely medical one based on objective medical facts demonstrated through scientific and clinical methodology. However, the reality is that, for most, disability embraces a specific context and frame of reference: disability from work in the labor market. The United States Institute of

Medicine has supplied a more comprehensive and nuanced description of the meaning of disability as employed in the SSA's programs:

> Disability determination is a complex process, inescapably involving some interpretive judgment about capacity for work. At a minimum, making such decisions requires clinical determination of the extent of a claimant's physical, mental, or sensory impairments; analysis of the degree to which such impairments limit the claimant's functional capacity relevant to work roles; and consideration of the interaction of the claimant's physical, mental, or sensory impairments with the person's age, education, and work experience to provide an overall picture of the claimant's future capacity for any sort of work. Finally the disability decision process requires a means for comparing those capacities with the capacities demanded by work roles in all jobs in the national economy that provide substantial gainful activity (SGA) earnings level.[11]

As described by the former Seventh Circuit chief judge and legal scholar Richard Posner, "[T]he medical (disability) question and the economic (vocational) question are not readily separable[;] [t]his is implicit in the concept of listed impairments—medical conditions that are deemed totally disabling without inquiry into labor-market conditions."[12] Moreover, medical science alone has never been directed to the study of work environments or been able to provide a reliable means to demonstrate the inability to adjust to and function sufficiently and consistently in a work setting.

Under the Social Security Act, with limited exceptions, claimants are disabled if, after considering their age, education, work history, and medical limitations, they are unable to perform their past relevant work (PRW) or make an adjustment to substantial and gainful "work which exists in significant numbers either in the region where [the claimant] lives or in several regions of the country."[13] The Act, however, provides no further elaboration on the meaning of "work which exists in significant numbers."[14]

Accordingly, the disability inquiry requires either a presumptive or more individualized determination of whether medically demonstrated conditions, combined with certain vocational characteristics and limitations, preclude meaningful participation in the labor market.

This statutory standard behind the inquiry takes into account some politically and socially approved vocational factors deemed relevant to making workplace adjustments, such as age, education, and prior work experience, while excluding others, such as employer preferences or structural discrimination, the prevalence of actual job openings, or distance of work from one's home. In that sense, the Act and disability standard more realistically embody the recognition that there are circumstances in which individuals should be excused from the social obligation of work.[15] Thus, the disability definition is a product of political compromise and reflects a degree of social consensus.

* * * *

The chapters that follow analyze the history, evolution, judicial interpretation, empirical vulnerabilities, economic and labor market trends, and contemporary public policy issues generated from the American labor market side of substantive disability benefits law, policy, and adjudication. This inquiry is important because 40–50 percent of the millions of annual disability insurance decisions are based on determinations about ability to make adjustments to other jobs in the labor market.[16] The SSA has described its cases involving full evaluation of vocational and labor market work adjustment issues as the "most difficult" to adjudicate.[17]

It is at this stage where the agency must determine: (1) what jobs are available in the economy and performable by persons with various medical impairments; (2) whether such persons can make work adjustments to jobs they have not performed in the past and successfully adapt based on their mix of vocational limitations such as age, education, and work experience and medical impairments; and (3) whether such jobs exist in sufficient incidence in the economy.

This book delves deeply into the legislative, regulatory, and judicial history and interpretive construction of the labor market work adjustment assessment in the social security disability adjudicative system to try to demystify a complex inquiry (Part 1 sets the table). Parts 2 and 3 include granular examination of the administrative adjudication and judicial review stages of the agency's adjudicative processes to supply content and meaning to this elusive standard and to identify deficiencies, obsolescence, inequity, and inconsistencies in practice and application. That further entails analysis of the use of the administrative notice doctrine and vocational expert (VE) testimony and their limitations in identifying jobs in individual cases; the unique medical-vocational or "grid" guidelines and their work adjustment matrices and decisional rules and conclusions; and the proper use of the grid's adjudicative framework in grid exception cases. Part 4 explores efforts to update the empirical foundation and occupational taxonomy for labor market work adjustment assessments by vocational experts and the grid rules alike, to better reflect twenty-first-century American labor market conditions.

Finally, Part 5 examines the many public policy currents and proposals to alter the labor market work adjustment component of the disability standard since its most recent alteration in the Social Security Amendments of 1967 to the present day. Much has been written about how the Act's disability benefit standard and program is antiquated—that it is essentially based on a mid-twentieth-century industrial view of the economy and the nature of work. However, on closer analysis the program's core focus and infrastructure remain valid, and many of the attempts to more dramatically "modernize" the program to reflect suggested and select labor market and disability program trends and evolving perceptions are often attempts to restrict and reduce program participation without careful consideration of the impact on current and potential program beneficiaries.

Moreover, while it may seem counterintuitive, the transformation from an industrial economy to a twenty-first-century service economy in the information age and resulting diminished demand for work requiring arduous physical labor have not meaningfully reduced the relevance of, or need for, the disability benefits programs. Indeed, they have created new and different obstacles to work adjustments based on the need for other skills and capacities in the new economy—especially for the significant portion of persons with cognitive, psychiatric, neuropsychological, or other mental impairments.[18] Therefore, while the disability program is in need of empirically supported updating and measures to remedy some identified deficiencies, inequities, and inconsistencies in application, this book argues that the program's framework is sufficiently broad and enduring to remain relevant and faithful to the Act's congressional purposes and aspirations. As such, it should be "mended, not ended" as outlined in the chapters that follow.

PART ONE

The History and Evolution of Labor Market Considerations in the Social Security Disability Benefits Programs

1

The Disability Category and the Congressional Ideal

The American social welfare system is based on notions of categorical eligibility and moral worthiness, with its genesis in the Poor Laws of Elizabethan England.[1] The receipt of public benefits generally requires inclusion in a subgroup of persons deemed "worthy" of assistance due to some status or situation that provides a socially acceptable justification for poverty or government assistance.[2] The disability category has long been among such worthy categories.[3] Nevertheless, the most sweeping social welfare law in the United States, the Social Security Act of 1935, failed to include the disability category.[4]

This obvious omission was due in part to Congress's inability to determine whether disability benefits should be distributed in the form of "welfare"—that is, as means-tested public assistance, as social insurance benefits, or as both.[5] As a political matter, there are considerably fewer obstacles to the substantial restriction or even elimination of public assistance programs due to transient or evolving public sentiments of recipient worthiness.[6] Yet, President Franklin Roosevelt sought to characterize the social security program as untouchable because benefits were earned in the sense that they were provided only in return for having paid for them. He famously declared that "with those taxes in there, no damn politician can ever scrap my social security program."[7] The omission of the disability category from the Act was also due to a second concern that the definition of "disability" could not be sufficiently cabined to restrain program costs within manageable and predictable limits.[8]

In the 1950s, Congress addressed this first concern by adding disability categories to both the joint federal-state public assistance (or "welfare") program, and then, a few years later, to the federal social insurance (or "social security") program.[9] Congress had added a disability category to the joint federal-state welfare program through amendments to the Social Security Act in 1950, which added the Aid to the Permanently and Totally Disabled (APTD) welfare program.[10] Under APTD, which SSI replaced, Congress simply defined benefits eligibility as available to "needy individuals eighteen years or older who are permanently and totally disabled."[11] However, Congress left to the states the creation and implementation of more meaningful disability eligibility standards for APTD.[12]

In the Social Security Amendments of 1972, Congress created the SSI program for adults and children and transferred the responsibility for welfare benefits for aged, blind, and disabled persons from a joint state-federal scheme to the federal Social Security Administration.[13] The states' varying APTD eligibility standards were often less strict and more flexible than the uniform federal SSI standard.[14] Nevertheless, the SSI program has provided many advantages over the APTD program for low-income disabled persons. SSI utilizes the SSA's procedures and processes developed for a more valued and privileged segment of society—disabled persons with significant work histories and "earned rights" from years of social security contributions.[15] Thus, SSI recipients are relieved of the obligation regularly to demonstrate continuing moral worthiness for assistance in a closely supervised welfare agency context as is present in most state-run welfare programs.[16] SSI also removed much of the stigma associated with participation in a "welfare" program, as recipients would receive a check from the SSA like most retirees.[17] Finally, SSI benefits, unlike state welfare benefits, are subject to regular cost-of-living increases.[18]

Congress in the 1950s addressed its second concern regarding the elusive definition of "disability" by adopting what it believed to be an objectively limited, medically centered definition of that word for its Social Security Disability Insurance program, which it then applied to the federal Supplemental Security Income program when it created SSI in 1972.[19] The narrower, medically centered disability definition reflected a retreat from broader conceptions of disability pursued during earlier stages of the Social Security program. As initially proposed in 1941 by Arthur Altmeyer, the chairman of the Social Security Board,[20] a disability insurance component to the Social Security program was to be inclusive and address economic loss and inability to perform actual work, rather than strict medical definitions of impairment severity.[21] Altmeyer and his colleagues sought a disability definition that would take into account "personal, economic and social circumstances,"[22] "regional economic conditions,"[23] a claimant's age and training, and even a claimant's "sex, race, urban or rural residence, occupation and experience."[24]

Further, they rejected the idea of basing disability determinations solely on a fixed schedule of medical findings and impairments as in the workmen's compensation program.[25] Altmeyer concluded that, while such a schedule might provide some useful guidance, disability methodology should include the broader range of individual circumstances.[26] Thus, vocational factors and labor market considerations would have played an explicit and quite substantial role under the early conceptions of the disability category.

However, major opposition developed in Congress to this broader disability conception based on fears of inundation from an inability to distinguish disability from more general unemployment and the potential for disincentives to both rehabilitation and the social obligation to work.[27] The experience of insurance companies handling private disability insurance policies during the Great Depression, when disability claims soared due to abysmal labor market conditions, bolstered this fear.[28] Many individuals who satisfied various medical definitions of disability still managed to find and maintain employment. Yet, when the economy contracted, many with severe impairments lost their jobs and applied for—and were granted—private disability insurance benefits.[29]

In addition, because doctors would be required to distinguish disability from unemployment cases, the medical profession opposed a social security disability program, fearing it would mandate a government medical corps that would signal the first step toward socialized medicine. As Deborah Stone described:

> The party line of organized medicine was that a federal program of disability insurance would be the entering wedge of socialized medicine. If the program were to require medical certification, so the logic went, then the government would have to provide free medical examinations to applicants. The government would therefore use government-employed physicians, such as those working for the Veterans Administration and the Public Health Service, to conduct the examinations. More and more physicians would come to be employed by government; government employment meant socialized medicine.[30]

Because of these concerns, proponents of the program retreated to a more medically based disability conception when Congress adopted its first modest inclusion of disability in the social insurance program through the disability freeze program in 1954.[31] Under the disability freeze program, periods of time during which one is not working and deemed disabled—which would otherwise reflect zero earnings in retirement benefits calculations and produce reduced benefit payments—would be removed from these benefits calculations.[32] Put another way, "individuals who became disabled were made eligible for retirement benefits at age sixty-five as if they had continued to work between the onset of disability and age 65."[33] Their eligibility for retirement benefits would thus be "frozen" in place from the onset of disability, although they would not receive cash benefits until retirement age.

Even though the disability freeze program did not realize the goal of providing cash benefits to claimants based on disability, Congress still expressed significant fear of program expansion and uncertainty due to the malleable nature of the disability category. This motivated the agency to convene a panel of medical experts to develop administrative medical guidelines to implement the freeze program that would assess impairment severity.[34] These guidelines provided a catalogue of impairments and conditions with specified medical findings deemed sufficient to establish disability.[35]

Thus, when Congress finally added a disability insurance cash-benefits provision to the Social Security Act in 1956—by an essentially bare one-vote majority in the Senate[36]—proponents of the disability initiative were able to point to the medical panel's guidelines to support the claim that medical science could sufficiently circumscribe a statutory disability standard.[37] The standard enacted was also touted as a "strict" standard that denied coverage for temporary or partial disabilities and provided benefits only for "permanent and total" disabilities.[38]

To effectuate a "permanent and total" disability requirement, Congress defined "disability" as the "inability to engage in any substantial gainful activity by reason of any medically determinable physical or mental impairment which can be expected to result in death or to be of long-continued and indefinite duration."[39] Congress also provided that "[a]n individual shall not be considered to be under a disability unless he furnishes such proof of the existence thereof as may be required."[40] The House Ways and Means Committee report that accompanied the disability amendment observed:

> Your committee has designed a conservative program for disability insurance benefits. . . . [A]n individual who is able to engage in substantial gainful activity will not be entitled to disability insurance even though he is in fact severely disabled.[41]

The Act also contained a number of other provisions designed to ensure its passage and to support the assertion of the disability standard's strictness. After Senator Walter George of Georgia withdrew his long-held opposition to the legislation, he became a strong supporter of the program and touted its strictness.[42] Senator George also referenced the Act's language as imposing a "very conservative requirement."[43] George emphasized other restrictive aspects of the legislation, along with the strict medically centered disability definition, as collectively imposing seven separate eligibility requirements to ensure its stringency and limited scope.[44] The seven requirements included the following: (1) the test of work history and contributions to social security; (2) the "unable to engage in substantial gainful activity" test; (3) the "medically determinable impairment" test; (4) the six-month waiting period; (5) the "age fifty or over" requirement; (6) the "proof of existence" test, wherein the applicant must furnish proof of his or her impairment; and (7) the willingness to accept rehabilitation test.[45] The statute then delegated to the agency the difficult and controversial task of determining when a medical impairment would be deemed the cause of an individual's inability to work under this disability definition.[46]

Perhaps ironically, in relying heavily on assertions that medical professionals could largely ascertain the parameters of permanent and total disability under this medically centered disability definition, Congress essentially ignored the overwhelming testimony of representatives from the medical community. Medical associations offered congressional testimony that medical science, while generally capable of objectively determining whether a person suffered from a medical impairment, was incapable of reliably extrapolating from an isolated impairment to the individual's functional capacity for ongoing work performance in the U.S. labor market.[47] As one physician from the American Academy of General Practice stated, the varying physical and mental requirements across jobs made concrete determinations of disability uncommonly difficult:

> Unfortunately, medical science has not reached the point of being able to unerringly state whether or not a man is totally and permanently disabled. . . . Is the delivery boy who loses both legs totally and permanently disabled? Or is the certifying doctor supposed to point out that he can still run a drill press and probably make more money?[48]

Other physicians stressed the elusive nature of various medical conditions that lack objectively or medically demonstrable symptomatology, such as backaches and other forms of physical pain, or a variety of psychiatric conditions, such as anxiety and neuroses.[49] Still other physicians pointed to the nonmedical "social," "psychological," and even "philosophical" elements inherent in work capacity determinations, including consideration of how much pain or medical risk one should be expected to endure in the workplace and the extent to which the availability of benefits might lessen a person's residual will to overcome medical handicaps and continue working.[50]

Because the physician lobby had originally expressed strong opposition to disability insurance legislation on economic grounds by calling it the first step toward socialized medicine,[51] Congress perceived these physicians' newfound professional modesty as insincere and self-interested and dismissed their concerns.[52] For example, Senator George expressed his view that the medical community was quite capable of creating appropriate, definitive medical criteria for disability determinations:

> Doctors have less confidence in themselves than I have. . . . I think more of the medical profession in this country than to believe that they cannot determine when a man or a woman worker has a permanent and total disability. That fact must be medically determined, for, if not medically determined, the worker cannot receive any benefit.[53]

Despite an emphasis on strict medical standards and previously developed guidelines of objectively determinable and presumptively disabling impairments, Congress and the agency did not fully abandon Chairman Altmeyer and the early disability insurance advocates' desire to provide for some consideration of individual circumstances and vocational and labor market factors.[54] Indeed, some degree of labor market evaluation was inherent in the statutory definition of "disability"; the standard referenced an inability to perform "substantial gainful activity" (SGA), which was defined as work activity garnering remuneration above certain minimum earning levels.[55] In addition, agency representatives indicated to Congress during legislative debates that the statutory definition would require some evaluation of the reasonableness of labor market work adjustments in light of a claimant's age, education, and experience. Sumner Slichter, a Harvard labor economist and the first associate chairman of the Social Security Advisory Council,[56] noted that the legislation's disability definition required that the claimant "be disabled not only for the occupation which he ha[d] been pursuing but [for] any occupation which he might be reasonably expected, by reason of education, experience, general background, age, and so forth, to pursue."[57] This inquiry would inevitably entail at least some evaluation of the availability and characteristics of such occupations or jobs in the U.S. labor market.

Consideration of these nonmedical vocational and labor market factors had the potential to cut both ways in the disability evaluation process. Some claimants with relatively strong vocational profiles who met the presumptively disabled criteria under the medical schedule could conceivably be found not to be disabled based on their ability to make adjustments to other work in the labor market. Meanwhile, other claimants who did not meet the presumptive medical criteria could still be found disabled based on a determination that their relatively weak vocational profiles precluded the ability to make labor market work adjustments.[58] Thus, the Act's proponents could reasonably assert that consideration of these limited labor market and vocational factors would more closely reflect a claimant's ability to perform meaningful work without necessarily loosening the strict disability standard. In short, although proponents of disability programs touted the objective medical aspects of the disability standard, notwithstanding overwhelming medical testimony to the contrary, proponents also plainly intended to include some vocational and labor market considerations.

To explain the disability insurance statute, its regulations, and the State Disability Insurance Manual (designed to guide adjudication at the state disability agencies), the SSA in 1958 prepared a booklet titled "Disability and Social Security."[59] The publication provided "a description of the method of disability evaluation," including "the weight to be afforded the nonmedical factors."[60] Under the heading "Other Factors in Evaluating Disability," the agency's 1958 booklet provides:

> The following are additional factors that influence the extent of handicap imposed by an impairment.
>
> Age
>
> An impairment may be more limiting for an older person than for a younger person. The aging process affects healing, prognosis, psychologic adaptability, general health, speed and efficiency. As indicated above, a person generally suffers physiological impairment due to the aging process. In addition, employers may have prejudice against hiring older workers. This prejudice may cause a man to be unemployed, but it does not make him unable to do substantial work by reason of a medical impairment. The medically determinable impairments are the primary facts the evaluation team considers in evaluating handicaps.
>
> Education
>
> The amount of education a person has is a factor in determining his adaptability to other occupations if he should become unable to perform his usual occupation. However, lack of schooling is not necessarily proof that applicant is uneducated or not adaptable.
>
> Experience
>
> A person who all his life has done simple unskilled work may find it difficult to adjust to a different occupation if he acquires a handicap which interferes with his ability to carry on the work in which he is experienced. Limitation to unskilled work, especially when paired with limited education, may indicate limited vocational adaptability. On the other hand, an educated person who has varied experience very often is able to make adjustments more readily.[61]

In 1961, in response to congressional calls for the SSA more fully to address the application of nonmedical factors in the disability program,[62] the agency promulgated regulations requiring consideration of the claimant's age, education, and work experience in determining his or her ability to make labor market work adjustments unless the claimant had only a "slight" medical impairment.[63] The 1961 regulations also generally exempted persons from making work adjustments to less-strenuous work if they had only a marginal education, performed arduous physical labor for thirty-five years or more, and had become medically unable to perform such work.[64] Thus, in the SSA's disability determination process, claimants who received benefits could be apportioned among three categories: (1) those who satisfied the precise medical criteria in the schedule of automatically disabling impairments; (2) those who fit into the unique category for persons with a marginal education who were unable to perform their previous arduous work of thirty-five years; and (3) those not in either of the first two categories who could not perform their past work and possessed more than a slight impairment.[65] The focus of the SSA's labor market work adjustment determinations centered on claimants in this third category and their combinations of medical and vocational adversities.

2

The Judicial Gloss

While the Social Security Administration's approach justified evaluation of certain labor market work adjustment considerations in the disability evaluation process such as the impact of age, education, and work experience, it simultaneously excluded others such as actual employment openings, job prevalence, regional economic circumstances, and employers' hiring practices.[1] Even as to age, education, and work experience, the agency did not consider evidence of the impact of these select vocational factors on the ability to make work adjustments; instead, it used various presumptions drawn from nonpromulgated agency guidelines, which militated heavily against finding disability.[2] Thus, despite these early administrative attempts to add some adjudicative guidance for the difficult questions entailed in determining when persons become medically disabled from work, the early 1960s was also a period when the courts felt compelled to address large, unanswered labor market adjustment questions stemming from the disability definition and the agency's approach.

The most prominent of those court decisions was the Second Circuit's 1960 opinion in *Kerner v. Flemming*.[3] In *Kerner*, the SSA hearing examiner had denied benefits to Kerner, a sixty-year-old self-employed furniture repairman, after concluding he could make a work adjustment to less demanding and unspecified light or sedentary work.[4] The hearing examiner had specifically rejected the suggestion that such work might not be "attainable" for a claimant with Kerner's profile—a sixty-year-old severe diabetic with an acute cardiac condition.[5] In setting aside the agency's decision, Judge Henry Friendly, writing for a three-judge appellate panel of the United States Court of Appeals for the Second Circuit, found two substantial deficiencies, one substantive and one procedural, in the SSA's approach to the evaluation of disability based on presumed labor market adjustments.

First, Judge Friendly interpreted the substantive disability standard as requiring more than a "[m]ere theoretical opportunity to engage in substantial gainful activity . . . if no reasonable opportunity for this is available."[6] Rather, he found the "determination requires resolution of two issues—what can applicant do and what employment opportunities are there for a man who can do only what applicant can do?"[7] Second, Judge Friendly held that, while the ultimate statutory burden of persuasion remained with the claimant based on express provisions in both the Social Security Act and the Administrative Procedure Act (APA),[8] where a claimant "has raised a serious question and the evidence affords no sufficient basis for the Secretary's negative answer[,] . . . the Secretary's expertise should enable him readily to furnish information as to the employment opportunities . . . or the lack of them, for persons of [the claimant's] skills and limitations."[9]

Kerner and its progeny were not without both academic and judicial detractors. For example, one commentator argued that *Kerner* and later interpretations following it "thwart congressional intent and fly in the face of statutory language" and that "[s]hort of an ideal government program which recognizes a generalized interest in unemployment, disability, rehabilitation, job retraining and relocation, there must be a limit on the duty of the Secretary to produce [such] evidence."[10] Dissenting in a 1967 case before the Fifth Circuit, Judge Minor Wisdom also strongly criticized *Kerner* and its progeny, arguing that the emerging post-*Kerner* labor market work adjustment court decisions were improperly "converting the disability insurance provisions of the Social Security Act into an unemployment compensation law" and noting that Congress intended a "strict" and "conservative" disability definition and "thought a rational determination (of disability) was possible without such evidence of employment opportunities."[11]

Earlier, another federal judge had construed *Kerner* narrowly, emphasizing the elusiveness of open-ended work adjustment assessments and the belief that "Judge Friendly did not intend straight-jacket formalism by the [ALJs]" and that "there is no necessity to delve into the mysteries of employment opportunities."[12] The judge stated:

> As a fact of life, employment is a matter of fortune. Surplus labor areas and types of available employment differ in most sections of the country.

> In this progressive and scientific age, government agencies alone or in combination may have the know-how to survey such situations with reasonable certainty of prediction. But to particularize that a certain human being with individualistic impairment and limitation may or may not have employment opportunity in a certain area, in my inexperienced judgment, may require an elite group of soothsayers superbly trained to probe the many intangibles.[13]

Despite some criticisms of *Kerner*, the federal courts largely embraced and extended both the substantive and procedural prongs of Judge Friendly's analysis. Courts extended *Kerner*'s substantive prong by setting aside nondisability work adjustment findings that did not evaluate the availability of specific jobs in the labor market to which a claimant could adjust:[14] the actual existence of and openings for such jobs,[15] the presence of such jobs in the claimant's community,[16] the potentially preclusive and discriminatory hiring practices of employers in the region and the impact of those practices on the claimant's opportunity to secure a position,[17] or some combination of these considerations.[18] Courts also extended *Kerner*'s procedural holding by expressly shifting the burden of proof to the agency to demonstrate the availability of other jobs to which claimants can make a work adjustment in all cases where claimants demonstrated the inability to perform their former work.[19] Thus, by the mid-1960s, to meet its new burden of proof in labor market work adjustment cases, the agency relied heavily on vocational expert testimony to supply the requisite evidence in adjudicated hearings.[20] As described in a comprehensive study of the SSA hearings and appeals process by the National Center on Administrative Justice and led by Professor Jerry Mashaw:

> The Secretary[,] after failing to convince the Solicitor General to petition for certiorari in *Kerner*, moved promptly to comply. In 1962, a nationwide program of vocational experts was established to provide testimony at the hearing level; a year later *Kerner* was published as a Social Security Ruling implying the Administration's acquiescence; and interpretive materials related to vocational factors in disability were distributed to the state agencies.[21]

To implement the Vocational Expert Program, the SSA entered into contracts with 600 vocational experts to provide services at administrative hearings.[22]

While the courts are credited with a significant role in the expansion of the disability program's focus on labor market and vocational factors, they, too, occasionally "bought into the myth" that disability from work could be largely ascertained solely through objective medical evidence.[23] For example, in *Mathews v. Eldridge*, the United States Supreme Court declared:

> In short, a medical assessment of the worker's physical or mental condition is required. This is a more sharply focused and easily documented decision than the typical determination of welfare entitlement. In the latter, a wide variety of information may be deemed relevant, and issues of witness credibility and veracity are often critical to the decisionmaking process. . . . By contrast, the decision whether to discontinue disability benefits will turn, in most cases, upon routine, standard and unbiased medical records by physician specialists.[24]

Indeed, even Judge Friendly—the author of the *Kerner* decision who is largely credited with initiating the agency's obligation to supply labor market evidence that led to the Vocational Expert Program's launch—later suggested that the SSA eschew expert hearing testimony altogether. He recommended instead the use of an expert medical board to adjudicate all disability cases.[25]

3

The Congressional Response

The post-*Kerner* era up through the mid-1960s marked a period of tension between the differing approaches to labor market adjustment determinations by the agency, on the one hand, and the courts on the other. Although the agency accepted and "acquiesced" in the *Kerner* decision, it specifically "non-acquiesced" in, and refused to follow, some of the post-*Kerner* labor market adjustment decisions that had expanded the scope of labor market considerations in the disability standard.[1] Congress tried unsuccessfully to enact legislation that would have expanded eligibility by providing an occupational definition of "disability" that extended benefits to claimants who could no longer "engage in the occupation or employment last performed on a regular basis before the onset of such impairment."[2]

These proposals would have avoided many of the complex issues of more open-ended potential labor market work adjustment determinations and would have broadened the program in a manner analogous to disability programs in other developed Western nations, where a medical inability to return to one's economic or social class or local position in the labor market is a more decisive factor.[3] It also would have brought the general work adjustment standards of the disability program closer to the largely occupational standards used for two other socially constructed groups: older "legally blind" claimants,[4] and claimants whom Robert Dixon has described as "worn-out manual laborers"—those in the previously discussed category comprising marginally educated individuals who have performed arduous, unskilled work for thirty-five years or more.[5] This congressional effort was unsuccessful.

A few years later, the Social Security Administration sought and obtained from Congress amendments to the Social Security Act that moved in the other direction and narrowed program eligibility by expanding the labor market work adjustment inquiry. The Social Security Amendments of 1967 provided, in relevant part, that

> [a]n individual shall be determined to be under a disability only if his physical or mental impairment or impairments are of such a severity that he is not only unable to do his previous work but cannot, considering his age, education, and work experience, engage in any other kind of substantial gainful work which exists in the national economy, regardless of whether such work exists in the immediate area in which he lives, or whether a specific job vacancy exists for him, or whether he would be hired if he applied for work. For purposes of the preceding sentence . . . "work which exists in the national economy" means work which exists in significant numbers either in the region where such individual lives or in several regions of the country.[6]

This provision's legislative history reflects significant congressional equivocation and the absence of a clear rationale for what Congress ultimately enacted. The initial Presidential Administration Bill made other changes to the Social Security program, such as inclusion of Medicare eligibility, but did not change the disability standard at all.[7] The House Ways and Means Committee then replaced that bill with its own bill, which introduced a redefinition of disability that expanded the work adjustment inquiry to the national labor market.[8] This bill was approved by the full House of Representatives.[9] The prior definition was then restored through a Senate amendment by Senator Lee Metcalf of Montana, who pointed out that eight witnesses had testified against the new definition, including George Meaney, president of the AFL-CIO, while only one witness, Paul Henkel from the Council of State Chambers of Commerce, had testified in its favor.[10]

Metcalf also chided the SSA for seeking a definitional amendment because "it lost a lawsuit."[11] He pointed to the only specific case that the committee report had identified and condemned—*Leftwich v. Gardner*—a case in which the United States Court of Appeals for the Fourth Circuit awarded benefits even though the claimant was regularly working.[12] Senator Metcalf noted that the courts had rejected the agency's attempted redefinition, appearing in the House bill at the time, and had been guided by disability definitions employed in the veterans and workmen's compensation programs.[13] The Senate adopted Metcalf's amendment to the bill by a vote of 34–20.[14]

However, the conference committee restored the redefined disability standard to reconcile the House and Senate versions.[15] The final version included a compromise whereby the phrase "work which exists in the national economy" would be explained to at least require the work adjustment inquiry to focus on work either in the claimant's home region or in several regions of the country. This would preclude a work adjustment finding based on jobs in isolated or remote regions.[16]

The congressional commentary on the need for the redefined standard suggested that the House Ways and Means Committee "was forced to conclude" that "subtle changes" in the concept of "disabled worker" had produced program allowances in excess of predictions.[17] However, the commentary then listed a series of circumstances, which had nothing to do with expansive court decisions yet the committee deemed "in large part the reasons" behind the program expansion. Those reasons included: "(1) greater knowledge of the program to increasing numbers of qualified people; (2) improved methods of developing evidence of disability; and (3) more effective ways of assessing total impact of an individual's impairment on his ability to work." As one legal scholar pointed out, "[W]hat the Committee [on Ways and Means] may have been 'forced to conclude' about relationships between the Administration's estimates, the list of reasons for the errors, and the court decisions expanding the disability definition, is left to conjecture."[18]

If one motivation behind the 1967 redefined standard was to correct court decisions awarding benefits to claimants who had been actually performing substantial gainful activity (as in *Leftwich*—the one case specifically referenced in congressional deliberations), a much simpler fix would have been sufficient, such as denying eligibility to persons engaged in significant work. The committee's reason for seeking a broader amendment to the disability definition to reverse many of the post-*Kerner* work adjustment cases from 1960 to 1967 appears to have been fear that, while these decisions were not yet major factors in the above-cited program growth, they might eventually lead to further program expansion.[19] The committee offered no analysis of those court decisions' merits but only the conclusory statement that "[i]t is and has been the intent of the statute to provide a disability definition which can be applied with uniformity throughout the nation, without regard to where a particular individual may reside, to local hiring practices or employer preferences or the state of the local or national economy."[20]

This statement failed to acknowledge the many ways in which the disability definition would still vary nonuniformly based on individualized factors that are affected by employer practices and the local economy and culture. For example, the definition mandates consideration of work experience and education in the work adjustment inquiry, and these factors are heavily influenced by the local economy and culture.[21] Moreover, the redefinition ultimately adopted still expressly incorporated some local variation because the work adjustment inquiry looked to the ability to adjust to jobs in either the unique labor market in the claimant's specific region or that of several regions.

This important 1967 amendment to the social security disability standard restricted *Kerner*'s substantive component by permitting more benefit denials based on a broader definition of "work" (to which an impaired claimant might adjust) than that recognized in *Kerner* and its progeny. However, the amendment also provided express congressional ratification of vocational and labor market considerations as unquestionable components of the Act's disability standard.[22] Furthermore, through the requirement in the 1967 amendments that such other work "exists in . . . significant numbers," Congress established, for the first time, a job incidence or job prevalence requirement for labor market work adjustment assessments. Although Congress has passed a number of amendments to the Social Security Act's disability benefit programs since 1967,[23] its disability definition has retained the labor market work adjustment standard adopted in the 1967 amendments.

Within a few years of the restrictive 1967 labor market work adjustment amendments, the Social Security Advisory Council twice recommended, to no avail, that Congress further amend the Act to broaden eligibility by applying to older disability claimants the more liberal "occupational" labor market work adjustment standard used for older claimants in the blindness program and extending eligibility to such claimants who are unable to perform their past relevant work.[24] In 1981, the Ronald Reagan administration proposed moving in the opposite direction and simplifying disability determinations through a far stricter disability standard based solely on medical considerations that did not include the 1967 amendments' limited vocational and labor market factors.[25] By 1983, the administration had withdrawn this proposal.[26] However, a proposal to restrict the disability definition through elimination of vocational and labor-market factors was revived and advocated by the SSA's Deputy Commissioner of Retirement and Disability Policy Mark J. Warshawsky (appointed to the agency during the Trump administration), along with Ross Marchand.[27]

* * * *

The 1967 amendments narrowed the substantive construction of the disability definition; however, they did not purport to alter the judicially created limited shift in the burden of proof from the claimant to the SSA derived from *Kerner*'s procedural holding. Although the judicial burden shifting to the SSA on the labor market work adjustment issue was mentioned in a report provided to Congress in 1967 about judicial interpretations of the disability standard (presumably those interpretations about which the agency harbored disagreement), the amending provision did not propose language to overrule those cases.[28] However, the 1967 amendments *did* include other language that could be interpreted as further mitigating the agency's evidentiary burden concerns by reemphasizing the claimant's burden to supply medically acceptable evidence of an impairment. The amendments also provided that

> "physical or mental impairment" is an impairment that results from anatomical, physiological, or psychological abnormalities which are demonstrable by medically acceptable clinical and laboratory diagnostic techniques. . . . An individual shall not be considered to be under a disability unless he furnishes such medical and other evidence of the existence thereof as the Secretary may require.[29]

Courts interpreting the 1967 amendments continued to expect the agency to shoulder a burden of producing labor-market evidence.[30] That burden was redefined based on the substantive provisions in the 1967 amendments as a burden of producing evidence of "work which exists . . . in significant numbers" either in the claimant's regional economy or in "several regions of the country."[31] This agency burden is triggered by the claimant's demonstration of a prima facie case: showing an inability to perform "past relevant work" or, for SSI claimants with no relevant work history, showing a lack of past relevant work.[32] Over time, every court of appeals[33] and the Supreme Court[34] adopted this burden-shifting process. Eventually, whether phrased as a burden of proof or of production, the agency ceased its opposition to the burden-shifting formulation and created regulations and accompanying commentary that explained this process.[35] It stated:

> This burden shifts to us because, once you establish that you are unable to do any past relevant work, it would be unreasonable to require you to produce vocational evidence showing that there are no jobs in the national economy that you can perform, given your RFC [residual functional capacity]. However, as stated by the Supreme Court, "It is not unreasonable to require the claimant, who is in a better position to provide information about his own medical condition, to do so." Thus, the only burden shift . . . is that we are required to prove that there is other work that you can do, given your RFC, age, education, and work experience.[36]

Before the promulgation of the medical-vocational regulations and their charts or "grid" in 1978, the SSA attempted to meet its burden of proof in two ways: "(1) through the use of the official notice doctrine often coupled with notice of the U.S. Department of Labor (DOL) Dictionary of Occupational Titles (DOT) and other government job market publications; and (2) through the vocational expert [(VE)] program with a particular focus on the use of live vocational 'expert' testimony at administrative hearings." The following part examines each of these methods in detail in chapters 4 and 5.

PART TWO

Labor Market Work Adjustment Assessments and the Social Security Administration's Basic Adjudicative System

4

The Official Notice/Administrative Notice Doctrine

Even though judicial support existed for the proposition that vocational experts were almost always necessary to supply evidence to satisfy the agency's labor market work adjustment burden in the post-*Kerner*, pre-grid time period,[1] several courts found that some form of properly implemented official or administrative notice could suffice under appropriate circumstances as well.[2] In agency adjudication such as claimants' disability hearings, "official notice" is the administrative-law analogue to "judicial notice."[3] (Courts and legal scholars also use the terms "administrative notice" and "official notice" interchangeably in this context.) Put simply, official notice is "a method for getting information into the [administrative] record somewhere between proof and simple recognition of a fact so well accepted as to be beyond debate."[4]

In perhaps the most significant early interpretation of the official notice doctrine prior to the Administrative Procedure Act's passage in 1946,[5] the United States Supreme Court in *Ohio Bell Telephone Co. v. Public Utilities Commission of Ohio*[6] recognized procedural due process limits on the doctrine's application. In *Ohio Bell*, the Ohio Public Utilities Commission had adjusted the utility's property value downward for ratemaking purposes to reflect the Great Depression, which had commenced in the middle of the ratemaking. Although the Court approved the commission's notice of the Depression and the general decline in market values as "one of its concomitants,"[7] it rejected the agency's use of the data because the general decline did not demonstrate "[h]ow great the decline has been for this industry or that, for one material or another, in this year or the next."[8]

In addition, "[f]rom the standpoint of due process—the protection of the individual against arbitrary action—a deeper vice" committed by the agency was its failure to disclose the particular evidence on which it had relied.[9] Thus, the party against which the officially noticed facts were taken was denied the opportunity to "see the evidence or hear it and parry its effect."[10] The Court explained that "[official] notice, even when taken, has no effect than to relieve one of the parties of the burden of resorting to the usual forms of evidence. 'It does not mean that the opponent is prevented from disputing the matter by evidence if he believes it disputable.'"[11]

Courts in SSA cases as well as others, have interpreted *Ohio Bell* as establishing two prerequisites for the use of official notice, one substantive and one procedural. First, the information must be substantively appropriate for official notice as a matter of common knowledge. Second, the agency must follow proper procedures in using the information, such as providing advance notice and a meaningful opportunity to rebut or contest its application by the agency in the adjudication.[12] With respect to *Ohio Bell*'s first requirement, the official notice doctrine has not been meaningfully expanded beyond matters of common knowledge or to facts "not subject to reasonable dispute," as is the limit of the judicial notice doctrine.[13] Rather, the academic debate over the official notice doctrine's substantive scope has centered on varying attempts to categorize the type of facts that can be officially noticed.[14]

The United States Attorney General's Committee on Administrative Procedure has posited a distinction between *litigation* and *nonlitigation* facts. Litigation facts arise from investigation of a pending case and should be adduced only from the usual adjudicative processes. Nonlitigation facts are those that "develop[] in the usual course of business of the agency," "emerge from numerous cases," and "become part of the factual equipment of the administrators."[15] Such facts are appropriate for official notice because they fall within the acquired technical or scientific expert knowledge of the agency and are as "obvious and notorious" to such expert agency administrators as facts susceptible to judicial notice are to judges.[16]

A similar but more far-reaching distinction that Professor Kenneth Culp Davis first articulated in 1942 is that between *adjudicative* and *legislative* facts.[17] Adjudicative facts are those pertaining to the parties, their activities, and their properties.[18] Legislative facts "are those a tribunal seeks in order to assist itself in the legislative process of creating law or determining policy."[19] They are "ordinarily general and do not merely concern the immediate parties."[20] Davis pointed out that some facts do not fit into either category and are not clearly adjudicative or legislative.[21] Nevertheless, Davis argued that obvious legislative facts need not even be noticed or brought into the record; where critical and debatable, they can normally be subject to challenge through briefs and arguments.[22] By contrast, adjudicative facts must be brought into the record either through direct proof or by official notice. Whether adjudicative facts can be officially noticed or must be proven directly depends on three variables: "[H]ow close the facts are to the center of the controversy; the extent to which the facts are adjudicative or legislative; and the degree to which the facts are certain."[23] As the facts "move closer to the basic issues of the hearing, relate to the parties, and are disputed, the usual methods of proof must be observed; as they move in the opposite direction, official notice is permissible."[24]

The 1946 enactment of section 7(d) of the APA codified the due process rebuttal rights within the second prong of *Ohio Bell* by providing that "[w]hen an agency decision rests on official notice of a material fact not appearing in the evidence in the record, a party is entitled, on timely request, to an opportunity to show the contrary."[25] Despite Rule 201 of the Federal Rules of Evidence's reliance on the adjudicative-versus-legislative fact distinction and its implication of relatively unrestricted judicial notice of legislative facts in federal court proceedings,[26] the APA does not include any such exemption from its provisions for federal administrative adjudications. In 2000, the Supreme Court recognized that official notice of even facts characterized as legislative must include the opportunity to respond to the facts noticed.[27]

Ernest Gellhorn has criticized both the Attorney General's and Kenneth Davis's reliance on categories or labels to ascertain the proper application of the official notice doctrine.[28] He argued that the central focus should be on the question of fairness: Is it fair with respect to costs and situational equities in the particular hearing to take official notice and transfer the burden of proof to a party?[29] He also suggested that, if proof burdens are to be altered, "it should be accomplished openly through a shift in substantive policy rather than covertly by manipulation of procedural devices."[30]

Regardless of the interpretive approach to the doctrine employed, the SSA's use of the official notice doctrine to meet the work adjustment burden in the post-*Kerner* era has received a mixed, and often highly critical, reception from the courts. Some courts have found that either the explicit or implicit taking of official notice is not appropriate and have demanded more individualized proof of jobs or of the claimant's ability to perform or adapt to them, in light of medical and vocational limitations.[31] For example, merely taking administrative notice of unspecified light or sedentary occupations does not meet the agency's burden because the agency must show that the "claimant has the physical and mental capacity to perform specified jobs, taking into consideration the requirements of the job as well as the claimant's age, education, and background."[32] Similarly, simply taking administrative notice of the existence of specific custodial or security jobs does not satisfy the agency's burden where "there was no 'job description clarifying the nature' and requirements of such jobs, . . . and no showing whatever that [the claimant] would have been able to perform such jobs."[33]

Other courts have pointed to the lack of specialized expertise by the lay agency adjudicators taking notice. The United States Court of Appeals for the Fourth Circuit explained the rationale behind its rejection of administrative notice on this ground:

> [W]e expressly rejected the contention that the Secretary may establish specific vocational ability solely through medical evidence or by "administrative notice." . . . [T]he ALJ is not qualified to provide affirmative vocational evidence. Such evidence, rather, should be provided by persons who have, through training and experience in vocational counseling or placement, an up-to-date knowledge of job requirements, occupational characteristics and working conditions, and a familiarity with the personal attributes and skills necessary to function in various jobs. An ALJ who has heard a multitude of disability claims and vocational experts, and therefore feels knowledgeable in vocational matters, must resist the temptation to dispense with vocational expert testimony in favor of his own experience. Aside from the ALJ's lack of formal qualification and actual contact with the working community, it is manifestly unfair for the ALJ to rely on assumptions and "facts" which the claimant cannot, without reading the ALJ's mind, test or rebut.[34]

Furthermore, some courts have found such notice appropriate under the first, substantive *Ohio Bell* step of an official notice analysis but rejected agency decisions under the second procedural step, where the agency adjudicators failed to provide sufficient opportunity to confront and rebut noticed facts.[35] Indeed, based on related process concerns, the agency more recently issued an internal memorandum, clarifying that its ALJs may not take administrative notice of vocational expert interrogatories offered in prior hearings for use in subsequent ones.[36] The agency reasoned that, since prior VE opinion does not fit within *Heckler v. Campbell*'s legislative rule promulgation in the grid regulations' enactment,[37] and has not gone through rulemaking's "procedural safeguards to ensure the accuracy of the facts contained therein," subsequent administrative notice of prior VE testimony would violate the requirement that decisions be "based on evidence adduced at a hearing."[38] The agency also noted substantive problems with noticing prior VE opinions: the "data about the work that exists in significant numbers . . . can change over time" and would not, in any event, be "individually tailored" to the claimant's unique confluence of medical and vocational adversities.[39]

Those courts that approved use of official notice in this context did so without meaningful analysis or application of either *Ohio Bell* requirement. These courts tended to approve notice in cases where claimants possessed the capacity to perform an unrestricted range of lighter work,[40] or where adjudicators identified specific jobs in the United States Department of Labor's Dictionary of Occupational Titles or other government labor market publications, that adjudicators deemed relatively less restricted claimants capable of performing.[41] On this latter point, the first Mashaw-led comprehensive study of SSA hearing and appeal processes (for the National Center for Administrative Justice) drew a distinction between official notice with a "documentary basis" on the work adjustment issue and official notice attempted without such a basis.[42] Mashaw and his coauthors suggested that the latter was the cause of restrictive court decisions on the doctrine's use.[43]

Thus, they reasoned that greater permissible official notice could be accomplished in this context if the notice were based on the DOT and similar publications and not merely the ALJs' intuitions.[44] Shortly thereafter, the SSA promulgated a regulation (apart from the broad, across-the-board grid regulations adopted later)[45] authorizing agency adjudicators to take administrative notice of "reliable job information" from the DOT and other government labor market publications in determining job availability and incidence.[46]

However, a flaw in the agency's approach, including through its administrative notice regulation, is the failure to identify the precise purpose and limits on the noticeable use of the DOT and other government labor market materials.[47] The post–1967 amendments' work adjustment inquiry devolves into at least three distinct inquiries that present obstacles for the use of government publications for official notice of work adjustment facts: (1) job performability; (2) job adaptability; and (3) job incidence. *Job performability* considers the ability functionally to perform alternative occupations and jobs in light of the claimant's medical restrictions and statutory vocational limitations (education, training, and work experience to some degree). This inquiry asks: Is the claimant actually able to perform the specific job tasks demanded in the job(s)/occupation(s)?

Job adaptability is a somewhat less concrete inquiry that addresses a claimant's ability to adjust to a new work environment and job functions and to sustain employment in that environment on a competitive basis regardless of the medical, educational, or acquired-skill abilities to perform the specific tasks involved in the work. For example, the inclusion of age as a mandatory factor in the statutory criteria is presumed to affect only adaptability and not performability in any manner that is independent from one's medical limitations. When the SSA finally promulgated clarifying regulations on how to evaluate the statutory age factor, it stated that "'[a]ge' refers to how old you are (your chronological age) and the extent to which your age affects your ability to adapt to a new work situation and to do work in competition with others."[48] In 2000, the SSA "incorporat[ed] the principle intended in this statement" into a new clause providing that, in determining the extent to which age affects a person's ability "to adjust to other work, we consider advancing age to be an increasingly limiting factor in the [person's] ability to make such an adjustment."[49] Indeed, in the earlier promulgation of the grid regulations, the agency found that age references physiological factors that "diminish a severely impaired person's aptitude for new learning and adaptation to new jobs."[50]

Adaptability is evaluated largely through the age factor in the statutory standard, even though the precise manner in which age affects adaptability has been difficult to ascertain. The concept of adaptability reflected in the age regulations may be seen as a limited component of what Robert Dixon referred to as "the key factor" in work adjustment determinations—the claimant's "set." Dixon uses the term "set" to reference such issues as a claimant's pain threshold, willingness to try to learn new skills, willingness to adjust lifestyle to accommodate the need for greater off-the-job rest, "residual zip in general," and pride.[51] Other studies have found or suggested that older workers "are typically limited in certain abilities such as flexibility, acceptance of new technology, and ability to learn new skills"[52] or reveal a "reduced capacity to adapt to stress . . . [which is deemed] to result from the loss of complexity with aging."[53]

Thus, fifty-five-year-old, high school–educated workers, who have performed unskilled medium work throughout their careers but can no longer physically perform such tasks, may not be deemed sufficiently adaptable to adjust to unskilled light or sedentary work, even if medically and educationally capable of handling all of the tasks involved in a wide range of light and sedentary occupations and jobs.[54] In addition, the SSA, from its very first vocational factor regulations in 1961, recognized the specific adaptability problems confronting claimants whom Robert Dixon has characterized as "worn-out, manual laborers"—marginally educated workers with a long history of arduous physical work.[55] SSA regulations authorize nonadaptability presumptions for such claimants even where proven medically capable of performing lighter employment.[56] (Application of the adaptability provisions and assumptions utilized in the grid [medical-vocational] regulations and related subregulatory guidance are discussed in Part 3).[57]

Finally, the third discrete labor market inquiry, *job incidence* (or "numerosity"), derives from the 1967 amendments. It is the inquiry about the existence of a significant number of jobs either in the "region" where the claimant lives or in "several regions of the country." The 1967 act clarified that such jobs need not exist in the immediate area in which the claimant lives, or whether specific vacancies for such jobs exist, or whether the claimant would be hired after applying for such work.[58]

Assuming that the DOT could be deemed both methodologically and temporally reliable, it would still present significant limitations for the use of the official notice doctrine to meet the labor market work adjustment burden of proof on all three of the work adjustment inquiries. The DOT is merely a catalogue of jobs and occupations accompanied by basic descriptions and duties that take into account some of a claimant's medical and vocational restrictions (i.e., residual functional capacity and certain educational and skill levels). First, the DOT does not particularize the job criteria to any given claimant's combination of restrictions. Accordingly, if that precise mix of medical and vocational restrictions is not apparent from the job description, then a performability conclusion cannot properly be derived from the DOT. For example, in a case where the Fifth Circuit was asked to decide "whether administrative notice of the Dictionary of Occupational Titles constitutes evidence similar to expert vocational testimony," the court reasoned:

> The [DOT] differs from expert vocational testimony in many ways. The Dictionary does not define the occupations of hand-lacer and pencil inspector as repetitive, low-stress jobs. Nor does the dictionary describe the particular skills or qualifications needed for the positions. It also fails to identify the unique requirements of the positions, such as the pace at which one must work or the environment in which the work is performed. Instead, it simply gives a general description of the duties involved. The fact that Fields may be able to inspect a pencil or lace a football does not necessarily mean she can function as a pencil inspector or hand-lacer. The ALJ's determination that Fields can perform those jobs is mere speculation.[59]

Second, the DOT provides no information whatsoever on adaptability and the relevance of work adjustment factors like age and the confluence of adverse age and limited work history and education. Third, it also provides no information on job incidence, much less incidence that is particularized to the claimant's region or to "several" specific regions in the nation.[60] Thus, whether official notice is government document–based (as advocated by Mashaw) or otherwise, it would be only the rarest of situations where notice of facts of all three work adjustment inquiries could be deemed a matter of common knowledge or "so obvious and notorious" to agency adjudicators—taking into account whatever expertise can be attributed to such lay decision makers—as to justify proof without any conventional evidence.[61] Even then, advance notice and the right to rebut such facts would be compelled under section 7(d) of the APA, 5 U.S.C. § 556(e), and *Ohio Bell*'s second prong.

Finally, Ernest Gellhorn's admonition on considering fairness and the situational equities of using official notice to reshift a burden of proof or production has particular resonance when applied to the work adjustment burden in SSA disability cases. Gellhorn observed that, while some courts had upheld official notice based on scientific data, technical facts, and academic articles, "many courts contend that this places too great a burden on the opponent to refute the 'noticed evidence.'"[62] Indeed, in support of this proposition, he cited a string of SSA disability cases.[63] The courts shifted the work adjustment burden of proof in disability cases to the government in express recognition of the manifest unfairness of requiring disabled, unemployed, mostly lower-income claimants to prove a broad negative proposition about the absence of suitable alternative work in the labor market when this job market information is more readily available to the government. The burden-shifting rule "is consistent with the recognition that information as to the availability of jobs in the national economy is sophisticated information that most individuals do not have the resources to prove or disprove."[64] By contrast, the government "has vast resources and information at [its] disposal" so "considerations of fairness and policy require that the [agency] bear the risk of non-persuasion on the element of disability on which the [agency] is in a better position than the claimant to introduce evidence."[65]

That even the agency has openly acknowledged these fairness considerations in its burden-of-proof regulations[66] further counsels against reshifting this burden back to claimants through the device of official notice.[67] As Ernest Gellhorn argued, if such a reshifting of the burden is justified by countervailing policy concerns, such as agency efficiency or mass justice considerations, it should be accomplished openly though legislative processes designed to address substantive policy rather than covertly through procedural devices.

5

Vocational Expert Evidence and the Vocational Expert Program

In response to significant resistance by the courts to the use of the official notice doctrine for individual labor market work adjustment decisions, and perhaps taking cognizance of some of the problems discussed, the agency eventually recognized a virtually presumptive need for vocational expert testimony in SSA disability work adjustment assessments at hearings prior to the grid's adoption.[1] At hearings, ALJs typically elicit VE testimony by means of hypothetical questions, which include all of the claimant's various medical limitations supported by the record and the claimant's age, education, and previous work experience.[2] The VE then indicates whether jobs are available, to which such a hypothetical claimant can make a work adjustment, and the incidence of those jobs in the economy.[3] The agency has always relied heavily on the VE's use of DOT descriptions to identify job requirements.[4] However, since the DOT provides only limited descriptions and characteristics of jobs and no information about adaptability or job incidence,[5] VEs must base more claimant-particularized job descriptive, adaptability, and incidence testimony on other sources.

As a practical matter and particularly in the post-*Kerner*, pre–grid era, VE testimony varied widely and was usually decisive because it was seldom challenged, even in cases where claimants were represented.[6] Thus, decisions and benefits eligibility sometimes turned on the disposition and perspective of the VE, leading to perceptions of adjudicative inconsistency and arbitrariness.[7] The degree of inconsistency in the pre-grid period was further exacerbated by the absence of adjudicative guidance on the interaction of the statutory vocational factors (age, education, and work experience), the application of the adaptability concept as particularly reflected through the non–medically duplicative evaluation of the age factor, or the criteria for determining job incidence under the "significant numbers" statutory criteria.

On these first two issues, some VEs tended to fold the other jobs inquiry solely into the question of job performability. That is, regardless of the negative synergistic mix of adverse vocational factors or, in particular, the adversity of older age, these VEs found claimants not disabled if deemed functionally capable of performing the requirements of specific jobs.[8] They reasoned, for example, that "while older workers are generally less adaptable to change than younger workers, it is virtually impossible to apply that generalization to specific situations."[9] In addition, they relied on the non-empirical bromide that "if necessity requires, most individuals will adapt to new situations and new jobs."[10]

On the job incidence question of how many jobs are required to meet the statutory "significant work in the economy" standard, there were very few reported decisions in the pre-grid era, as courts tended either to find other problems with VE testimony or sustain significant numbers findings without analysis, however large or small the numbers might be.[11] A few early pre-grid reported decisions found that the incidence of 200 to 1,000 appropriate jobs from the claimant's region was insufficient.[12] These court decisions did not attempt to determine how the mix of statutory vocational factors and adaptability issues might affect the bottom-line "significant numbers" conclusion.

As in the pre–grid era, the approach that has emerged in VE cases during the post–grid era (where the grid does not provide a rule of decision) has been simply to ascertain whether the number of jobs identified by the VE seems significant from a "common sense" perspective. As the Sixth Circuit described:

> We know that we cannot set forth one special number which is to be the boundary between a "significant number" and an insignificant number of jobs. . . . A judge should consider many criteria in determining whether work exists in significant numbers, some of which might include: the level of claimant's disability; the reliability of the vocational expert's testimony; the reliability of the claimant's testimony; the distance claimant is capable of traveling to engage in the assigned work; the isolated nature of the jobs; the types and availability of such work, and so on. *The decision should ultimately be left to the trial judge's common sense in weighing the statutory language as applied to a particular claimant's factual situation.*[13]

Judicial decisions on this issue reflect that "common sense" varies significantly from court to court. Courts have found as few as 174 regional jobs and 25,000 national jobs sufficient while finding as many as 1,800 regional jobs and 120,350 national jobs insufficient.[14] The court finding 120,350 jobs insignificant reasoned that, because the total number of jobs in the economy was 150,606,000, the identified 120,350 jobs comprised only .080 percent of the total number of jobs, which was not a "significant number of jobs."[15] However, the court did not specify a percentage of the labor market bright-line that would necessarily reflect a "significant" number of jobs in the economy. Apart from supporting ad hoc and inconsistent adjudicative results, these decisions have sanctioned a "significant numbers" approach in VE hearing cases that still largely fails to consider the statutory age criteria and adaptability considerations based for the most part on age and the synergistic mix of statutory vocational adversities.

There are also numerous problems with the current-day use of VE testimony to satisfy the SSA's burden of production on the work adjustment assessment from the standpoint of meeting even minimal requirements of legal evidentiary sufficiency and reliability. First, there are no readily available published standards for VE certification, selection, or training. Although agency guidelines provide some rather sparse bases for identifying and qualifying medical experts based on requirements of the doctor's medical or comparable degree, license, and type of practice,[16] there is no corresponding guidance or requirements on what types of careers or degrees qualify one as a VE. A study of SSA adjudication by Professor Mashaw found that "[t]here is, indeed, no clear definition of what a vocational specialist or expert is. . . . [It] is in some sense a legal invention and includes persons whose training ranges from rehabilitation therapy through psychology to high school counseling."[17] The SSA's Vocational Expert's Handbook, provided to VEs, provides some minimal guidance and lists the nondefinitive requirements for an "ideal VE" as someone possessing:

> Up-to-date knowledge of, and experience with, industrial and occupational trends and local labor market conditions. An understanding of how we determine whether a claimant is disabled, especially at steps 4 and 5 of the sequential evaluation process. . . . Involvement in or knowledge of

> vocational counseling and the job placement of adult, handicapped workers into jobs. Knowledge of, and experience using, vocational reference sources of which the agency has taken administrative notice under 20 CFR 404.1566(d) and 416.966(d), including [the DOT].[18]

There is no examination, certification, licensing, apprenticeship, or other identifiable process even for demonstrating proficiency or knowledge in the above nondefinitive SSA qualification functions for so-called ideal (or any other) VEs. The Seventh Circuit's comments in *Donahue v. Barnhart* reflect a growing cynicism about the expertise of VEs and an "emperor's new clothing"[19] perception sometimes attendant to VE assessments in SSA cases:

> We asked the parties at oral argument what makes a vocational expert an "expert" (and where the information in the [DOT] came from). They did not know. Maybe both the authors of the [DOT] and the vocational expert in this case are talking out of a hat.[20]

In contrast, federal law requires that non-attorney representatives must possess a bachelor's degree or equivalent qualifications, pass a written examination administered by the SSA, secure professional liability insurance or equivalent, undergo a criminal background check, and regularly complete continuing education courses in order to represent claimants and receive compensation for services rendered sent directly by the SSA from claimants' retroactive disability awards.[21]

Second, VEs often rely on assertions of "personal knowledge" or "experience" to justify job incidence conclusions or to describe jobs whose requirements deviate from their DOT classifications and descriptions. When questioned, VEs often fail or decline to supply specific bases for the bottom-line conclusions supportable by "knowledge or experience." As described by the longtime social security disability lawyer and authority Barbara Samuels, the VE's "personal experience" justification raises many questions:

> Is the VE's experience recent or remote? Is it based on actual placement of individuals with disabilities? How many placements does it involve? Does it involve placement of people with the kind of impairments from which

> the particular claimant suffers, or a different population? Has the VE actually placed impaired individuals in the same occupations the VE now testifies the claimant can perform? What personal knowledge does the VE have of those particular placements? What is that personal knowledge based on (site visits? reports from some other source? etc.).[22]

One might add to that list the questions of how the VE extrapolated from personal placement experience to job incidence numbers in the entire economy[23] and several regions within it, or to considerations of adaptability based on age in this work adjustment assessment.[24]

Assuming a particular VE is established as having significant expertise relevant to SSA labor market work adjustment assessment inquiries, the courts have recognized in other contexts that "merely demonstrating that an expert has experience . . . does not automatically render every opinion and statement by that expert reliable."[25] In the more formal setting of federal judicial proceedings, for example, advisory notes to the relevant Federal Rules of Evidence on expert testimony (Rule 702) provide a common sense maxim:

> If the witness is relying solely or primarily on experience, then the witness must explain how that experience leads to the conclusion reached, why that experience is a sufficient basis for the opinion, and how that experience is reliably applied to the facts. The trial court's gatekeeping function requires more than simply taking the expert's word for it.[26]

Some courts have rejected VE testimony grounded solely or largely on VE experience, especially on job incidence testimony where the VE "didn't explain how impressions from unspecified past experience and 'knowledge' could enable him [or her] to determine numbers of particular jobs."[27] On a related issue, ALJs used to find that, in situations where the VE's testimony conflicts with the DOT—for example, where a VE finds that a claimant can perform a significant number of jobs in a DOT-defined occupation but without being medically or vocationally capable of performing various DOT-required tasks for the occupation in question—the VE's testimony and experience simply trumps the DOT and prevails. Many courts rejected that position causing the agency to alter policy.[28] The trending position of the courts, at least tacitly approved by the Supreme Court,[29] reflects further skepticism of the agency's naked reliance on VE experience or expertise; it recognizes a duty imposed on ALJs to identify and resolve apparent conflicts between DOT information and VE testimony. This duty "is not fulfilled simply by taking the VE at his word that his testimony comports with the DOT when the record reveals an apparent conflict between the VE's testimony and the DOT."[30] Instead, "the ALJ has an affirmative obligation to identify any 'apparent' conflict and to resolve it [and] the failure to properly discharge this duty means the ALJ's decision is not supported by substantial evidence."[31]

Third, there are no prescribed standards for assessing the reliability of the methodological bases required for validating job incidence numbers or non-DOT job characteristics evidence, and this evidence is often produced through questionable job data, statistics, and methodologies. As Judge Posner observed in his 2016 book:

> I recently became curious about the source of the statistics that vocational experts trot out in social security disability hearings. I discovered to my surprise that there is no reliable source of such statistics—in fact, . . . vocational experts' estimates of the number of jobs of different types in different parts of the country appear to be made out of whole cloth.[32]

Although the current approach to ensuring reliable expert testimony in federal judicial proceedings based on Rule 702 of the Federal Rules of Evidence[33] and the Supreme Court's opinion in *Daubert v. Merrell Dow Pharmaceuticals, Inc.*[34] and its progeny is not categorically binding in administrative adjudications,[35] the principle that expert testimony should be based on reliable methodology also enjoys solid grounding in administrative law. The Seventh Circuit in *Donahue v. Barnhart* has explained that, in evaluating the substantiality of VE testimony under the substantial evidence standard of review applied to SSA and most other agency adjudications,[36] "[e]vidence is not substantial if . . . conjured out of whole cloth."[37]

The SSA and vocational experts face a particular methodological challenge in supplying the job incidence testimony to meet the agency's work adjustment burden. The SSA's established occupational taxonomy for work in the U.S. labor market, the DOT, has not been updated in more than thirty years and has been deemed obsolete by the U.S. Department of Labor.[38] As mentioned previously, the DOT only supplies occupational titles with job duties and requirements; it does not supply job incidence data. Therefore, an additional data source is needed for such job incidence estimates.

In addition, and partially as a result of the DOT's obsolescence, there are no known data sources available for identifying the number of jobs within the economy and in various regions strictly by DOT-defined occupational codes that utilize DOT descriptions of and requirements for jobs. The principal source of job number data is the Occupational Employment Statistics (OES) produced by the U.S. Department of Labor's Bureau of Labor Statistics (BLS), which relies on a non-DOT classification system known as the Standard Occupational Classification (SOC).[39] Whereas the DOT's classification system contains more than 13,000 occupational codes and titles for work in the economy, the SOC system contains only 867 such codes.[40] Although there are various crosswalks for locating the far more numerous 13,000-plus DOT code occupations within the 800-plus broader SOC-coded occupational groups to which job numbers are maintained,[41] the methodology of simply extrapolating from one to the other has significant shortcomings.

For example, if there are 1.4 million jobs listed through Department of Labor statistics data as pertaining to a single SOC occupational group and ten different DOT occupational codes are identified as falling within that specific SOC group, how many jobs can be properly attributed to any one of the ten DOT occupational codes within that single SOC group? Can one simply assume that one-tenth of those jobs (140,000) are attributable to the single DOT occupation in question, from that group of ten, where a VE has identified that single occupation as the one to which an SSA claimant can make a work adjustment? The methodology of assuming that jobs within the DOT-coded occupations are evenly distributed within a broader SOC occupational grouping has been referred to as the "equal distribution" method and has received some pushback from the courts. A leading decision on the topic from the Seventh Circuit,[42] *Chavez v. Berryhill*,[43] explained some of the problems with this methodology:

> The use of one system to supply the job titles and another to provide the number of jobs creates a matching problem: *a one-to-one correlation does not exist.* When a VE identifies an SOC code and the number of jobs in that code, that number approximates (at best) the number of positions within a DOT job group—not the specific DOT job title that the VE identified as suitable for a particular claimant. Vocational counselors have recognized that this crude data matching is highly inaccurate and thus are advised not to perform this analysis in other areas of their practice (when they are not testifying in a disability hearing).[44]

The court also pointed out some of the obviously anomalous results of this methodology. Borrowing largely from an example in *Chavez*, the separate DOT occupations of "Cook" (DOT# 313.361.014—cook at restaurants and hotels) and "Chef de Froid" (DOT# 313.281–010—designs "artistic food arrangements for restaurants" such as "molding butter into artistic forms") might fall under the same SOC occupational group of "Cooks, Restaurants" (SOC #35–2014), and there are ten DOT occupations included in this single SOC group.[45] BLS data in the OES reports that there are approximately 1.4 million jobs in the cooks, restaurants SOC (35–2014) occupational group.[46] It does not take much intricate or sophisticated knowledge of the labor market to know that, of the 1.4 million cook/restaurant jobs, it is unlikely in the extreme that there are an equal number of "Chefs de Froids" as there are ordinary cooks in regular restaurants and hotels or that each would represent approximately 10 percent of the 1.4 million total or 140,000 such jobs each under this broader SOC occupational group.

In *Chavez*, the court proceeded to reject the VE's application of such an equal distribution methodology to find 108,000 unskilled, light work, bench assembler/small parts assembler (DOT #706.684–010) jobs in the economy. The court pointed out that a software program (JobBrowser Pro) using a form of "occupational density" analysis found that only 800 such jobs remained in the entire national economy and that the VE's rejection of the 800-job estimate as significantly low in the VE's opinion—without any other reasoning other than his "experience" and consultation with unidentified others—was insufficient to support the 108,000 job number obtained though the equal distribution method.[47]

As such, the court set aside this decision because of "the possibility that the VE's job numbers were conjured out of whole cloth."[48]

Another problem with this methodology is matching the DOT job descriptions with the current job data linked to the SOC codes in light of the DOT's staleness and declared obsolescence. Do the current jobs really include the DOT job requirements and only such requirements when these DOT code descriptions have not been updated in more than thirty years and, in many cases, in more than forty years? The SSA's regulations on past relevant work specify that jobs performed more than fifteen years from the onset of disability are no longer "relevant" because "[a] gradual change occurs in most jobs so that after 15 years it is no longer realistic to expect that skills and abilities acquired in a job done then continue to apply."[49] Although not part of the identified issues raised in *Chavez*, can one assume that the bench assembly DOT occupational code, last updated in 1979,[50] reflects the current skills and demands of such work in today's labor market? This position is largely an automobile assembly-line position requiring

> repetitive tasks on assembly line to mass produce small products, such as ball bearings, automobile door locking units, speedometers, condensers, distributors, ignition coils, drafting table subassemblies, or carburetors: Positions parts in specified relationship to each other, using hands, tweezers, or tongs. Bolts, screws, clips, cements, or otherwise fastens parts together by hand or using handtools or portable powered tools.[51]

More than forty years later, there is a significant possibility (if not likelihood) that much of this work has been altered by computerization requiring additional worker skills. Additionally, other functions have likely been fully automated, thereby eliminating many such jobs, and some of the remaining work has likely been outsourced and otherwise substantially diminished in the current American economy.[52]

Indeed, the bench assembler occupation is one of the ten most utilized jobs in SSA decisions to deny benefits based on determinations of ability to make a successful work adjustment.[53] The other DOT occupations on this SSA ten-most-utilized list include such obviously altered if not obsolete occupations such as the number-one go-to occupation used in almost 10 percent of all work adjustment (step 5) agency benefit denials: unskilled, sedentary "Addresser" (DOT #209.587-010—addressing envelopes, cards and packages *by hands and typewriters*).[54] This job has not been updated since 1977.[55] This list also includes such occupations as unskilled photocopy machine operator (the third most used), which has likely been automated to oblivion as full-time work, and (the fifth most used) unskilled, sedentary "surveillance system monitor," for which there is much literature describing that this occupation has become a more skilled and physically demanding position after 2001 (post-9/11).[56]

A further problem is the process for confronting and questioning VE methodology and source materials at SSA disability hearings. VEs rarely supply the bases of their job incidence and work adjustment testimony and are typically not questioned on or requested to disclose such source materials by the ALJs. In the approximately 60 percent of SSD or SSID cases when claimants are represented by attorneys[57]—that is to say, persons with some skill (or with the reasonable expectation of skill) in cross-examination of witnesses (as opposed to hearings in cases with claimants who appear without representation or with non-attorney or lay representatives)—sometimes claimants' counsel request VE supporting materials in order to question or cross-examine the bases of the VE testimony.[58] In such circumstances, ALJs rarely order disclosure of VE source materials or grant requests for administrative subpoenas seeking such materials.[59] The VE's bottom-line job incidence numbers conclusion provides the basis for the ALJ's denial decision, and the VE's methodology and data supporting that job incidence testimony remain undisclosed.[60]

A split among the U.S. courts of appeals developed on the question of what to do in these circumstances. The Court of Appeals for the Seventh Circuit held that claimants represented by counsel who question the VE's bases are entitled to have the ALJ "make an inquiry (similar though not necessarily identical to that of Rule 702 [of the Federal Rules of Evidence]) to find out whether the purported expert's conclusions are reliable."[61] More specifically, the Seventh Circuit has held that while the VE "is free to give a bottom line, . . . the data and reasoning underlying that bottom line must be available on demand."[62] Otherwise the ALJ's decision predicated on that VE testimony cannot be said to be supported by substantial evidence.

However, the Seventh Circuit has also held that the failure to question the VE's methodology or bases for testimony at the hearing would ordinarily preclude raising the issue of inadequate support for the VE's testimony or conclusions on appeal of that hearing decision when seeking judicial review by a federal district court.[63] Presumably, the Seventh Circuit's "raise it or waive it" approach to VE testimonial reliability is limited to cases where the claimant is represented by counsel, as it is predicated on the opportunity to cross-examine an expert on the methodological reliability of his or her testimony. This is a task that a lay representative or lay claimant cannot reasonably be expected to undertake. Thus, in self-represented ("pro se") or non–attorney representation cases, the heightened duty to develop the record on behalf of unrepresented or underrepresented claimants should compel ALJs to specially inform the claimant of the VE reliability issues and even question the VE's supporting methodology and bases on the claimant's behalf.[64] For example, in one case where the ALJ asked only one question of the VE—whether the jobs were consistent with the DOT—and did not elicit the VE's methodology for reaching his job numbers testimony, the Seventh Circuit found that the ALJ failed to meet "the duty to develop a full and fair record" on behalf of an unrepresented claimant and had "no reasoned basis to accept the VE's jobs number estimates."[65]

Moreover, in *Sims v. Apfel*, the Supreme Court held that the SSA's informal, nonadversarial, inquisitorial adjudicative model is inconsistent with the prudential requirement that claimants raise or "exhaust" issues to the SSA appeals council in order to preserve those issues from waiver upon judicial review, regardless of whether claimants are represented.[66] Although the Court in *Sims* reserved the question of the application of "issue exhaustion" at the ALJ hearing stage,[67] its reasoning applies with greater force at the hearing level, where the inquisitorial adjudicative model is at its apogee given that the ALJ has a duty to raise issues for the claimant and government alike and because the SSA's hearing-level regulations do not require issue exhaustion.[68] Thus, the Seventh Circuit's approach to VE reliability arguably did not go far enough and is inconsistent with the Supreme Court's issue-exhaustion reasoning in *Sims*, even as applied to represented claimants. However, the circuit courts remain divided on the potential applicability of ALJ hearing-level issue exhaustion on issues that could be identified at the hearing stage, although this general exhaustion issue is pending before the Supreme Court at the time of this writing.[69]

Other federal appeals courts have also expressly rejected the Seventh Circuit's broader approach to VE testimony as going too far and have accepted contested VE testimony despite the VE's failure to supply, or the ALJ's refusal to compel, such supporting evidence or methodology.[70] Those courts have reasoned that, because admissibility of expert testimony and evidence in administrative hearings is not governed by *Daubert*, *Kumho*, or Rule 702, "no additional foundation is required" for the VE's testimony other than the VE's "recognized expertise."[71] Accordingly, for substantial evidence purposes, the ALJ may reasonably credit the VE's testimony without articulation of methodology or the requested disclosure of supporting materials but simply "on the basis of the expert's professional experience and clinical judgment."[72]

The Supreme Court granted certiorari to resolve this circuit conflict in *Biestek v. Berryhill*.[73] In *Biestek*, the claimant was a former construction worker whose degenerative disc disease and other impairments prevented him from continuing that work.[74] His disability benefits application for the contested time period was denied after an ALJ determined he could make a successful adjustment to other work. At the hearing on this claim, the VE testified that Biestek could perform alternative, less demanding unskilled sedentary work in the occupations of bench assembler (for which there were 240,000 jobs in the economy) and sorter (for which there were 120,000 such jobs).[75] When Biestek's attorney asked the VE for the source of those job numbers, the VE referenced the Bureau of Labor Statistics and "her own individual market surveys."[76] When the attorney then requested the opportunity to review the surveys purporting to support these job numbers, the VE refused, stating that the surveys were confidential because they were part of her client files.[77] When the attorney then suggested that the VE simply "take the client names out of the survey" to protect their confidentiality, the ALJ interjected and ruled that he would not require the VE to produce these surveys in any form.[78]

When Biestek's appeal of his benefits denial eventually reached the Sixth Circuit, the court expressly rejected the Seventh Circuit's rule that VE source material and data supporting the job incidence testimony must be provided when requested. The Sixth Circuit instead cited with approval the Second Circuit and Ninth Circuit positions that "a [VE]'s recognized expertise provides the necessary foundation for his or her testimony [and] no additional foundation is required."[79] Additionally, in the court's view, the ALJ weighed the objection to the VE's testimony by counsel yet accepted this testimony, and "responsibility for weighing the credibility of witnesses belongs to the ALJ, who in this case acceptably fulfilled that obligation."[80]

The Supreme Court accepted certiorari review on the question proffered by the petitioner (Biestek):

> whether a vocational expert's testimony can constitute substantial evidence of "other work" available to an applicant for social security benefits on the basis of disability, when the expert fails upon the applicant's request to provide the underlying data on which that testimony is premised.[81]

In opposing the petition for certiorari, the government reframed the question presented for review as

> [w]hether the administrative law judge in this Social Security disability benefits case erred in crediting the vocational expert's opinion, which was based upon the expert's professional experience, without requiring disclosure of the expert's confidential files.[82]

While the certiorari petition was pending, the SSA attempted to dissuade the Court from accepting review on the petitioner's broader issue by pointing to a then-new, 2017 version of the SSA's Vocational Expert's Handbook, which made clear that VEs "'should have available at the hearing, any vocational resource materials [on which they] are likely to rely' and that they 'should be able to thoroughly explain what resource materials [they] used and how they arrived at [their] opinions.'"[83]

In its 2019 decision affirming the Sixth Circuit's judgment, a majority of the Supreme Court answered in the negative the petitioner's question upon which certiorari was granted, but it did so without addressing the SSA's reframed question about the sufficiency of the VE evidence in Biestek's individual case. In so doing, the Court decoupled the procedural question of process fairness—basing decisions essentially on a secret record supporting the VE's testimony and denying access to that record to the claimant—from the substantive question of evidentiary sufficiency under the substantial evidence appellate review standard—whether VE work adjustment testimony could ever be deemed legally sufficient under such circumstances.[84]

Having framed the substantive evidentiary sufficiency inquiry as one involving such a broad categorical proposition, the Court then denied the necessity of the sought-after categorical VE source-material disclosure rule. It did so not based on any facts in Biestek's case but instead on a hypothetical claimant's case where the Court theorized sufficient support for the VE's testimony could be found without the nondisclosed evidence. It stated:

> Suppose an expert has top-of-the-line credentials, including professional qualifications and many years' experience; suppose, too, she has a history of giving sound testimony about job availability in similar cases (perhaps before the same ALJ). Now say that she testifies about the approximate number of various sedentary jobs an applicant for benefits could perform. She explains that she arrived at her figures by surveying a range of representative employers; amassing specific information about their labor needs and employment of people with disabilities; and extrapolating those findings to the national economy by means of a well-accepted methodology. She answers cogently and thoroughly all questions put to her by the ALJ and the applicant's lawyer. And nothing in the rest of the record conflicts with anything she says. But she never produces her survey data. Still, her testimony would be the kind of evidence—far "more than a mere scintilla"—that "a reasonable mind might accept as adequate to support" a finding about job availability.[85]

Because of the existence of this possible—albeit highly unlikely—hypothetical case, the petitioner's pursuit of a categorical absolute rule applicable in all situations was a bridge too far.

While the majority made clear that it had no opinion about the legal sufficiency of the VE evidence in Biestek's case as that specific question was not petitioned,[86] it offered some guidance for the case-by-case evaluation of VE evidence in future litigation. First, the Court found that "[o]f course, the [VE] testimony would be even better—more reliable and probative—if the [VE] had produced supporting data."[87] In so reasoning, the Court noted that in "the handbook given to vocational experts, the agency states: 'You should have available, at the hearing, any vocational resource materials that you are likely to rely upon' because 'the ALJ may ask you to provide relevant portions of [those] materials.'"[88] Therefore, providing such supporting data "would be a best practice for the SSA and its experts [a]nd of course, a different (maybe less qualified [than the hypothetical] expert) failing to produce such data might offer testimony that is so feeble, or contradicted, that it would fail to clear the substantial-evidence bar."[89] Second, the Court found that "[s]ometimes an expert's withholding of such data, when combined with other aspects of the record, will prevent her testimony from qualifying as substantial evidence [such as] if the expert has no good reason to keep the data private and her testimony lacks other markers of reliability."[90]

Third, the Court found that courts "may properly consider obstacles to such questioning [of VEs] when deciding how much to credit an expert's opinion."[91] Fourth, the Court pointed out that "even without specific data, an applicant may probe the strength of testimony by asking an expert about (for example) her sources and methods—where she got the information at issue and how she analyzed it and derived her conclusions"; it cited the Seventh Circuit's *Chavez* case (see above) with approval for that proposition.[92]

It is still too soon since the 2019 *Biestek* decision to gauge the decision's longer-term effects on VE work adjustment testimony in the SSA's hearing-level adjudicative processes. Despite the absence of a broad prophylactic rule mandating VE presentation of supporting source material and data in all cases under all circumstances, the guidelines articulated by the *Biestek* majority offer protection against simply accepting VE testimony based solely on "experience" or unidentified data and failing to discuss the methodology leading to bottom-line job incidence conclusions. The agency will be pressured by claimant representatives to comply with the now-declared VE "best practices" (in accordance with the SSA's Vocational Expert's Handbook) of ensuring that VEs bring to the hearing anticipated supporting materials for the VE's job incidence testimony.[93] The lack of good reasons for nondisclosure of these materials should be additionally held against the VE testimony, and the ALJ must permit questioning and cross-examination on the VE's methodology even when supporting data is not available. Specifically, that questioning can include inquiries along the lines of that outlined in *Chavez*, cited with approval by the Supreme Court, which had revealed deficiencies in job incidence testimony procured through equal distribution methodology. While the appellate standard of review is the deferential "substantial evidence" standard, at the hearing "the administrative law judge must base the decision on the *preponderance of the evidence* offered at the hearing or otherwise included in the record"[94] and the VE evidence must meet that preponderance requirement.

Moreover, while the majority declined to consider the merits of Biestek's individual case, the three dissenting justices (Neil Gorsuch, Ruth Bader Ginsburg, and Sonia Sotomayor) did so, and each found the VE's testimony in Biestek's case insufficient as a matter of law. Justices Gorsuch and Ginsburg would have reversed on the broad categorical proposition, as they reasoned that the reliance on secret evidence to support proof burdens in agency adjudication is tantamount to misuse of the official notice doctrine[95] (presumably because, at a minimum, official notice requires advance notice and a meaningful opportunity to rebut such officially noticed, otherwise unpresented evidence).[96] However, with respect to Biestek's specific case, Gorsuch and Ginsburg also interpreted the majority opinion and reasoning as reflecting the view that when lower courts decide the merits of "real world cases like Mr. Biestek's" they "may—or even should find the substantial evidence test unmet."[97] They reasoned:

> If clearly mistaken evidence, fake evidence, speculative evidence, and conclusory evidence aren't substantial evidence, the evidence here shouldn't be either. The case hinges on an expert who (a) claims to possess evidence on the dispositive legal question that can be found nowhere else in the record, but (b) offers only a conclusion about its contents, and (c) refuses to supply the evidence when requested without showing that it can't readily be made available. What reasonable factfinder would rely on evidence like that? It seems just the sort of conclusory evidence courts have long held insufficient to meet the substantial evidence standard. And thanks to its conclusory nature, for all anyone can tell it may have come out of a hat—and, thus, may wind up being clearly mistaken, fake, or speculative evidence too. Unsurprisingly given all this, the government fails to cite

> even a single authority blessing the sort of evidence here as substantial evidence, despite the standard's long history and widespread use.[98]

Similarly, Justice Sotomayor, in her separate dissenting opinion addressed only to Biestek's specific case, reasoned that

> the expert offered no detail whatsoever on the basis for her testimony. She did not say whom she had surveyed, how many surveys she had conducted, or what information she had gathered, nor did she offer any other explanation of the data on which she relied. In conjunction with the failure to proffer the surveys themselves, the expert's conclusory testimony alone could not constitute substantial evidence to support the ALJ's factfinding.[99]

Indeed, in issuing the first two major federal appellate decisions to explore *Biestek*'s implications in evaluating VE methodology to resolve an individual case on the merits, the Eleventh Circuit and Seventh Circuit appeared to offer an early vindication of the Gorsuch–Ginsburg *Biestek* dissent's prediction.[100] In *Goode v. Commissioner of Social Security*,[101] the Eleventh Circuit found the VE testimony deficient and insubstantial, and it vacated the decision and remanded the case for a new administrative decision.[102] The court specifically cited and quoted the Gorsuch–Ginsburg *Biestek* dissent to reject the SSA's position that the absence of binding federal evidentiary rules on the foundation for expert testimony supported testimony lacking ascertainable methodology.[103] It reasoned that "the fact that vocational expert testimony is admissible does not mean that it necessarily constitutes substantial evidence."[104]

Next, the Eleventh Circuit court, relying on the Seventh Circuit's *Chavez* decision, explained that the VE must have a reliable methodology.[105] In particular, the VE must address the "matching problem" from "using one system to supply the job titles [the DOT] and another . . . for the number of the jobs" based on the SOC.[106] This means that the VE, after figuring out the total number of jobs in a broad SOC occupational group, must take "an additional step in determining how many of those are the specific job or jobs that the claimant could perform."[107] In other words, the VE "must use some measure for associating SOC-based employment numbers to DOT-based job types."[108]

Because the vocational expert "did not take any further steps, or use any other methodology" to demonstrate the number of the 43,000 national and 1,000 regional jobs identified for the (very broad) "Food Processing Workers, All Others" SOC occupational grouping (SOC # 51–3099)—itself containing sixty-five DOT codes that were properly and approximately attributable to the VE-identified single DOT occupational code of bakery worker (DOT # 524.687–022)—in the VE's work adjustment assessment, the court held that the testimony was fatally deficient.[109] In short, "a finding based on unreliable vocational expert testimony is 'equivalent to a finding that is not supported by substantial evidence and must be vacated.'"[110]

Then, in *Brace v. Saul*,[111] the Seventh Circuit amplified its holdings in *Chavez* that a VE's job numbers estimate "must be supported with evidence sufficient to provide some modicum of confidence in its reliability" and that "the ALJ 'must require the VE to offer a reasoned and principled explanation of the method [the VE] used to produce it.'"[112] It also relied on its interpretation of the Supreme Court's majority opinion in *Biestek* as holding that VE "job-number testimony will survive review under the substantial-evidence standard as long as it rests on a well-accepted methodology and the expert describes the methodology 'cogently and thoroughly.'"[113] The Seventh Circuit further held that VE attempts to explain job numbers methodology that are "unintelligible," "jargon"-laden, "obscuring the process rather than elucidating it," or simply taking a "trust me" approach, fail to satisfy the substantial-evidence standard.[114] To underscore its holding, the appeals court quoted from the transcript a portion of the VE's explanation of his methodology for a job numbers estimate of 140,000 jobs in the occupations of call-out operator, semiconductor bonder, registration clerk, and counter clerk:

> Well, it's—it's that combination of, one, you are looking at the number of titles that are in that [OES] category[,] and then based upon the—my information that I have as far as how the frequency of those jobs are performed, then we do an allocation based upon weighting or re-weighting those allocations to get the estimates of the numbers.[115]

The Court found this passage of VE job incidence methodology testimony "entirely unilluminating," stating:

> Testimony that incants unelaborated words and phrases such as "weighting" and "allocation" and "my information that I have" cannot possibly satisfy the substantial-evidence standard. What allocations? How is the weighting and re-weighting performed? According to what criteria? And what is the unidentified "information" in the expert's possession?[116]

Finally, in reaching its determination that the ALJ's decision needed to be vacated and remanded due to the lack of substantial evidence in support of the VE's job numbers and the ALJ's work adjustment conclusion, the court also rejected the SSA's arguments that the claimant waived objection to the VE's methodology by stipulating and not objecting to the VE's qualifications and that, in light of the VE's large job numbers estimate, any methodological issues reflect only harmless error.[117] It reasoned that "a claimant need not object to an expert's *qualifications* in order to object to the expert's *methodology*,"[118] and "an unreliable job-number estimate cannot be considered reliable merely because it is large."[119]

PART THREE

The Conceptual and Adjudicative Structure of the Grid Regulations

6

"Gridding" the Labor Market Work Adjustment Assessment

The 1978 Mashaw-led study by the National Center for Administrative Justice that criticized the varying use and widely inconsistent outcomes of VE-laden SSA hearings and advocated greater use of government document–based official notice on a case-by-case basis[1] also suggested broader, more sweeping solutions. The agency "by regulation supported by appropriate administrative findings could specifically authorize the taking of official notice in designated cases."[2] It could also supply "better decisional standards . . . that reduce individual ALJ discretion by providing per se rules, presumptions or the like."[3] In commenting on this study's relationship to the agency's development of its medical-vocational regulations, the U.S. Court of Appeals for the Third Circuit in 1982 observed:

> In order to achieve greater uniformity in disability claim determinations, the Mashaw study considered three possible reforms. One was rejected out of hand as politically unacceptable and administratively cumbersome: namely, that each ALJ be instructed to make a finding of disability in only a certain percentage of the cases he reviews. The reform preferred by the authors was that a panel system be deployed—*i.e.*, three ALJs would consider the merits of each disability claim. As a purely statistical matter, the variance in outcomes between these panel decisions and the decisions presently rendered by ALJs sitting alone would be significantly less. Recognizing that such a three-judge approach might entail "quite staggering" administrative costs, the authors also recommended "the development and enforcement of better decisional standards . . . that reduce individual ALJ discretion by providing per se rules, presumptions, or the like." HHS, in developing the medical–vocational [grid] regulations, appears to have followed this last recommendation.[4]

The House Ways and Means Committee had also urged the agency to "explore the possibilities as to whether the definition of disability could be stated more specifically in the law or regulation[s], and whether more operational presumptions may be incorporated into its administration."[5] Thus, emboldened by Congress's "exceptionally broad" delegation of rulemaking authority,[6] the SSA responded to these calls for greater standardization, consistency, efficiency, and fairness in work adjustment determinations by promulgating the medical-vocational guidelines regulations[7] to accomplish this task. "Because parts are displayable as a simple chart or table, the medical-vocational guidelines are commonly called "the grid"—a usage [that], though technically limited to the tables themselves, commonly includes the attendant explanatory matter."[8]

The grid avoids both the obstacles to the use of official notice in case-by-case work adjustment adjudicative determinations and the shortcomings and burdens of producing reliable and supportable vocational expert evidence. It provides broad, across-the-board legislative rules based on non-rebuttable official or administrative notice of all three work adjustment inquiries for claimants who fit into certain medical-vocational profiles. In so doing, it satisfies the agency's burden of proof in such cases.[9]

The grid represents the agency's most concrete manifestation of Professor Mashaw's bureaucratic rationality model of administrative justice, articulated in his later comprehensive analysis of the SSA's disability adjudication process in his 1983 book *Bureaucratic Justice*.[10] Bureaucratic rationality elevates considerations of efficiency, consistency, and the pursuit of accuracy through hierarchical and rigid adherence to centrally formulated policies over fairness through greater, individualized evaluation. It thus privileges such centrally formulated bureaucratic decision making over more individualized approaches, such as standard judicialized adjudication processes or professional expert evaluation.[11]

In *Heckler v. Campbell*, the Supreme Court rejected a variety of challenges to the grid's validity. First, the Court clarified that properly empowered agencies may promulgate rules to resolve a class of factual issues in advance of individual adjudications:

> It is true that the statutory scheme contemplates that disability hearings will be individualized determinations based on evidence adduced at a

> hearing[,][] this does not bar the Secretary from relying on rulemaking to resolve certain classes of issues. The Court has recognized that even where an agency's enabling statute expressly requires it to hold a hearing, the agency may rely on its rulemaking authority to determine issues that do not require case-by-case consideration. A contrary holding would require the agency continually to re-litigate issues that may be established fairly and efficiently in a single rulemaking proceeding.[12]

Therefore, the grid rules conflict with neither the Social Security Act's requirement for individualized consideration of each claimant's case, contained in 42 U.S.C. § 423(d)(2)(A), nor the requirement that hearing decisions be based on evidence adduced at the hearing, contained in 42 U.S.C. § 405(b).[13]

Second, the Court also rejected assertions that the grid denied claimants the right to notice and the opportunity to rebut administratively noticed facts protected in explicit terms by the Administrative Procedure Act, 5 U.S.C. § 556(e),[14] and, more generally, by the Fifth Amendment's Due Process Clause.[15] It reasoned that the purpose of the rebuttal rights principle "is to provide a procedural safeguard: to ensure the accuracy of the facts of which an agency takes notice."[16] The rulemaking proceeding itself provided sufficient procedural protection to test the facts upon which the rule was based.[17]

Finally, the Court also observed that the plaintiff in *Campbell* did not challenge the grid's rulemaking proceeding itself or the sufficiency of the rulemaking record supporting the grid's work adjustment rules,[18] and the Court concluded that the record did not establish that the rule was arbitrary and capricious.[19]

The Sequential Evaluation Process

The grid is a component of the final step in the agency's promulgation of a five-step sequential evaluation process for disability benefits claims. The five-step process functions like a flow chart.[20] At each step, the process either resolves eligibility by finding that the claimant is disabled or not disabled, or it continues to the next step. The first step (step 1) evaluates whether the claimant is currently performing substantial gainful activity.[21] If claimants are engaging in SGA, then they are deemed not disabled and their claims are denied. If not, the process moves to step 2 for an evaluation of whether the claimant has a "severe" medically determinable physical or mental impairment, defined as an impairment that "significantly limits [the claimant's] physical or mental ability to do basic work activities."[22]

Step 2 is designed to distinguish disability applications from routine unemployment claims by denying benefits to persons who lack a true medical basis contributing to their unemployment. It allows denial of claims based on medical grounds alone to claimants found to be lacking a "severe" impairment. The courts have interpreted step two narrowly as a de minimis screening device or "slightness" standard to weed out frivolous or trivial claims since the Act generally requires consideration of more than merely medical factors—age, education, and prior work experience—in determining disability.[23] The agency must also consider the combined effects of claimants' impairments and limitations to determine if their cumulative effect is more than de minimis, or slight, under this step.[24]

If the claimant does have a severe impairment, the process continues to step 3 to determine whether the claimant's impairments are so severe that they meet or equal the criteria of the listings of impairments.[25] The listings are the successor to the administrative schedule or catalogue of automatically disabling impairments developed at the outset of the SSA disability program.[26] Because impairment severity for the listing is set at a very high level,[27] it is employed by the agency as a presumptive screening device to lock in claims the agency deems likely indicative of an inability to perform SGA, and it preserves administrative resources required for a fuller evaluation of such cases.[28] Thus, if the impairment meets or is equivalent in severity to the requirements of the listings, SSA grants the claim. If not, the process continues to step 4.

Steps 4 and 5 involve claims that cannot be resolved through medical evidence alone "and address the more complex medical–vocational aspects of the disability standard."[29] These last two steps both rely on the agency's assessment of the claimant's "residual functional capacity." RFC is a measure of how claimants' medical limitations affect their ability to perform work functions.[30] The RFC assessment first requires an assessment of the claimant's exertional, or strength-related, limitations. The agency's exertional RFC assessment corresponds to the DOT's classification of jobs by exertional requirements (sedentary, light, medium, heavy, and very heavy) and is based on limitations that restrict an individual's ability to do strength-related work activities: walking, standing, sitting, lifting, carrying, pushing, and pulling.[31]

Nonexertional limitations are all restrictions that are not strength-related as described above.[32] They include limitations that are sensory (visual, auditory, tactile); postural (stooping, climbing, kneeling, crouching, balancing, crawling); manipulative (fine/gross dexterity, reaching); environmental (restrictions from dust, gas, heat, cold, moisture, allergens, mold, chemicals, heights, or dangerous machinery in the work environment); and mental (cognitive or psychiatric restrictions).[33] While regulations and case law often use "impairment" terminology, agency guidance clarifies that "medical impairments" and symptoms, including pain, are not intrinsically exertional or nonexertional. The functional limitations or restrictions caused by medical impairments and their related symptoms are categorized as exertional or nonexertional.[34] Nonexertional limitations must also be factored into RFC; for example, even a claimant with an exertional RFC for very heavy work may lack the mental RFC for meaningful employment.

Step 4 then examines whether the claimants, given their RFC, are able to perform jobs or occupations that they had done in the past.[35] A claimant's past work is "relevant" if it was performed within the last fifteen years, has lasted long enough to be learned, and constituted SGA.[36] A claimant is capable of performing PRW, or past relevant work, if he or she retains the RFC to perform either the actual functional demands and duties of a particular past relevant job or the functional demands and job duties of the occupation as generally required throughout the economy.[37]

If the clamant can perform his or her PRW, the agency will deny the claim; if not, the process continues to step 5, the final step.[38] Only at step 5 does the process fully address the statutory medical-vocational disability standard and the labor market work adjustment inquiries. In step 5, the SSA determines whether work "exists in significant numbers" in the economy to which the claimant can make a work adjustment, considering his or her age, education, work experience, and RFC.[39] If so, the claimant is not disabled; if not, the claimant is disabled and entitled to benefits.[40] The sequence utilizes the grid and sometimes VE testimony to facilitate step 5's "other work" determination.

The grid is a series of matrices providing decisional rules based on administrative notice of the availability or nonavailability of a significant number of jobs to which the claimant can make a work adjustment. The grid's rules directly apply and supply rules of immediate decision only to claimants with solely exertional medical limitations and only in situations where a claimant's medical-vocational profile coincides precisely with the criteria of a rule.[41] In such situations, the grid's rules provide the work adjustment decisional result and may not be rebutted through contrary VE testimony or otherwise.[42]

The Grid Tables and Methodology

The grid includes three tables based, respectively, on RFCs for sedentary, light, and medium work with decisional rules based on the combination of those RFCs with various permutations of age, education, and work experience. Age is divided into four categories: closely approaching retirement age (sixty to sixty-four); advanced age (fifty-five to fifty-nine); closely approaching advanced age (fifty to fifty-four); and younger individuals (below fifty).[43] Education is also apportioned into four categories: high school or above, limited (seventh to eleventh grade), marginal (sixth grade or below), and illiterate.[44]

A 2020 Social Security Ruling (SSR 20-1p) provides further internal guidance on "illiteracy" and the educational categories.[45] Persons should fall into the "illiteracy" category if they "cannot read or write a simple message such as instructions or inventory lists even though [they] can sign [their] name"; in the "marginal education" category if they have the "ability in reasoning, arithmetic, and language skills that are needed to do simple, unskilled types of jobs"; in the "limited education category" if they have "ability in reasoning, arithmetic, and language skills, but not enough to allow a person with these educational qualifications to do most of the more complex job duties needed in semi-skilled or skilled jobs"; and in the "high school or above" category if they have the "abilities in reasoning, arithmetic, and language skills acquired through formal schooling at a 12th grade level or above."[46] The illiteracy category reflects the "inability to read or write a simple message" in any language."[47] SSA "will generally find that an individual who completed fourth grade is able to read or write a simple message and is therefore not illiterate" unless the individual can provide "relevant evidence" of illiteracy from various delineated categories to counter this presumption.[48]

The illiteracy category in the past embraced either illiteracy or the inability to communicate in English. However, effective April 27, 2020, the SSA eliminated the inability to communicate in English as an educational factor when evaluating disability claims. The SSA suggested that there have been changes in the national workforce because the inability to communicate in English was first included in the grid rules in 1978 and various research and data "led us to conclude that this category is no longer a useful indicator of an individual's educational attainment or of the vocational impact of an individual's education for the purposes of our programs."[49] The agency also indicated that social security programs have an increasingly "international reach," and the elimination of inability to communicate in English as a vocational factor is an acknowledgment that, because "education in any language may provide vocational advantage," it "is no longer a useful indicator of an individual's educational attainment or of the vocational impact of an individual's education because of changes in the national workforce."[50]

It is unclear what data supported the conclusion that lack of English-language communicative ability no longer affects ability to retain unskilled work in the increasing service sector of the economy or for some of the top-ten most commonly cited occupations cited by VE's in work adjustment assessments in SSA decisions denying benefits that require regular telephone communication. Those occupations include: (#5) unskilled, sedentary, Surveillance System Monitor, DOT #379.367–010 ("notifies authorities by telephone of need for corrective action[;] . . . telephones police or other designated agency to notify authorities of location of disruptive activity") and (#10/tie) unskilled, sedentary, Call-Out Operator, DOT #237.367–014 ("fulfill subscribers' requests, using telephone[;] . . . [t]elephones subscriber to relay requested information").[51]

Work experience is categorized as "none," "unskilled," "semi-skilled," or "skilled." Claimants in the latter two categories will be placed into a different grouping, presuming greater work adjustment potential, if deemed to possess transferable skills to other skilled or semiskilled work. The semiskilled and skilled categories can be categorized further, maximizing presumptive work adjustment ability at the fully skilled level.[52] Where a claimant's characteristics (i.e., RFC, age, education, and work experience) "exactly" meet the combination of those in a grid rule, the rule directs a decision in the case.[53] Table 6.1 is displayed as an example:

TABLE 6.1. Residual Functional Capacity: Maximum Sustained Work Capability Limited to Light Work as a Result of Severe Medically Determinable Impairment(s)

Rule	Age	Education	Previous work experience	Decision
202.01	Advanced age	Limited or less	Unskilled or none	Disabled.
202.02	......do	......do	Skilled or semiskilled—skills not transferable	......Do.
202.03	......do	......do	Skilled or semiskilled—skills transferable[1]	Not disabled.
202.04	......do	High school graduate or more—does not provide for direct entry into skilled work[2]	Unskilled or none	Disabled.
202.05	......do	High school graduate or more—provides for direct entry into skilled work[2]	......do	Not disabled.
202.06	......do	High school graduate or more—does not provide for direct entry into skilled work[2]	Skilled or semiskilled—skills not transferable	Disabled.
202.07	......do	......do	Skilled or semiskilled—skills transferable[2]	Not disabled.
202.08	......do	High school graduate or more—provides for direct entry into skilled work[2]	Skilled or semiskilled—skills not transferable	......Do.
202.09	Closely approaching advanced age	Illiterate	Unskilled or none	Disabled.
202.10	......do	Limited or Marginal, but not Illiterate	......do	Not disabled.
202.11	......do	Limited or less	Skilled or semiskilled—skills not transferable	......Do.
202.12	......do	......do	Skilled or semiskilled—skills transferable	......Do.
202.13	......do	High school graduate or more	Unskilled or none	......Do.
202.14	......do	......do	Skilled or semiskilled—skills not transferable	......Do.
202.15	......do	......do	Skilled or semiskilled—skills transferable	......Do.
202.16	Younger individual	Illiterate	Unskilled or none	......Do.
202.17	......do	Limited or Marginal, but not Illiterate	......do	......Do.
202.18	......do	Limited or less	Skilled or semiskilled—skills not transferable	......Do.
202.19	......do	......do	Skilled or semiskilled—skills transferable	......Do.

TABLE 6.1. Continued

Rule	Age	Education	Previous work experience	Decision
202.20	......do	High school graduate or more	Unskilled or none	......Do.
202.21	......do	......do	Skilled or semiskilled—skills not transferable	......Do.
202.22	......do	......do	Skilled or semiskilled—skills transferable	......Do.

1 See 202.00(f)
2 See 202.00(c)

The grid also concretely resolves both the somewhat elusive adaptability and job incidence inquiries (also known as adjustment to the statutory "work which exists in significant numbers" inquiries) that have vexed the courts and commentators based on the calculus of factors and categories for exertional RFC, age, education, and work experience described above. Social Security Ruling 83-10 explains how the grid resolves these issues:

> When the medical-vocational rules were promulgated, administrative notice was taken of the fact that it was possible to identify, at the unskilled level, approximately 200 sedentary occupations; approximately 1,600 sedentary and light occupations; and approximately 2,500 sedentary, light and medium occupations, each representing numerous jobs in the national economy. (By "administrative notice" we mean our recognition that various authoritative publications identify occupations which exist in the national economy; these sources are listed in sections 404.1566 and 416.966 of the regulations.) Thus, as related to RFC, the occupational base considered in each rule consists of those unskilled occupations identified at the exertional level in question. . . .
>
> The Issue of Work Adjustment
>
> In the situations considered in the numbered table rules (those indicating decisions of "Disabled" as well as "Not disabled"), an individual has the RFC to perform a full range of the unskilled occupations relevant to the table. Each of these occupations represents numerous jobs in the national economy. *However, the individual may not be able to adjust to those jobs because of adverse vocational factors.*
>
> The issue of whether a work adjustment is possible involves a determination as to whether the jobs whose requirements can be met provide an

> opportunity for adjusting to substantial and gainful work other than that previously performed. Accordingly, *the issue of work adjustment is determined based on the interaction of the work capability represented by RFC (the remaining occupational base) with the other factors affecting capability for adjustment—age, education, and work experience.*
>
> Each numbered rule in Appendix 2 includes an administrative evaluation which determines whether a work adjustment should be possible. In each instance, the issue is decided based on the interaction between the person's occupational base as determined by RFC with his or her age, education, and work experience.[54]

Close examination of the grid's methodology, coupled with the addition of occupational base job data, more fully elucidates how the adaptability and job incidence questions are resolved within the contours of the grid's adjudicative framework. The grid tables are predicated on the existence of 200 unskilled sedentary occupations, 1,400 unskilled light occupations, and 900 unskilled medium occupations for a total of 2,500 unskilled occupations in the national economy at these RFC levels.[55] There is a quantum of jobs within the national economy for each particular occupation.[56] SSA regulations and guidance contain no estimates of the number of jobs within the occupations that are administratively noticed in the grid but do state that the job figures were derived from a variety of publications.[57] The precise number of jobs within the various respective unskilled occupational bases is difficult to ascertain partly because job numbers change each day with the elimination or addition of individual job positions. However, a common source of job data utilized by vocational experts—the Occupational Employment Quarterly II (OEQ), prepared by the U.S. Publishing Company using SOC data—estimates that there were 749,661 unskilled sedentary, 9,371,638 unskilled light, and 7,768,451 unskilled medium jobs in the national economy in the fourth quarter of 2018.[58] Thus, as a rough estimate, in light of the OEQ methodological data uncertainties described herein,[59] the "not disabled" conclusions based on the grid rules for claimants who can perform a full range of sedentary, light, or medium work reflect determinations that the presence of approximately 750,000, 10,000,000, or 17,770,000 jobs, respectively, is insufficient. Those job numbers do not represent "work which exists in significant numbers" in the national economy to which such claimants can make a work adjustment in light of their particular combinations of RFC, age, education, and work experience.

Take the situation under the grid of a fifty-five-year-old, high school–educated claimant, with an unskilled heavy work history, who can no longer perform the exertional demands of that work but can perform a full range of both sedentary and light work, and the actual job tasks of the millions of jobs in the combined unskilled sedentary and light work job bases. If the only question is job performability, the claimant would lose; this claimant can perform the job tasks involved in the full range of light and sedentary occupational bases representing millions of jobs in the economy. However, grid rule 202.04 reflects administrative notice that the claimant cannot adapt or make work adjustments to a large enough number of those jobs to meet the "significant numbers" statutory standard in light of the confluence of adverse medical and vocational limitations. Such a claimant is therefore disabled.[60]

The grid, therefore, reflects administrative notice that the approximately 10 million jobs, derived from the 1,600 combined light and sedentary occupations, are not a sufficiently significant number of jobs in the economy to which this claimant can make a work adjustment. However, a claimant with the identical vocational profile, if exertionally limited to an RFC for a full range of medium work, would be found not disabled under grid rule 203.14.[61] In that scenario, the grid takes administrative notice that the addition of the medium work occupational base to the light and sedentary job base—for a total of 2,500 occupations reflecting approximately 17.7 million jobs—would represent a significant number of jobs to which this claimant could make a work adjustment. Accordingly, for this claimant's profile, 1,600 occupations and 10 million jobs are not sufficiently significant to permit a work adjustment under the grid; however, 2,500 occupations and 17.7 million jobs are sufficient.

7

Gaps in the Grid

The Grid's Adjudicative Framework and Occupational Base Erosion Approach for Work Adjustment Assessments in Grid Exception Cases

Writing for the Seventh Circuit Court of Appeals in 1989, Judge Richard Posner described how "[t]he grid has simplified the determination of social security disability claims and brought about a modicum of uniformity in the adjudications of almost a thousand administrative law judges. But it has the characteristic flaws of mechanical rules, and one of them is that it abounds in gaps."[1] Posner suggested that in the grid's "gaps"—grid exception cases—the ALJs will need to "get off their grids" and call vocational experts to address work adjustment determinations.[2]

While the grid provides a direct and immediate rule of decision in claims involving only exertional restrictions, the agency's regulations and rulings provide that the grid's adjudicative framework should still be employed in cases where the grid's per se rules are not directly applicable. This includes cases where the administratively noticed grid occupational and job bases are eroded by the presence of nonexertional limitations, falling between two exertional RFC categories or lacking the exertional RFC for even a full range of sedentary work. It also includes the situation where the grid's unskilled occupational bases are not eroded, but are instead enhanced, by a claimant's possession of transferable skills. In this situation, a claimant otherwise deemed disabled under the grid's administratively noticed unskilled occupational bases might be presumed capable of making a work adjustment to the larger occupational base reflected by the addition of semiskilled or skilled occupations to the unskilled bases.[3]

In any of these four grid gap (or grid exception) situations, additional vocational evidence or administrative notice would usually be required to determine the extent of the erosion or enhancement of the job base in order to decide the ultimate question of whether a claimant could make a work adjustment to a significant number of jobs in the economy. In these grid exception cases, agency guidance mandates use of the grid as a "framework" to determine the extent of erosion or enhancement of the applicable grid labor market occupational bases in making the "off the grid" work adjustment/significant numbers assessment. Thus, for example, in the situation of a common grid exception—claimants with both exertional and nonexertional limitations—the grid regulation's explanatory section provides:

> (2) . . . [W]here an individual has an impairment or combination of impairments resulting in both strength limitations and nonexertional limitations, the rules in this subpart are considered in determining first whether a finding of disabled may be possible based on the strength limitations alone and, if not, the rule(s) reflecting the individual's maximum residual strength capabilities, age, education, and work experience provide a *framework for consideration of how much the individual's work capability is further diminished in terms of any types of jobs that would be contraindicated by the nonexertional limitations.*[4]

Further guidance is supplied in a 1983 Social Security Ruling (SSR 83-14), which provides:

> The Exertionally Based Rules as a Framework for Evaluating Additional Impairments of a Non-Exertional Nature
> Where a person cannot be found disabled based on strength limitations alone, the rule(s) which corresponds to the person's vocational profile and maximum sustained exertional work capability (Table No. 1, 2, or 3) will be the starting point to evaluate what the person can still do functionally. The rules will also be used to determine how the totality of limitations or restrictions reduces the occupational base of administratively noticed unskilled sedentary, light, or medium jobs.
>
> A particular additional exertional or nonexertional limitation may have very little effect on the range of work remaining that an individual can perform. The person, therefore, comes very close to meeting a table rule which directs a conclusion of "Not disabled." On the other hand, an additional exertional or nonexertional limitation may substantially

> reduce a range of work to the extent that an individual is very close to meeting a table rule which directs a conclusion of "Disabled." . . .
>
> The Disability Determination or Decision Based on a Combination of Exertional and Nonexertional Impairments. . . .
> In reaching judgments *as to the sufficiency of the remaining exertional job base (approximately 2,500 unskilled medium, light, and sedentary occupations, approximately 1,600 unskilled light and sedentary occupations, and approximately 200 unskilled sedentary occupations)*, there are three possible situations to consider:
>
> 1. Where it is clear that the additional limitation or restriction has very little effect on the exertional occupational base, the conclusion directed by the appropriate rule [in Tables] would not be affected.
> 2. Where it is clear that additional limitations . . . have significantly *eroded* the exertional job base set by the exertional limitations alone, the remaining portion of the job base will guide the decision.
> 3. Where the adjudicator does not have a clear understanding of the effects of additional limitations on the job base, the services of a V[E] will be necessary.[5]

Taking the previous example of a fifty-five-year-old, high school–educated, unskilled claimant with an exertional RFC for medium work, suppose that the claimant is further limited due to nonexertional limitations and is moderately limited in following even simple instructions, using judgment, and working at an efficient pace due to borderline intellectual functioning; has environmental restrictions precluding work around heat, cold, moisture, dust, or certain allergens due to severe asthma; and has a postural restriction on any reaching over the shoulder with the dominant arm due to the residuals of multiple rotator cuff injuries. Suppose further that a VE testifies that this claimant can perform twenty occupations, reflecting 400,000 jobs in the economy notwithstanding these limitations. Under the ad hoc approach of ascertaining significant numbers without reference to the grid's occupational and job base numbers (and without considering issues of adaptability based on age and the combination of adverse statutory vocational factors), the claimant would likely be found not disabled.[6] However, if the grid framework approach described in the agency guidance above is interpreted as requiring analysis of the extent to which the grid's occupational and job bases are eroded by the nonexertional limitations and the comparative size of the remaining bases, then this claimant would be found disabled.

If limited to an RFC for the full range of light work, this claimant would be determined unable to make a work adjustment to a significant number of jobs under the grid. The ability to perform 1,600 occupations, reflecting approximately 10 million jobs, would not be enough. Since the claimant would be found not disabled if capable of adjusting to 2,500 occupations, reflecting 17.7 million jobs under the medium work grid table and applicable rule, there has been quite substantial erosion of the applicable occupational and job bases due to the non-exertional limitations. Thus, using the grid as a framework and the grid's administratively noticed work adjustment conclusions and job bases as the parameters for this inquiry, the claimant, capable of performing only twenty occupations and 400,000 jobs, must be found disabled.

Indeed, agency guidance suggests that, if the remaining occupational and job bases identified by the VE after erosion due to nonexertional limitations are significantly closer to the light work bases under which the claimant would be found disabled than to the medium work occupational base under which the claimant would be denied, then the claimant should be found disabled. Although drafted to address the grid exception for claimants who fall between two exertional categories, another 1983 Social Security Ruling (SSR 83-12) further clarifies the framework approach for using the various occupational bases as principled and consistent comparison points for the "significant numbers" work adjustment inquiry. It provides:

> 2. If the exertional level falls between two rules which direct opposite conclusions, i.e., "Not disabled" at the higher exertional level and "Disabled" at the lower exertional level, consider as follows:
>   a. An exertional capacity that is only slightly reduced in terms of the regulatory criteria could indicate *a sufficient remaining occupational base* . . . for a finding of "Not disabled."
>   b. On the other hand, if the exertional capacity *is* significantly reduced . . . , it could indicate *little more than the occupational base for the lower rule* and could justify a finding of "Disabled."

c. In situations where the rules would direct different conclusions, and the individual's exertional limitations are somewhere "in the middle". . . . for exertional ranges of work, more difficult judgments are involved as to *the sufficiency of the remaining occupational base* to support a conclusion as to disability.[7]

Similar regulatory language and Social Security Rulings set out this approach for using the grid's adjudicative framework to assess erosion of the applicable occupational and job bases and the comparative size of the remaining job base for other grid exceptions. This includes the exceptions for claimants with solely nonexertional impairments/limitations,[8] those with exertional RFCs in between applicable exertional categories as discussed,[9] or those younger individuals lacking the RFC to perform even a full range of sedentary work.[10]

Despite the apparent clarity of the agency subregulatory guidance and principled consistency generated from using essentially the same occupational and job bases and identical adaptability considerations to determine the significant numbers/work adjustment issue in grid and grid exception cases alike, courts and agency ALJs have only occasionally invoked it.[11] Whether applying a form of the grid framework occupational base erosion approach in the Social Security Rulings (SSRs) or categorically rejecting it, the courts have rarely evinced full understanding of this methodology. A series of Ninth Circuit cases reveals the adjudicative confusion surrounding the collision of the SSRs' grid framework erosion approach to labor market work adjustment determinations in grid exception cases, and the perseverant ad hoc, inconsistent approach that predated the grid.

In *Swenson v. Sullivan*,[12] a grid exception case involving a claimant with exertional and nonexertional limitations, the Ninth Circuit appeared to embrace the above grid framework job base erosion approach. In *Swenson*, a claimant with an exertional RFC for light work would have been found disabled based on the sedentary work grid but not on the light work grid based on exertional capacity along with his age, education, and work experience. Because the claimant possessed nonexertional limitations, a VE testified. The VE found, however, that the combination of the claimant's nonexertional and exertional limitations eroded the remaining job base to less than the number of jobs in the grid's light work job base under which the claimant would be found not disabled based on exertional capacity alone.[13] However, after also finding that there were several thousand jobs that the claimant could perform, the VE "expressly concluded that such jobs existed in significant numbers."[14]

The court remanded the case, finding the VE's testimony contradictory.[15] The court first noted that when the grids are "not fully applicable" because of the existence of nonexertional limitations, they nonetheless provide "a framework for consideration of how much the individual's work capability is . . . diminished . . . by the nonexertional limitations."[16] It then held, in what it determined to be an issue of first impression, that the grid framework continued to apply, even in cases involving grid exceptions where a VE has testified about job numbers.[17] It stated:

> Regulatory language supports the position that an ALJ *may not find* from vocational testimony that a claimant, deemed disabled under the grids, nonetheless could perform a substantial number of jobs and not be disabled. . . . *We interpret the regulations to require the Secretary to reject vocational testimony that is inconsistent with the grids' overall framework*. . . . If an expert testifies that a claimant would be disabled under the grid best approximating the totality of his exertional and nonexertional limitations, the Secretary must reject, or specify reasons for accepting, any significantly inconsistent testimony, such as that the claimant nonetheless could perform a substantial number of jobs.[18]

A few months after *Swenson*, the Ninth Circuit clarified the binding nature of the grid's adjudicative framework and the importance of the adaptability assumptions that are quantified through the grid's work adjustment/significant numbers methodology. Based on the record in *Cooper v. Sullivan*,[19] the ALJ's primary error was the failure to acknowledge that a claimant's nonexertional "manipulative impairment" based on osteoarthritic changes in one hand, the lower back, and both wrists also limited the claimant exertionally to light work.[20] However, by the time the claimant's case had proceeded to the hearing stage, she had exceeded age fifty-five. Thus, for part of the adjudicative period in question, she was under fifty-five years old, and for part of it she was older.[21]

Because the ALJ had characterized the claimant's condition as entirely nonexertional, he had procured VE testimony in lieu of the grid.[22] Based on VE testimony that the claimant could perform "several jobs" whether she was fifty-five or under, the ALJ utilized the ad hoc, "common sense" significant numbers approach and concluded that the claimant was not disabled.[23]

The Ninth Circuit reversed the ALJ's decision, finding that the grid's light work rule mandated a finding of disability for the period after her fifty-fifth birthday.[24] It then remanded the remainder of the case for a determination of the extent of the light work job base's erosion due to the claimant's nonexertional manipulative limitations for the period in which she was under age fifty-five.[25] It observed that different grid-based job adaptability assumptions applied to the pre- and post-fifty-five period.[26] The court observed that the claimant would be found disabled based on the sedentary grid rule and not disabled under the light work grid rule for the adjudicative period in which she was between fifty and fifty-five years old.[27] The court then offered a rare judicial explanation of the grid's methodology and adaptability assumptions. It stated the following:

> Moreover, we note that the ALJ erred when he disregarded the assumptions which underlie the grids. Based on the vocational expert's testimony, the ALJ concluded that Mrs. Cooper was not disabled because "[c]onsidering the types of work which the claimant is still functionally capable of performing in combination with her age, education and work experience, *she can be expected to make a vocational adjustment to work which exists in significant numbers in the national economy.*" However, *the regulations stress that the most difficult problem that a claimant such as Mrs. Cooper faces is that of adapting to a new job.* Indeed, that is the reason that the grids direct the conclusion that claimants like Mrs. Cooper are disabled. "[F]or individuals of advanced age [i.e., age 55 or older] who can no longer perform vocationally relevant past work and who have a history of unskilled work experience . . . the limitations in vocational adaptability represented by functional restriction to light work warrant a finding of disabled." Just as the ALJ may not disregard the grids' conclusion of disability, he also may not disregard the assumptions which underlie the grids.[28]

Several years later, a different panel of the Ninth Circuit in *Moore v. Apfel*[29] rejected the grid framework erosion approach entirely and returned to the ad hoc "common sense" methodology in a case similar to *Swenson* involving a claimant whose nonexertional limitations reduced his remaining job base. In *Moore*, the record established that the job base erosion from nonexertional restrictions would place the remaining job base closer to the sedentary work grid job base under which the claimant would be deemed unable to make a work adjustment as opposed to the light work grid job base under which he would lose.[30] Nevertheless, the court rejected the erosion argument and did so without even mentioning *Swenson*. It reasoned that SSR 83-12 merely required that the ALJ obtain VE testimony when a claimant's nonexertional limitations "put him between two [grid] rules."[31] Once the VE testifies that "a person with [the claimant's] profile [can] perform substantial gainful work in the economy," that is all that is required.[32] Since the number of jobs the VE identified (125,000 nationally and 7,700 regionally) was consistent with prior numbers the court had accepted as "significant" under the ad hoc approach to this issue, no comparison to the job bases in the grid and use of the grid's adaptability presumptions were required.[33]

A few years later, in *Lounsburry v. Barnhart*,[34] the Ninth Circuit appeared to return to the grid framework approach and rejected the ad hoc "common sense" approach in a case where it cited *Cooper* and *Swenson* but not *Moore*. *Lounsburry* concerned a claimant with transferable skills, so the issue involved the potential expansion of the grid's unskilled job bases due to these skills rather than erosion. Without sufficient transferable skills, the grid would deem the claimant unable to make a work adjustment.[35] A VE testified that the claimant's skills transferred to only one occupation representing 65,855 jobs in the national economy.[36] The ALJ found that these numbers reflected a sufficiently "significant number" of jobs to justify a nondisability decision.[37]

In analyzing the ALJ's reasoning, the Ninth Circuit was forced to confront a potential conflict in the language of different sections of the agency's regulations and the question of whether the phrase "significant range of work" under Section 202.00(c) of 20 C.F.R., Pt. 404, App. 2, and the SSRs, referenced the significance of the range of occupations administratively noticed in the grid or the significance of an ad hoc "range of jobs" untethered to the grid's occupational or job bases. Section

202.00(c) provides that "for individuals who are of advanced age . . . who have only skills that are not *transferable to a significant range of unskilled or semi-skilled work* that is within the individual's [RFC], . . . the limitations in vocational adaptability represented by a[n] [RFC for] light work warrant a finding of disabled."

However, the agency's general regulation implementing the 1967 amendments' "significant numbers" requirement provides that "[w]ork exists in the national economy when there is a significant number of jobs (*in one or more occupations*) having requirements which you are able to meet."[38] In reconciling these provisions, the court also applied SSR 83-10 and its reference to a "full range of work" reflecting "substantially all *occupations* within that exertional range." In reversing the agency, the court stated the following:

> SSR 83-10 defines the phrase, "Range of Work," as "*Occupations* existing at an exertional level." It defines the related phrase, "Full Range of Work," as: "All or substantially all *occupations* existing at an exertional level." *Id.* at *16 (emphasis added). We thus construe the phrase "significant range of . . . work" in Rule 202.00(c) to require a significant number of occupations. The record in this case establishes that Lounsburry's skills would transfer to precisely one occupation at her [RFC]. One occupation does not constitute a significant range of work. Rule 202.00(c) directs a finding of disability for Lounsburry.[39]

While the court in *Lounsburry* found strong support for looking to the grid's "occupational" bases to determine whether the VE's testimony supported the claimant's ability to make a work adjustment, a grid framework analysis based on the SSRs, as described above, and the grid's job bases would have led to the same conclusion. The VE's identification of only 65,000 additional skilled jobs to the unskilled job base (10,065,000 jobs) would not be deemed to sufficiently expand the light work job base away from the approximately 10 million jobs under which the claimant would prevail to a close enough point on the continuum to the 17.7 million jobs in the medium work job base under which the claimant would lose. Thus, under either a grid occupational or job base approach, the claimant should prevail. This claimant would lose only under an ad hoc approach in which an adjudicator is free to find any number of jobs or occupations sufficient to meet the significant numbers or "significant range of work" requirements and no adaptability work adjustment assessment based on grid-noticed presumptions need be undertaken.

A few years later, the Ninth Circuit limited *Lounsburry* to its facts and applied the ad hoc approach in another case involving expansion of the grid's occupational base due to the presence of transferable skills. In *Tommassetti v. Astrue*,[40] a VE testified that the claimant's transferable skills expanded the applicable grid sedentary occupational base by only one occupation (semiconductor assembler) reflecting 100,000 jobs nationally.[41] The ALJ concluded that this testimony established a significant number of jobs sufficiently to augment the unskilled sedentary base and found the claimant not disabled.[42] The claimant argued that one single additional occupation could not establish a "significant range of skilled work" to infer sufficient grid occupational base expansion under *Lounsburry*.[43] The court, however, explicitly rejected *Lounsburry*'s applicability and implicitly rejected the entire grid adjudicative framework by reasoning simply that the light work rule uses different language than the sedentary rule.[44]

Although the claimant pointed out that the analogous grid sedentary work explanatory provision, § 201.00(e) in 20 C.F.R., Pt. 404, App. 2,[45] also requires that a claimant's skills be transferable to "a significant range of skilled work" within the claimant's RFC,[46] the court inexplicably dismissed the argument in one sentence as "not persuasive."[47] The court concluded its opinion with the observation that the grid was adopted "to increase consistency and promote uniformity" in step 5 disability determinations.[48] Thus, the claimant's efforts to "graft" the light work rules onto the sedentary work rules "would lead to the confused and arbitrary application of grid rules from one exertional category to other exertional categories and might in effect . . . defeat the goal of consistency and uniformity in decision-making that the particularized grids serve."[49]

The *Tommassetti* decision reflects manifest error in two respects. First, the court misread the common "significant range" language in both the sedentary and light work grid transferable skills explanatory sections (202.00(c) and 201.00(e)). More fundamentally, the court—in the name of consistency and uniformity—rejected the grid adjudicative framework's significant numbers/work adjustment approach from the

SSRs that is based on consistent and uniform, grid-derived occupational and job bases. Ironically, instead it applied an ad hoc, arbitrary approach that varies dramatically from case to case, bears no relationship to the occupational and job bases used for all claimants who fit within the grid's criteria, and fails to incorporate any considerations of adaptability based on age.

In 2020, the Ninth Circuit re-embraced *Lounsburry* without even mentioning *Tommassetti*. In *Maxwell v. Saul*,[50] the court found that a fifty-five-year-old claimant limited to light work who would be disabled under the grid if unskilled, and who possessed skills transferable to only two occupations according to the VE, was disabled because two occupations did not reflect a "significant range of work" under *Lounsburry* and Section 202.00(c).[51] The court expressly rejected the agency's argument that these two occupations contained "numerous jobs" that should be viewed as independently meeting the "work which exists in significant numbers" requirement in the Social Security Act under an ad hoc approach to the work adjustment inquiry.[52] The court had "considered and rejected that argument in *Lounsb[u]rry*."[53] While declining to announce a bright-line rule of how many occupations reflect a significant range of work under Section 202.00(c), it reasoned that because, by definition, "range requires more than one occupation, a significant range must require more than two."[54]

The Seventh Circuit Court of Appeals has been somewhat less equivocal in its continued adherence to the ad hoc approach. In *DeFrancesco v. Bowen*, that court first expressed solicitude for the grid framework and described the occupational base erosion process under SSR 83-12.[55] Later in this opinion, however, the court appeared to embrace the ad hoc approach based on VE testimony of jobs that was untethered to the grid's framework, "spirit," or "formula" for ascertaining whether the jobs identified are sufficiently significant in number under the Act where a case falls within the grid's "gaps."[56]

Then, in *Fast v. Barnhart*, the Seventh Circuit more definitively rejected the grid framework erosion approach in a case involving a claimant with solely nonexertional limitations.[57] In so doing, the court construed provisions of the applicable SSR narrowly and in isolation, misinterpreted the facts in the Ninth Circuit's decision in *Swenson* (and thereby misconstrued its holding), and expressly reaffirmed the validity of an ad hoc work adjustment approach. First, the court rejected the plaintiff's request to use the grid as a framework for decision-making under the regulations and, in so doing, distinguished this case, which solely involved nonexertional impairments and limitations, from other cases where claimants suffered both exertional and nonexertional restrictions.[58] It reasoned that, in such a solely nonexertional case, SSR 85-15 and grid Section 200.00(e)(2) only require "that the grids should be given consideration."[59]

The Seventh Circuit similarly rejected reliance on the Ninth Circuit's *Swenson* decision to support use of the grid as a framework. In so doing, the court reasoned that *Swenson* was merely a distinguishable case where the claimant was disabled based solely on exertional limitations and the applicable grid rule and that the ALJ erred on that point by attempting to rebut the grid with vocational testimony contrary to the grid's conclusion.[60] Finally, the court rejected the plaintiff's attempt to have the court overrule an earlier case, *Lee v Sullivan*,[61] which had utilized an ad hoc approach to the work adjustment job incidence inquiry and sustained an unfavorable ALJ decision finding adjustment to 1,400 regional jobs in the economy sufficient.[62] The court concluded that the plaintiff's "rather odd argument that the grids must somehow be used as a framework has no support, and it conflicts with the common-sense rule that where the grids do not address a particular problem, the ALJ is entitled to rely on [VE] testimony."[63]

Although clarifying *DeFrancesco*'s ambiguities, at least in cases involving solely nonexertional limitations, the court's reasoning in *Fast* fails to supply a credible interpretation of SSR 85-15 and the SSR grid framework scheme. The court first incorrectly assumed that SSR 85-15 only "addresses the situation" in which a claimant suffers both exertional and nonexertional limitations. It then provides only that the grid "should" be "considered" in cases involving solely nonexertional limitations.[64] However, SSR 85-15's title expressly references the agency's methodology for using "[t]he [grid] rules as a framework for evaluating *solely nonexertional* impairments"[65] and mandates that decision makers *must* consider the grid "[ta]ble rules for specific case situations" in assessing whether "the person can be expected to make a vocational adjustment considering the interaction of his or her age, education or work experience."[66]

The court's decision expressly eschews reference to the grid rules in any fashion and also provides no mechanism for "consideration" of adaptability or "vocational adjustment" based on age and the interaction of other vocational factors as interpreted through the grid rules. Furthermore, the court failed to examine the framework methodology set out in the other Social Security Rulings discussed or cross-referenced in SSR 85-15 (such as 83-10, 82-41, and 83-12), which further clarify the applicability of the grid framework in grid exception cases.[67] The Seventh Circuit also misinterpreted the Ninth Circuit's decision in *Swenson* in its effort to distinguish it. *Swenson* did not involve a claimant who was deemed disabled based on exertional limitations alone. Rather, the Ninth Circuit in *Swenson* had set aside the agency's decision because a VE testified that the additionally limiting effects of the claimant's nonexertional restrictions eroded the claimant's remaining job base to a point where she might be found unable to make a work adjustment with reference to the grid's job bases.

More fundamentally, the Seventh Circuit in *Fast* reaffirmed its earlier ad hoc approach in *Lee*, which had held that 1,400 jobs was a significant number of jobs in a decision that did not even mention the grid's framework, adaptability issues, or any relevant SSRs. Thus, under the court's approach, a fifty-five-year-old claimant without transferable skills, who would be deemed disabled because he is unable to make a labor market work adjustment on the grid if exertionally limited to the grid's light work job base of 10 million jobs, could still be found not disabled and capable of making a successful work adjustment in an ad hoc grid exception analysis if not exertionally limited to light work but still able to adjust to only 1,400 jobs—reflecting 0.014 percent of that 10-million grid job base—due to other medical limitations. In other words, a claimant could be deemed capable of making a work adjustment with a severe mental impairment and a limitation to only 0.014 percent of the job base under which a claimant with an identical vocational profile, but suffering only the exertional consequences of arthritis, would be found disabled.[68] In summary, the Seventh Circuit's approach—using the grid's job bases only for cases involving strength-related impairments and limitations and the ad hoc approach for mental and other nonexertional impairments and limitations—sanctions significantly discriminatory, disadvantageous, and arbitrary treatment of claimants in the latter category based solely on disability type.

A few other circuit courts of appeals have discussed the general grid framework approach in grid exception cases with somewhat less relevant analysis than the Ninth and Seventh Circuits. The Third Circuit has offered further variation on this issue. It has interpreted the grid framework erosion approach and the ad hoc approach as alternative approaches that may be applied in the same case.[69] The Sixth Circuit, much like the Seventh Circuit but with less reasoning, has interpreted the Social Security Rulings narrowly to support continuation of an ad hoc approach.[70] The Tenth, Eighth, and Eleventh Circuits have adopted the ad hoc approach without giving extended relevant consideration to either the Social Security Rulings' grid framework erosion approach or the relationship of the VEs' ad hoc job numbers to the grid's job bases.[71]

The emerging case law on the grid framework reflects significant inter- and intra-circuit variation. Because the predominant ad hoc significant numbers approach to the work adjustment determination in grid exception cases conflicts with agency guidance, fails to accord full effect to statutory vocational factors (especially issues of adaptability based largely on age), and produces profound adjudicative inconsistency and markedly unequal treatment between grid and grid exception claimants, its usage should be curtailed by the agency and the courts. Part of the courts' confusion on this issue may reflect some degree of uncertainty over the legal significance of the Social Security Rulings implementing the grid framework. Although Social Security Rulings are not promulgated through APA rulemaking,[72] the agency, by promulgating an APA rule, has made SSRs binding on itself.[73] The agency is thus bound to follow Social Security Rulings in individual cases and cannot disregard them on an ad hoc basis.[74]

Furthermore, for the agency to disregard its own Social Security Rulings in this context, or to interpret them narrowly so as to permit an ad hoc approach in grid exception cases that is completely untethered from grid occupational and job base numbers and adaptability considerations based on age, would produce other administrative law and constitutional infirmities. Since the ad hoc approach sanctions the use of widely varying job numbers for each case—even for cases with highly similar facts—it is systemically arbitrary. The Third Circuit, commenting on the entirely ad hoc pre-grid work adjustment assessment process, explained:

> An agency that makes thousands upon thousands of individualized determinations as to disability each year will inevitably at times treat similarly situated persons differently. It is not surprising, therefore, that [the Department of Health and Human Services] was subjected to considerable criticism with respect to what some perceived to be the agency's failure to "produce predictable and consistent results." One academic study concluded, for example, that "(t)he inconsistency of the disability process is patent. Indeed, it is widely believed that the outcome of cases depends more on who decides the case than on what the facts are." Such a state of affairs, of course, is difficult to accept: "Perhaps no characteristic of a procedural system is so uniformly denounced as a tendency to produce inconsistent results. When disposition depends more on which judge is assigned to the case than on the facts or the legal rules, the tendency is to describe the system as lawless, arbitrary, or the like, even though the case assignment is random.[75]

Perhaps more significant, the use of dramatically lower and disadvantaging job numbers for labor market work adjustment assessments for persons with nonexertional limitations or other non-grid factors under the ad hoc approach raises arguable equal protection concerns.[76] Consider the following example: two construction workers performing heavy labor tasks for the same employer for the previous twenty years are seriously injured driving home from the construction site one day. They are each fifty-five years old, have an eleventh-grade education, and identical work histories characterized as semiskilled experience but without transferable skills to other work. One worker suffers a permanent mild spinal injury from the accident, preventing continuation of previous heavy construction work and producing exertional limitations to light work but with no other restrictions. The second worker suffers a concussion and permanent brain injury from the accident with the permanent loss of some cognitive functioning reflected in a significant drop in full-scale IQ to 69 and mental limitations in areas such as concentration, pace, judgment, and understanding instructions but no exertional restrictions. Both workers are unable to return to and perform their past construction work after the accident.

Both workers then apply for SSDI benefits. The first worker is immediately granted benefits based on grid rule 202.02 at step 5. Even though he is potentially capable of performing all the approximately 10 million jobs in the light work base, the grid directs the conclusion of the inability to make a successful labor market work adjustment to "work which exists in significant numbers" based on the claimant's age, education, work experience, and limitations. The second worker proceeds to an ALJ hearing, where a VE determines that the worker can perform only 20,000 jobs in the national economy based on the worker's severe brain injury, cognitive impairment, and limitations. An ALJ, utilizing the ad hoc or common-sense work adjustment approach at step 5 in this second case, and not the grid because the second worker suffers from nonexertional mental impairments and limitations, denies the claim based on finding the ability to make a work adjustment to "work which exists in significant numbers" in reliance upon the VE's testimony. Are these two agency determinations on claims by persons with identical vocational profiles with injuries from the same accident reconcilable? Are they supported by labor market data on the substantially greater adaptability to new jobs by persons with cognitive limitations and brain injury as compared to persons with spinal impairments and exertional limitations? Indeed, one might surmise that the second worker's identified cognitive limitations would impose greater impediments to learning and adapting to new work tasks and work environments than the first worker's exertional limitations to light work—that is, lifting no greater than twenty pounds and standing or walking no longer than six hours in a workday.[77]

At a minimum, government classifications must bear a rational relationship to a legitimate governmental interest under equal protection principles.[78] Neither the agency adjudicators that have employed the ad hoc approach to labor market work adjustment assessments nor courts that have sustained it have proffered rational means or legitimate ends for the widely disparate and disadvantaged adjudicative treatment of claimants in grid exception cases. A rational justification to support the comparative labor market work adjustment assessments for the two workers in the above example is not apparent. However, the use of the grid framework work adjustment approach in grid exception cases, in reliance on the agency's SSRs and utilizing the same vocational adaptability assumptions and occupational and job bases as are used in exertional limitation cases through the grid rules, would produce the same result for the first and second workers in the above example and supply greater consistency and fairness to this inquiry.

8

The Adjudicative Use of the Official Notice/Administrative Notice Doctrine in Grid Exception Cases

Another grid-interpretive issue that appears to have vexed the Social Security Administration and federal courts is the question of when or how limiting a potential grid exception–producing nonexertional restriction or impairment must be to mandate an "off the grid"[1] work adjustment assessment.[2] Because the grid's direct application is limited to claimants' exertional or strength-related medical impairments and limitations, adjudicators must determine when the presence of a nonexertional or non–strength related (i.e., mental, sensory, environmental, postural, or manipulative) impairment or limitation should preclude direct grid rule application. This issue expressly or implicitly also requires determination of the extent to which agency adjudicators may take official notice that a claimant's nonexertional limitation or impairment does not meaningfully erode the base of jobs in the grid's occupational base so as to mandate a more individualized work adjustment assessment beyond mere application of the grid tables and usually conclusive rules. Even before determining job base erosion due to nonexertional limitations or other grid exceptions, the agency is required to determine in the first instance whether a claimant possesses limitations that can potentially erode the relevant exertional job bases in a nontrivial way and thereby preclude direct application of the grid's per se rules when used to "lock-out"[3] and deny claims.

The grid regulations make clear that the vocationally limiting effects of nonexertional limitations have not been administratively noticed through the grid's legislative rules, and thus their presence precludes a conclusive determination of nondisability based on the grid tables' direct application. However, agency regulations provide scant guidance for determining how adjudicators should evaluate whether such nonexertional restrictions are sufficiently limiting to preclude direct application of the grid to deny claims. For example, when a claimant possesses nonexertional limitations such as blindness in one eye (monocular vision) or borderline cognitive limitations (IQ in the high 70s), are such impairments significant enough to preclude direct application of the exertional-based grid to deny benefits and to require VE testimony to determine the erosion of the grid's occupational and job bases and provide an individualized work adjustment assessment?

The grid has proven to be a tempting device for a busy agency confronting pressing mass-justice realities. The agency often attempts to shoehorn claimants with nonexertional limitations into a fully exertional category within a grid table to deny the claim by asserting—without vocational or labor market evidentiary basis—that the nonexertional limitations have no meaningful erosive impact on the grid's exertional occupational and job bases. Therefore, the agency determines that the grid rules may still be given direct and decisive effect to deny claims in such cases. Direct grid application averts the time and resources required to provide individualized VE work adjustment determinations based on the varied and less definable effects on jobs and the occupational base from nonexertional limitations. Where the grid applies directly, vocational expert testimony followed by either the grid job base erosion approach under the SSRs or an ad hoc approach to work adjustment is thus unnecessary.

The federal circuit courts of appeals are even more clearly divided on their approaches to the question of determining when nonexertional limitations preclude direct application of a grid exertional rule than they are on the appropriate step 5 labor market work adjustment approach in grid exception cases for determining whether "work exists in significant numbers" discussed above in chapter 7. The courts are in conflict on several basic questions: (1) Under what circumstances *may* adjudicators presume or take administrative notice of the extent of diminution or erosion of the grid's job bases due to the presence of nonexertional limitations without additional vocational or labor market evidence to support their non-erosion conclusions? (2) Under what circumstances *must* adjudicators utilize vocational testimony or other vocational or labor market evidence to support non-erosion conclusions? and (3) If the adjudicators take administrative notice of the lack of sufficient grid job base erosion due to nonexertional or other grid exception limitations, when must they provide claimants notice and the opportunity to rebut the non-erosion work adjustment conclusions?

The Ninth Circuit has held that agency adjudicators may determine, without vocational or labor market evidence, that even otherwise medically severe nonexertional limitations (i.e., limitations that have a significant or nontrivial impact on work-related functions)[4] do not meaningfully erode the occupational bases administratively noticed in the grid to which a claimant is deemed capable of making a work adjustment.[5] The First Circuit has adopted a similar approach.[6] While not announcing it as such, the Ninth and First Circuits have, in essence, authorized adjudicators to take unannounced and nonrebuttable administrative or official notice that even medically severe nonexertional limitations do not meaningfully erode the grid's labor market work adjustment conclusions that were developed for claimants with only exertional limitations. It reflects a form of official notice because the agency adjudicator is assuming a vocational or labor market fact—that a claimant's severe nonexertional limitations have a trivial erosive impact on grid's occupational base—without any direct proof of that fact through record evidence. Under this approach, the agency may simply rely on the grid's per se nondisability work adjustment rules as if the severe nonexertional limitations did not exist. Such is the case whether the adjudicator purports to have relied on direct application of the grid rule or to have only used the grid as a "framework" in this manner.[7]

In contrast, the Eighth Circuit has held that, where a claimant has a severe nonexertional impairment, "the Commissioner's use of the grids at step five, as opposed to VE testimony," reflects error.[8] The Fifth Circuit announced a similar rule, requiring that, where a claimant's nonexertional impairments or limitations have more than a "slight" or "minimal effect" on work activities, the agency may not satisfy its step 5 work adjustment burden of proof through reliance on direct application of the grid's rules.[9] The Eleventh,[10] Seventh,[11] and D.C.[12] Circuits appear to incorporate elements of the Eighth Circuit's approach of mandating resort to other vocational or job base evidence where a claimant's nonexertional limitations exceed a designated minimal medical "significance" threshold.

The Second,[13] Fourth,[14] Sixth,[15] and Tenth[16] Circuits have relied on standards that appear closer to those of the Ninth and First Circuits but are difficult definitively to categorize. They each purport to permit sole reliance on the grid's conclusive work adjustment rules unless adjudicators make the essentially vocational determination that nonexertional limitations significantly erode the applicable grid jobs bases (or the availability of the full range of work at the most applicable exertional level). However, these circuits frequently reject agency decisions for making grid framework non-erosion conclusions without any supporting vocational evidence from which non-erosion could be inferred.[17] These circuits have also not explicitly rejected the Eighth Circuit's explicit—or the Fifth, Seventh, Eleventh, and D.C. Circuits' implicit—requirement that vocational work adjustment evidence be produced in all cases where nonexertional limitations are deemed medically significant or nontrivial.

The Third Circuit is the only court of appeals that has consistently identified that this inquiry involves an analysis of the proper scope of the official notice doctrine.[18] In *Sykes v. Apfel*, the court analyzed the agency's sole reliance on a per se grid rule to determine that a claimant with a nonexertional impairment deemed "severe"[19]—one-eyed blindness (monocular vision)—could make a work adjustment to a significant number of jobs. The court first observed that "[th]e Social Security Administration has not conducted a rulemaking establishing either that the lack of binocular vision does not significantly diminish the occupational base for light work or more generally establishing common facts applicable to individuals with Sykes's set of impairments."[20] Accordingly, "[t]he grids do not purport to answer this question, and thus under *Campbell* the practice of the ALJ determining without taking additional evidence the effect of the nonexertional impairment on residual functional capacity cannot stand."[21]

The court then analyzed the propriety of the ALJ's de facto application of official notice of that non-erosion fact as a substitute for record evidence. In its official notice/administrative notice analysis, the court reiterated the two basic substantive and procedural "prerequisites" for application of the official notice doctrine under *Ohio Bell*: "First, the information noticed must be appropriate for official notice. Second, the agency must follow proper procedures in using the information, disclosing it to the parties and affording them a suitable opportunity to contradict it or 'parry its effect.'"[22] On the first substantive requirement, the court found that the doctrine "allow[s] adjudicators to take notice of commonly acknowledged facts, but official notice is broader than judicial notice insofar as it also allows an administrative agency to take notice of technical or scientific facts that are within the agency's area of expertise."[23] Nevertheless, the court declined to decide whether official notice of the lack of meaningful grid light work occupational base erosion from monocular vision met this substantive requirement.[24] It concluded that even if official notice were substantively appropriate, it would be procedurally inappropriate. "[T]he ALJ would have had to provide Sykes with notice of his intent to notice that fact and, if Sykes raised a substantial objection, an opportunity to respond."[25] The court concluded:

> On remand, if the ALJ intends to rely on official notice rather than additional vocational evidence to establish that Sykes's nonexertional impairment does not diminish his occupational base for light work, the ALJ must provide notice to Sykes that he intends to notice that the lack of binocular vision causes no diminution in the occupation base and give Sykes an opportunity to respond.[26]

The Third Circuit's approach further highlights the nonuniformity and conflict among the circuits on this issue. Indeed, the court in *Sykes* expressly interpreted several of the other circuits' approaches to the grid's nonexertional exception as more narrow than its own.[27] It has also admonished the agency to apply the *Sykes* standard in cases in the Third Circuit and to refrain from continuing to cite the Second Circuit's more ALJ speculative approach in *Bapp v. Bowen*.[28]

The agency has issued an acquiescence ruling in *Sykes* that also reveals ambiguity and confusion in the SSA's approach to this issue.[29] The agency issues so-called acquiescence rulings only where it determines that a "Court of Appeals holding conflicts with [its] interpretation of a provision of the Social Security Act or regulations and the Government does not seek further judicial review or is unsuccessful on further review."[30] The agency notes that *Sykes* differs from national policy in that agency adjudicators can presume non-erosion of the relevant grid occupational base without either vocational evidence or the procedural protections of the official notice doctrine—notice and rebuttal rights—in a wider variety of situations than *Sykes* permits.[31] Other than pointing to the "instance" where subregulatory adjudicative guidance in a Social Security Ruling supports a conclusion that a particular nonexertional limitation does not significantly erode the job base—an issue the agency also noted was expressly reserved in *Sykes* and thus not decided contrary to agency policy[32]—the agency offered no further clarity on adjudicators' authority to make non-erosion determinations.

The *Sykes* Acquiescence Ruling (as it is officially known in the SSA operations manual[33]) suggested only one way that agency policy differs from the *Sykes* holding: the agency does not "always consult" a vocational expert or other vocational evidence in nonexertional limitation grid exception cases.[34] However, neither does *Sykes* command such a result; it requires vocational evidence or the proper invocation of the official notice doctrine. Thus, with the possible exception of reserving the right to invoke de facto official notice of job base non-erosion without complying with the doctrine's due process and APA-based prerequisites, the agency has not identified any specific way in which *Sykes* is contrary to the SSA's national policy and adjudicative approach to the issue. In short, there is perhaps no substantive Social Security disability law issue for which there is greater adjudicative confusion and nonuniformity at present among courts and the agency alike, and the *Sykes* acquiescence ruling deepened that confusion.

Finally, in *Allen v. Barnhart*,[35] the Third Circuit addressed the issue reserved in *Sykes* concerning the use of the agency's examples of the potential erosive impact of various nonexertional limitations in its Social Security Rulings. The claimant in *Allen* had been found previously disabled based solely on severe psychiatric impairments, including bipolar disorder and manic-depressive disorder with "schizoid" features.[36] The ALJ had found that the claimant's condition had improved to the point that he had the capacity to perform "simple, routine repetitive work." Then, in reliance on the grid and Social Security Ruling 85-15, and without any vocational testimony, the ALJ determined that a restriction to "simple, routine repetitive work" would not erode the job base in any of the applicable exertional grid rules and thus justified terminating the claimant's benefits.

On appeal by the claimant, the agency asserted explicitly that it could rely on SSR 85-15 in lieu of record vocational evidence (and, implicitly, without proper invocation of the official notice doctrine) to determine that the claimant's nonexertional psychiatric restrictions did not erode the grid's occupational or job bases.[37] In rejecting the agency's argument, the court set two prerequisites for the use of Social Security Rulings in this context: one substantive and one procedural. First, "if the [agency] wishes to rely on an SSR as a replacement for a vocational expert, it must be crystal-clear that the SSR is probative as to the way in which the nonexertional limitations impact the ability to work, and thus, the occupational base."[38] Second, where use of a ruling is substantively proper, the claimant should ordinarily be provided "advance notice" and the opportunity to contest the ruling's suggested non-erosion conclusion.[39] The court reasoned that "the claimant should have the opportunity to consider whether it wishes to attempt to undercut the agency commissioner's proffer by calling claimant's own expert. Obviously, this requires notice in advance of the hearing."[40] It added some degree of ambiguity to this conclusion, stating:

> We think it only appropriate to give close scrutiny to the ALJ's reliance on a Ruling as satisfying the Commissioner's burden at Step 5 where the Commissioner has not previously advised or argued the clear applicability of the Ruling in advance of the hearing. In this way, while the Commissioner has the ability to satisfy its burden in this way, its doing so does not constitute an ambush whereby the claimant, who assumed he would have the opportunity to cross-examine a vocational expert, is left as a practical matter to merely argue against a Ruling in response to the Commissioner's proof.[41]

Typically, a claimant first learns that the ALJ has relied on an SSR when the ALJ issues a written decision denying benefits through application of the relevant grid rule. At that stage, there is obviously no opportunity to rebut the ALJ's official notice and/or application of the SSR and its applicability. The lower (district) courts within the Third Circuit are divided on whether the above final passages in *Allen* on advance notice and right to rebut grid SSRs reflect a mandatory or hortatory right to advance notice and the opportunity to rebut reliance on an SSR to satisfy the SSA's step 5 evidentiary work adjustment burden.[42] Basic principles of administrative law and constitutional law support the mandatory rebuttal right interpretation.

First, apart from this passage in *Allen*, the right to advance notice and opportunity to rebut official notice of the non-significant erosion of the occupational base in reliance on SSRs is compelled by the Fifth Amendment's Due Process Clause and the Administrative Procedure Act as well as the constitutional and legal requirements that agency decisions be based on evidence adduced at (not after) the hearing.[43] In upholding the grid regulations in *Campbell*, the Supreme Court recognized only a limited exception to the procedural protections guaranteed by the APA and the Due Process Clause for notice and rebuttal rights under the official notice or administrative notice doctrine as is long established in Supreme Court cases such as *Ohio Bell*. The *Campbell* Court found that the APA legislative rulemaking proceeding in which the grid regulations were legislatively promulgated itself provided sufficient procedural protection through notice and comment to test the facts on which the grid rules were based.[44]

The Supreme Court's reasoning in *Campbell* does not extend to Social Security Rulings that have not been promulgated through an APA legislative notice and comment process with procedural protections that provide a mechanism to test the facts on which subsequent non-rebuttable administrative notice is based. Accordingly, advance notice and the right to rebut administrative notice pursuant to a Social Security Ruling should still be compelled by the APA and the Due Process Clause, and this source of "evidence" of step 5 labor market, work adjustment information must be "adduced at the hearing" and not after the hearing for the first time in a final decision.

Indeed, based on related process concerns, the agency issued an internal memorandum clarifying that its ALJs may not take administrative notice of vocational expert interrogatories offered in prior hearings for use in subsequent ones. The agency reasoned that, since prior vocational expert opinion does not fit within *Campbell*'s legislative rule promulgation and has not gone through rulemaking's "procedural safeguards to ensure the accuracy of the facts contained therein," subsequent administrative notice of such prior vocational expert testimony would violate the requirement that decisions be based on "evidence adduced at the hearing."[45] It follows a fortiori that SSRs—which (unlike vocational interrogatory answers) may not even have been written by persons with vocational expertise, are not supplied under oath, have never been subject to cross-examination, do not include reference to any data or materials in support of their conclusions, and also have not been tested through the legislative rulemaking process—may not be used or "administratively noticed" in lieu of vocational evidence to satisfy the agency's step 5 burden of production without advance notice and the right to rebut such SSRs when "adduced" at the hearing.

Moreover, by using the SSRs as if they were formal, non-rebuttable, substantive rules of decision, or decisive "mini-grids" in nonexertional limitation cases, the agency would have effectively created legislative rules of decision in a class of cases without utilizing the legislative rulemaking process in the APA. This arguably reflects an unlawful end run on APA legislative rulemaking requirements in violation of the APA and administrative law principles. Rules with legislative effect may be adopted only through the notice and comment legislative process set out in the APA at 5 U.S.C. § 553 or through the even more formal "on the record" rulemaking requirements of the APA at 5 U.S.C. §§ 556, 557.[46]

In *Allen*, because the ALJ's mere conclusory reference to SSR 85-15 failed to supply the requisite "crystal-clear fit" between the non-erosion conclusions and the totality of the claimant's psychiatric limitations, the court set aside the agency's decision based on the first substantive prong without reaching the procedural notice and rebuttal rights issue.[47] However interpreted, *Allen* appears more clearly divergent from agency policy than *Sykes*, as it imposed plain limitations on the use of the agency's use of grid SSRs to deny claims that are contrary to national policy. Nevertheless, the agency has still failed to issue an acquiescence ruling in *Allen*.[48]

None of the Third Circuit cases has set a minimal medical threshold for use of its two-prong official notice approach to job base non-erosion.[49] The agency's authority to insist on such a threshold to winnow out frivolous or trivial nonexertional limitations and permit direct application of the grid in such situations is likely inherent in the authority supporting its nonseverity regulations.[50] However, just as the proper application of those regulations requires that even slight or minimal impairments and limitations must be considered in combination to evaluate whether they have a more than slight cumulative impact on basic work activities and permit a claim to proceed beyond step 2,[51] such a cumulative approach should also be employed to determine whether even slight nonexertional limitations can produce significant exertional job base erosion in the aggregate in making the step 5 work adjustment determination.

Coda

It is conceivable that an updated grid and duly promulgated grid regulations might be expanded to cover a larger range of circumstances than the grid's current exertional scope. This would be dependent on the presence and quality of methodologically reliable and accurate data supporting inclusion of such other restrictions in the grid's matrix format and presumptive rules. Perhaps a more sophisticated and multivariate calculus of factors and rules would be supported by the data. Unlike the attempts to manufacture "mini-grids" on nonexertional limitations through subregulatory guidance in the SSRs, the agency should pursue any such efforts at "gridding" nonexertional limitations into its rules that presume successful labor market work adjustments through transparent, participatory, and democratically accountable processes such as the notice and comment processes in the APA (5 U.S.C. §553 et seq.) utilized for agency regulations with full legal effect. This would avert the official notice doctrine and due process and APA violation issues emerging through the use of subregulatory guidance in non–APA notice and comment promulgated SSRs or ALJ speculation as evidence to support occupational base non-erosion conclusions.

For example, perhaps reliable data may permit the agency to quantify and generalize certain nonexertional postural or manipulative limitations to a degree comparable to the exertional limitations in the grid. Because mental impairments are so highly variable, it is less likely, however, that mental limitations could be sufficiently quantified in a manner that comports with the grid's matrix of generalized work adjustment presumptions. The SSA's past attempts at utilizing mental impairment findings and matrix rating systems to ascertain claimants' presumptive ability to perform unspecified, unskilled work were discredited by medical/psychiatric/psychological professionals and the courts alike and were specifically condemned in a class-action decision affirmed by a rarely unanimous Supreme Court.[52] This history counsels against removing mental limitations and other highly individualized and contextual nonexertional limitations from case-by-case assessments.

Any remaining "off the grid" assessments should still be informed by the grid's framework and by using, where needed, particularized vocational evidence on the extent of erosion of the grid's administratively noticed occupational bases attributable to these highly variable and individualized limitations. Use of the grid's framework in this manner promotes consistency and equity in adjudication as described above. In short, a properly updated and potentially expanded grid, and use of the grid's adjudicatory framework, can still provide consistent and nonarbitrary bases to circumscribe the labor market work adjustment assessment in mental impairment and other nonexertional or grid exception cases and promote the principles of greater bureaucratic rationality that its proponents lauded.

PART FOUR

The Empirical and Taxonomic Foundation for Labor Market Work Adjustment Assessments

9

The Dictionary of Occupational Titles in Work Adjustment Assessments

As established in Parts 2 and 3 of this book, both the grid and vocational expert work adjustment assessments are predicated on the DOT and on data sources purportedly linked to the DOT's occupational taxonomy. Indeed, whereas vocational expert assessments can be based on the most recent, albeit now thirty years old, edition of the DOT (the revised fourth edition of 1991),[1] the grid is predicated on an even more outdated 1960s-era version of the DOT and related publications when promulgated. The grid has not been meaningfully updated to reflect any of the fundamental structural changes in the U.S. economy over more than a half-century.

When the SSA promulgated the grid in 1978, the agency acknowledged that it had relied at least partially on the 1965 DOT third edition, which had been superseded by the fourth edition in 1977, even though the agency knew the 1965 data was no longer accurate in at least some areas.[2] The SSA's reasons for not incorporating material from the 1977 DOT were somewhat contradictory. The agency stated that the differences in "content and substance" between the 1965 and 1977 editions were so significant that they precluded "detailed analysis in the immediate future," or at least in time for the grid's promulgation.[3] At the same time, the agency declared that it "did not anticipate any major changes in job incidence or other occupational data."[4]

However, the 1977 DOT reflected some significant changes from the 1965 third edition. For example, the sedentary occupational base had diminished from 200 occupations in 1965 to only 137 occupations in 1977.[5] Also, while the grid still claims that 85 percent of the unskilled sedentary occupations are in the machine trades and benchwork categories,[6] the 1977 DOT edition noted "rapid changes in industrial technology."[7] With the advent of automation and computerization, the labor market landscape saw significant changes: "[T]he electronic computer came of age during this period with effects that were visible in virtually every sector of the economy."[8] Around this time, the U.S. labor force also experienced a substantial shift from manufacturing to service industries.[9] That the Department of Labor's 1977 edition of the DOT recognized these changes suggests that, by as early as 1977, the administration was aware that many of the machine trade and benchwork occupations administratively noticed in the grid were lost or altered due to labor market trends.

Nevertheless, the agency vigorously defended its use of 1960s-era DOT occupational titles and source data in the grid. Based on conversations with officials from the North Carolina Occupational Analysis Field Center—an organization that compiles data for Department of Labor publications—the SSA confirmed that there is "no precise updated data but that the regulatory estimate of approximately 200 sedentary unskilled occupations is still valid, because some of the 137 occupations in the [fourth] edition of the DOT comprise more than one of the separate occupations of which we take administrative notice."[10] In a 1982 decision authored by Judge (later Justice) Stephen Breyer, the First Circuit sustained the grid against claims that it was substantively invalid on account of its reliance on the 1965 DOT instead of the 1977 edition.[11]

While observing that "the numbers ha[d] declined from the [1965] to the [1977] edition," the First Circuit still concluded that "it ha[d] not been shown that the decline was so great that a rule premised on the earlier figures [wa]s now without foundation and that a failure to reconsider the rule [wa]s 'arbitrary.'"[12] Although not directly relating the issue to the grid's underlying data, the Second and Fourth Circuits have since invalidated the use of the 1965 DOT to support work adjustment assessments in grid exception cases.[13] Expressly labeling the 1965 edition "outdated," these courts explained that there are "substantial" differences between the two editions; the "[1977] Edition requires a much higher level of mathematical and verbal skills for most of the jobs at issue than d[oes] the [1965] Edition."[14]

Even so, the 1977 edition has also been questioned. As far back as 1980, the National Research Council (NRC) raised questions about the accuracy of the data and methodology underlying the 1977 DOT.[15] The NRC identified major deficiencies in the 1977 edition's source data and the occupational characteristics it created.[16] The NRC nevertheless concluded that, "[d]espite deficiencies" in several functions, the 1977 edition remained "the most comprehensive set of occupational characteristics currently available" and encouraged its continued use.[17]

By 1986, however, a Chicago-area study had obtained findings challenging the SSA's assumption of a significant unskilled sedentary occupational base.[18] The study found that only 2.4 percent of employers "reported having jobs that were sedentary, unskilled, and self-contained."[19] The study suggested that the discrepancy between the unskilled sedentary occupations identified in the grid and those found in the actual labor market was attributable to: (1) increasingly outdated source data; (2) significant transformations in the labor market due to decreases in the nation's manufacturing base due to international competition or otherwise; and (3) an increase in automation with a corresponding increase in the need for some particular skills in "almost all" of the clerical, technical, and professional occupations that represent the core of the "sit down" sedentary base.[20] The study concluded "that the existence and numbers of occupations claimed by the [SSA] [are] insignificant in the standard metropolitan statistical area of Chicago."[21] Although the study suggested that, based on the size and diversity of Chicago's business community, a similar inference could be drawn for the national economy, the study recommended that a comparable study be undertaken to analyze labor market conditions nationally.[22]

In 1991, the Department of Labor updated and revised the DOT. However, the 1991 version was only a partial revision and still relied mostly on job survey updates from the 1970s.[23] It still did not account for many of the broader labor market trends in the economy and was criticized for an overrepresentation of the manufacturing fields and an underrepresentation of the service sectors.[24] In 1998, the DOL replaced the DOT with a new occupational classification system known as the Occupational Information Network (O*NET).[25] An advisory panel to the DOL in 1993 provided the impetus for the O*NET by recommending the creation of a more accessible and flexible occupational taxonomy for meeting the DOL's primary goals of promoting "effective education, training, counseling and employment of the American workforce."[26] The O*NET was first released to the general public in December 1998.[27]

While the O*NET met the DOL's employment and policy concerns, it failed to meet the SSA's adjudicative requirements for work adjustment disability decisions.[28] The O*NET's most specific shortcoming as an SSA work adjustment tool was that it did not categorize jobs by exertional residual functional capacity.[29] The O*NET also utilized a different, more layered system for classifying skills and the required vocational preparation for various jobs than was contemplated in the SSA's transferable skills rules.[30]

The O*NET also presented aggregation and matching problems when used in conjunction with DOT-based systems. In the most recent version of the O*NET, the DOL aggregated the DOT's approximately 13,000 total occupations into only 800-plus occupations,[31] thus further obscuring the DOT's and the grid's occupational groupings and bases.[32] Although officials from the DOL have conceded that even the 1991 DOT has been "obsolete" for more than a decade,[33] the SSA continues to use the DOT and DOT-based adjudicative tools out of necessity because the O*NET is inadequate for SSA work adjustment assessments and because there are no other alternatives.[34]

10

Progress Toward a New Occupational Taxonomy for Work Adjustment Assessments

An Inter-Organizational Task Force (IOTF) that included the Social Security Administration and the Department of Labor set out to create a coordinated remedy for the ailing occupational classification system. From 2000 to 2004, the IOTF worked "to establish a common, objective, measurable, and reliable framework that c[ould] best describe the physical, mental, cognitive, training and environmental demands associated with occupations."[1] Early efforts were promising: the IOTF explored both updating the DOT and revising the O*NET to serve disability adjudication purposes.[2] According to the NRC, a pilot study funded by the DOL and based on the IOTF's work showed promise in creating O*NET–D, a version of the O*NET specifically designed for disability purposes.[3] However, while the SSA staff initially agreed with the O*NET–D approach, the SSA later withdrew its support.[4] The IOTF ultimately reached no agreement on a collaborative interagency approach to the problem.[5] As the National Research Council then observed, "[C]ommunication and collaboration between DOL and SSA regarding a common occupational database now appears quite limited."[6]

In 2009, the SSA's own advisory panel commenced work to evaluate and make recommendations on the creation of a new labor market taxonomy designed solely for the SSA's disability adjudication process.[7] The SSA panel responsible for developing the new approach, the Occupational Information Development Advisory Panel, did not include any representatives from the DOL or any of its divisions, such as the Bureau of Labor Statistics, and attempted to make recommendations without directly drawing on the DOL's labor market expertise and data or its insights into the contemporary U.S. labor market.[8]

Perhaps foreseeing the potential shortcomings of the SSA's independent project, the NRC issued a report recommending collaboration between the SSA and the DOL as the most efficient, cost-effective, and sensible approach to this problem.[9] The NRC report stated:

> Given public demand for budgetary restraint and efficient government, which acquire additional importance in times of economic recession and slow economic growth, duplication in government should be prevented. Therefore the development of parallel, possibly redundant, occupational information systems, one for general purposes termed O*NET and the other tailored to the needs of [the] SSA, is of concern to taxpayers. In addition dual data collection processes would seem unnecessarily expensive. . . . There are also some potential economies of scale to be derived from the development of a single occupational information system to be used by both agencies which may allow cost-sharing of resources in such functions as data collection and system maintenance.[10]

The NRC specifically recommended that the SSA and the DOL reconvene a joint task force to conduct "(1) an in-depth needs analysis of the occupational information required by the current disability determination process and (2) an interagency cost-benefit analysis and cost-sharing analysis of the additional resources that would be needed to make the O*NET suitable to the disability determination."[11]

Apparently accepting this general recommendation, the SSA since 2012 has discontinued its solo effort and has been working in conjunction with the DOL on a new occupational taxonomy for SSA adjudication in the Occupational Information System (OIS) project.[12] The OIS project utilizes the BLS Occupational Requirements Survey (ORS) as the principal instrument to survey and supply data to inform the new classification system.[13] The ORS, in turn, utilizes the Standard Occupational Classification occupational grouping taxonomy for its surveys.[14] Presumably, the OIS taxonomy will have stronger and more direct linkages to BLS jobs data collection systems based on SOC codes. The OIS will also utilize data from other sources, including the O*NET and the BLS Occupational Outlook Handbook.[15]

The ORS proposes to provide job-related information and data on occupations and jobs. It will include information on "physical demands; environmental conditions; education; training and experience; as well as cognitive and mental requirements for jobs in the U.S. economy."[16] The

ORS surveys since approximately 2015 have included reports on percentages of required tasks by broad occupational type based on exertional demands, including amount of time on exertional functions (such as sitting and standing and the need to alternate sitting and standing at will), fine and gross manipulation, education and training requirements, interaction with the general public and crowds, and speed or pace of work, among other areas.[17]

The job information sought and surveyed will include some additional areas and job requirements that were not surveyed in the DOT as described above. However, the ORS has been criticized by Professor Michael Handel for not utilizing "in-person observations of job performance by trained field analysts, which were a prominent part of the DOT," and instead relying on interviews of select employers.[18] This latter approach introduces "interviewer related variance" into survey measures due to "varying interviewer skills, styles, and perspectives."[19] Handel also criticized the ORS reliance on occupational groupings that would be much more aggregated and less granular than the DOT.[20] Handel's ORS critique recommended, among other measures, identifying the most common fifty or so job or occupational titles used in the "past relevant work" and "other work"/work adjustment (steps 4 and 5) of the SSA adjudicative process, as well as taking additional measures with that sampling to promote data integrity.[21] Those steps include additional data collection efforts ("e.g. personal visits by field economists") and subdividing some occupational groups "into finer codes to meet concerns regarding within occupation heterogeneity (true variance)" to supply a "limited expansion of the level of occupational detail."[22]

Although SSA earlier reported 2020 as the date of the new OIS's completion,[23] the most recent reports suggest that ORS survey data, including more complete mental and cognitive demand data intended to inform and be part of the new OIS for SSA work adjustment adjudication purposes, will not be available until 2024 at the "earliest."[24] Moreover, while the "OIS demonstration started with the goal of supporting current policy with minimal change,"[25] the SSA now reports that "larger changes to policy will be needed to support the data."[26] Although the ORS still has at least four or five more years of data-gathering to complete by its own admission, it also points out that these "larger policy changes" driven by the data happen to "coincide with the office of disability policy's plans to modernize the vocational regulations used in steps 4 [past relevant work] and 5 [other work/work adjustment] decisions."[27]

The SSA's OIS website does not elaborate on those potential policy changes. However, the agency has issued an advance notice of proposed rulemaking (ANPRM) on vocational factors in SSA determinations signaling potential policy changes on the treatment of labor market and vocational factors as follows:

> When we determine whether an individual can adjust to other work, we consider an individual's functional capacities and limitations, the occupational base in the national economy, and the vocational factors of age, education, and work experience. We have ongoing activities related to each of these considerations. Although complementary, our activities related to functional limitations and the occupational base are independent and are occurring on separate timeframes from our effort on the vocational factors. Accordingly, we are narrowing the scope of this ANPRM to solicit public comments on only the vocational factors. We are not soliciting public comments on how we assess an individual's functional limitations. We are also not soliciting public comments in this notice on sources of occupational data we use at step 5, such as the Dictionary of Occupational Titles, because we are working with the Bureau of Labor Statistics (BLS) to test the collection of updated occupational information that we intend to use to develop a new occupational information system.
>
> Specifically, given today's work environment and advances in technology and medicine, we are seeking public input, research, and data about the following:
>
> 1. Is the factor of age predictive in determining an individual's ability to work or to adjust to other work? If it is predictive, what are the vocationally significant age milestones we should consider? If it is not predictive, what data support that assertion?
> 2. When determining if age affects an individual's ability to work or to adjust to other work, what other factors or combination of factors should we consider?
> 3. Does an individual's educational level affect an individual's ability to do work or to adjust to other work? If so, how? What data support the

conclusion that an individual's educational level does or does not affect an individual's ability to do work or to adjust to other work? How does literacy affect an individual's ability to do work or adjust to other work?

4. Does the skill level of an individual's past work affect his or her ability to adjust to other work? If so, how? What data support the conclusion that the skill level of an individual's past work does or does not affect an individual's ability to do work or to adjust to other work? How does the skill level of an individual's past work considered along with an individual's educational level affect this adjustment?
5. Are there other vocational factors or combinations of vocational factors that we should consider when determining an individual's ability to do work or to adjust to other work?[28]

Several years later, the only implemented policy change specifically to follow from this ANPRM has been the repeal of the "inability to communicate in English" educational category and a restriction on the scope of the remaining illiteracy category in what used to be the grid's "unable to communicate in English or illiterate" category. These regulatory eligibility restrictions were adopted in 2020.[29] It is unclear if any ORS data supported these changes.

On the SSA's policy side referenced in the agency's comments on the OIS website, the Trump-appointed deputy commissioner for retirement and disability policy at SSA, Marc J. Warshawsky,[30] advocated for eligibility restrictions in the disability programs through elimination of the grid and all of the vocational factors utilized in step 5's work adjustment assessment. Prior to his SSA appointment, Warshawsky had coauthored a 2015 paper with Ross A. Marchand, who became director of policy for the Taxpayer Protection Alliance,[31] advocating for the complete or virtually complete elimination of the age, education, and (presumably) work experience and worker skills categories in the grid and the eventual elimination of the grid.[32] While acknowledging that legislation would be needed to fully eliminate the grid and vocational factors, this proposal calls for a "sole focus on residual functional capacity, combined with an evaluation of jobs available in the national economy and suitable to the claimant," without any consideration of age, education, or English-language skills and presumably any other considerations beyond RFC and job incidence.[33]

The merits of the Warshawsky/Marchand proposal are discussed below throughout Part 5. Whether that proposal will eventually lead to the Office of Disability Policy's suggested policy changes to "modernize the vocational factors" as supported by ORS data is as yet unclear.[34] However, the very fact that the Office of Disability Policy appears to have prejudged the data as supporting new "large policy changes" is troubling. The critique about the shortcomings of the current data-collection system and problems of interviewer bias—with the variations inherent in a system of data collection based on interviews instead of field observations, as well as the role of the subconscious and conscious perspectives and varying skills and styles of the interviewers—raises greater concerns about data accuracy and reliability in a situation where the agency has already determined that the data will match predetermined new policy directions. It is hoped that the agency, with a change in administration, will resist the temptation to attempt to make the data match proposed policy changes and instead allow the data to take policy wherever it leads.

As Professor Ernest Gellhorn suggested in eschewing changes in substantive result through the less transparent device of shifting process burdens through the official notice doctrine,[35] the same is true with policy driven by data shaped to match predetermined results. For example, if the agency seeks eligibility-restrictive substantive regulations for budgetary reasons, as is also argued in the Warshawsky/Marchand proposal, it should do so transparently and in a manner subject to full democratic accountability. It should also avoid placing the greatest burden of budgetary program contraction on the most vocationally disadvantaged claimants, which would be the result of program contraction through "vocational factor" elimination or reduction. As discussed below in Part 5, such a "large policy change" would produce disparate impacts on lower income claimants and would disproportionately disadvantage African American and Latinx claimants.

PART FIVE

Alternatives to the Current SSA Disability System, the Twenty-First Century Low-Skill Labor Market, and the Contemporary Call for Disability Benefits Reform

11

Introduction to the Debate Over Alternatives to the Current Disability Standard and Program

In light of the deficiencies in the vocational expert program and grid systems; the complexity of some work adjustment issues; and the conflicts, inconsistencies, and confusion within the SSA and among the courts, a case could be made for exploring alternatives to the current system and disability standard. As discussed in Part 1, the statutory disability definition does not create a precise, objective, or scientifically determined standard but one that is socially constructed. Despite some of the program's congressional framers' highest aspirations and faith in the guidance of medical professionals, medical science has never been directed to the study of work environments or been able to provide a reliable means to demonstrate the inability to adapt to and function sufficiently and consistently in a new work setting. The program more realistically embodies the recognition that there are circumstances in which individuals should be excused from the social obligation of work.[1] Thus, the disability definition is a product of political compromise and reflects a degree of social consensus.[2]

It includes some nonmedical factors that are relevant to the ability to obtain, perform, adapt to, and retain employment in the labor market, but it also excludes other potentially relevant factors. For example, the disability definition accounts for a claimant's age, education, and work experience, as well as the incidence of jobs to which claimants might make a work adjustment in the relevant labor markets. However, it excludes factors such as employer hiring practices and discriminatory biases, local economic conditions, and the presence of actual job openings. The compromise inherent in the current system has stirred debates over whether its calculus of medical, vocational, and labor market factors reflects the appropriate balance of considerations for determining disability from work in a manner that is consistent with American social values and norms.

The standard's propriety remains the subject of fierce debate. More than fifty years after the Social Security Amendments of 1967, a federal judge opined on the work adjustment assessment standard's stinginess:

> This definition of disability, written generations ago, has been called long obsolete by scientists and scholars. Under its cramped structure, the Administration says it "does not matter" if there is a "lack of work in [the] local area" for [the claimant's] body. Nor does it matter if he "would not actually be hired" for open jobs, even if the "hiring practices of employers" discriminate against him.[3]

More than twenty years after the grid's promulgation, an administrative law judge for the SSA published an article railing against this standard's leniency as implemented through the 1978 grid regulations:

> [I]f a person in the age group 55–60 can do sedentary work, he or she should not be deemed to be disabled. Indeed, this is a *non sequitur*—If a person can do sedentary work, he can work! In our new age of technology and computers, a person age 55–60 can, with a minimum of training and skill, perform all sorts of useful work, and should not be found disabled. The Dictionary of Occupational Titles contains the listings of numerous jobs that persons age 55–60 can do if they are limited to sedentary work and have a limited education and unskilled work background, and these jobs exist in significant numbers.[4]

As described in chapter 3, in the 1980s, the Reagan administration introduced legislation that would have made the Social Security Act much stricter by eliminating consideration of all labor market and vocational factors and thereby the entire work adjustment determination.[5] Under such a system, claimants would presumably either satisfy step 3 of the current five-step process or be denied benefits. An offshoot of this approach was more recently advocated by Marc Warshawsky and Ross Marchand and pursued in the Trump administration (see chapter 10).

In the 1960s, legislators introduced multiple bills to make the Act more inclusive by eliminating the work adjustment assessment and employing an occupational standard of disability.[6] Under such a standard, claimants who could prove an inability to perform past relevant work at step 4 in the process would be determined to be disabled. This also would eliminate the work adjustment assessment and all labor market factors independent of one's past work and would significantly expand eligibility. Other proposals seek to borrow principles from the 1990s welfare reform and attach various forms of mandatory work requirements to the program. Each of these ideas is discussed in chapters 12–16.

12

Amendments to Simplify Work Adjustment Assessments by Restricting Eligibility

The Elimination of Labor Market and Vocational Factors

The Reagan administration proposal in the 1980s would have imposed a nonindividualized "average person" concept on the program, which Congress and the SSA patently rejected from its inception.[1] It would have relied entirely on presumed employment-related reactions to various medical impairment findings regardless of substantial employment-related differences in vocational factors such as age, education, and work experience, as well as any relevant labor market realities. In addition, it would have failed to evaluate medical differences in physical and mental RFC and would not have considered pain, fatigue, and other potentially debilitating subjective symptoms that cannot be as effectively measured through objective tests and exams, except to the extent such symptoms were part of a listing.[2]

The Warshawsky/Marchand proposal purports to retain RFC but remove all other considerations relevant to making a successful adjustment to work such as the vocational factors of age, education, work experience, and work skills. Moreover, the Warshawsky/Marchand proposal also calls for the elimination of all "nonlisted conditions" (presumably all those not in step 3 of the SSA's list of automatic medical disabilities).[3] Such a result would leave no room for considering RFC because RFC comes into play only when a claimant is found not to have a listed impairment and the remaining non–listing level impairments are then evaluated for residual functional capacity to guide determination of return to past relevant work or adjustment to other work at steps 4 and 5.

On a basic level, both proposals would move the program "even further away from a concept of disability geared towards differentiating between those who can or cannot work."[4] This concept lies at the heart of the Social Security Act's disability standard. Each proposal would also have negative distributive consequences on the most economically vulnerable segments of the disabled population: older, less-educated, and less-skilled claimants.[5] Lower-income claimants would be disproportionately disadvantaged based on their inclusion in the above groups and due to disparate access to the health care resources necessary to establish listing-level severity from required medical procedures and testing or the requisite documented treatment histories.[6] Some racial minority groups, particularly African American and Latinx claimants, as well as other claimants who already confront inexplicably disparate outcomes in the adjudicative process,[7] would have suffered additional disparate ineligibility due to their greater inclusion in many of the categories above.[8]

In addition, each proposal would remove vocational factors that are long recognized as highly relevant to work and successful work adjustments. They would also reflect a substantial alteration of the Act, without meaningful data or evidence supporting the express or implied assumptions about the nonrelevance or substantially diminished relevance of these vocational and labor market factors. For example, the entire rationale in the Warshawsky/Marchand proposal for eliminating all educational considerations in the grid is contained in a single paragraph:

> Finally, as is well known, the American labor force is much more educated than it was in the 1950s. According to data from the United States Census Bureau (2015), in 1992, 12 percent of workers above age 25 had less than a high school education while almost 27 percent had at least a bachelor's degree. By 2014, these shares had changed to 8 percent and 38 percent, respectively. In the 1950s, having a college degree was relatively uncommon and represented a real and permanent advantage in the labor market. Therefore, it might have been reasonable to assume that even with some level of disability and aging, well-educated workers would be advantaged enough to find work. Now college degrees are common and no longer the advantage they once were. As proof, college graduates trying to enter the labor force were hit hard in the recent recession. The opposite is also true. If someone has been in the labor force for decades, even with only a high school education, one may presume that on-the-job and vocational training and years of experience and hard work give that

> worker skills and talents valuable in the labor force. It is hard to understand the justification for the discrimination in the medical-vocational grid based on educational attainment in the context of today's economy; this factor should be eliminated.[9]

However, 2019 ORS data reveals that 69 percent of jobs in the economy for civilian workers have minimum education requirements of at least a high-school diploma, with about the same percentage requiring a degree above high school (30 percent) as with no minimum educational requirements (31 percent).[10] This proposal would also eliminate the educational category of illiteracy. Yet numerous studies document a connection between employability and literacy skills, finding that those with the lowest literacy levels are more likely to be unemployed, lower-paid, not working in full-time work, and with more constricted opportunities within the labor market.[11] Even within the lowest-skill jobs with no minimum educational requirements or requiring even a high-school degree, many still require basic literacy.[12] For example, ORS data shows that only 3.7 percent of workers' jobs in production worker positions, food preparation or related food service, or office clerical or administrative assistant occupations still do not require literacy.[13]

Many jobs require basic language skills and communicative capacity with the ability to read and understand and speak and be understood. While it is true that the SSA in 2020 eliminated the vocational factor of "inability to communicate in English" from the grid regulations, albeit without supporting ORS data, this factor will still be part of vocational expert work adjustment assessments in grid exception cases. There remain bases for applying this factor in those individual adjudications, particularly with respect to specific popular occupations for vocational expert work adjustment assessments requiring telephone or other verbal communicative functions.[14]

Indeed, the SSA's 2020 position on the presumptive nonrelevance of ability to communicate in English for work adjustment assessments in the grid puts it at odds with 2018 regulations of another federal agency, the U.S. Department of Homeland Security (DHS). In listing lack of English-language facility as a factor to consider in determining whether an immigrant is likely to become a public charge—even without confining itself to the negatively synergistic work adjustment mix of a severe medical impairment combined with lack of English facility as in the SSA disability context—DHS represented that "[a]n inability to speak and understand English may adversely affect whether an [immigrant] can obtain employment."[15] It also found that "[p]eople with the lowest English speaking ability tend to have the lowest employment rate, lowest rate of full-time employment, and lowest median earnings."[16]

Moreover, the assumption that "years of experience and hard work give that worker skills and talents valuable in the labor force" fails to establish that those acquired "skills"[17] are all that is needed to make an adjustment to "other work" that a claimant has never previously performed and that involves different job requirements. Similarly, the observation that college graduates are having difficulty in the pandemic-depressed labor market or were "hit hard" during the earlier recession commencing in 2008 does not imply the converse: that noncollege or noneducated workers are having an easier time in the labor market or did not take even harder "hits" during the earlier recession.[18]

The Warshawsky/Marchand proposal's rationale for eliminating age as a factor in work adjustment assessments is similarly unsupported. The rationale for complete elimination of age, much like the fallback suggestion of considering age as a factor in some manner but only after age sixty,[19] is the greater life expectancy of average workers. The average worker at various ages now lives a longer lifespan by about five to seven years since 1960.[20] However, a series of studies reveal that "gains in life expectancy are concentrated among people with higher socioeconomic status."[21]

There is a 5.4-year gap in life expectancy between top-half earners and bottom-half earners,[22] and disability benefit recipients and claimants are assuredly concentrated in the bottom half. Indeed, 100 percent of SSI disability benefit recipients are low-income and live below or near the poverty line;[23] nearly 50 percent of SSDI recipients would be living below the poverty line in the absence of benefits, and many SSDI recipients remain in poverty even with benefits.[24] Average life and health vary widely based on other socioeconomic factors relevant to the core disability claimant population, such as lack of college education or access to higher-quality health care.[25] More fundamentally, the life expectancy gains for average workers who are experiencing the average health of the population and deemed to be healthier now at various ages bear no relationship to persons who are unhealthy now at those same target ages.

The age category also functions as the major factor in the job adaptability component of the work adjustment assessment.[26] While no sources have demonstrated a precise point when age denotes various levels of obstacles to adaptability to new occupations (and that is why the grid has always eschewed mechanical application in borderline age category situations), it is fairly well established that age bears some relationship to adaptability (although it is difficult to quantify). The grid age categories start to become more broadly salient at age fifty.

There is some support for recognition of a "fifties cliff"—a point when the decline in the ability to combine perception and action, known as perceptuo-motor skills, becomes more pronounced.[27] The greatest declines in the learning rate for new tasks are at age sixty, but at various testing levels "the 50 year olds showed a reduced performance level relative to younger participants and looked very similar to those in their 60s, 70s and 80s."[28] Other studies have found or suggested that older workers "are typically limited in certain abilities such as flexibility, acceptance of new technology, and ability to learn new skills"[29] or reveal a "reduced capacity to adapt to stress . . . [which is deemed] to result from the loss of complexity with aging."[30] Another study found that "older adults (typically those in their 60s and 70s) take roughly 50 percent to 100 percent longer than younger adults (those in their 20s) to perform any new task" and that "[g]eneral slowing is seen in all kinds of activities, both mental (learning) and physical (response time)."[31] A further study found that "[r]elatively few" disability insurance applicants aged fifty-one or older who are denied DI benefits based on presumed ability to work actually resume working.[32]

In addition, older workers suffer from a greater incidence of degenerative impairments such as various musculoskeletal and circulatory impairments. It may also be more difficult and frustrating to learn and adjust to new tasks and job functions with progressive worsening of one's previous functional capacities, as opposed to suffering impairment restrictions that are generally constant at the same or similar levels. The chart below reveals the distribution of impairment types by DI age group:

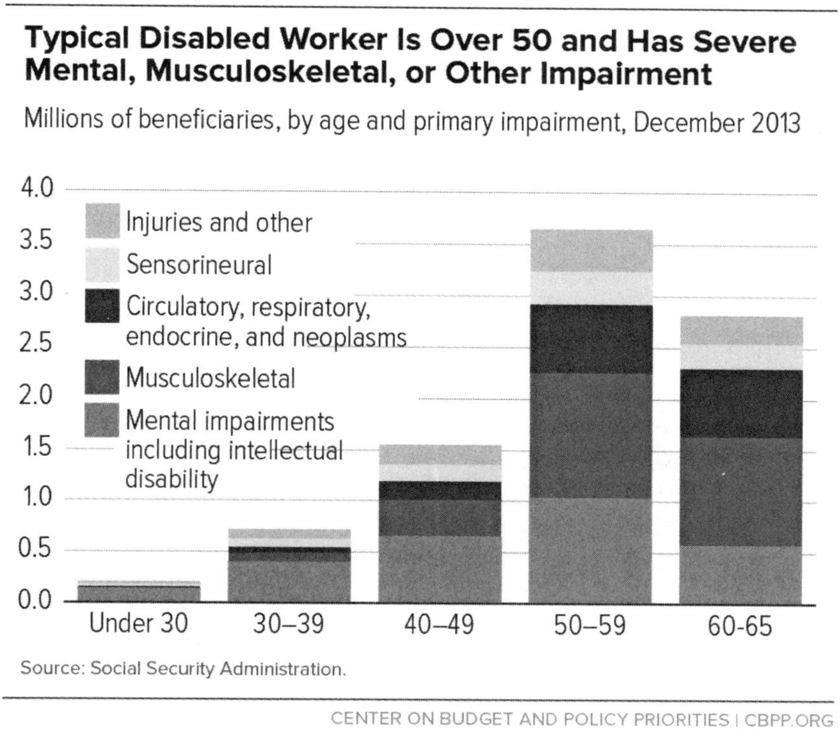

Figure 12.1. Chart from Center for Budget Policy Priorities (CBPP), Typical Disabled Worker Is Over 50 and Has Severe Mental, Musculoskeletal, or Other Impairment (2017), www.cbpp.org/typical-disabled-worker-is-over-50-and-has-severe-mental-musculoskeletal-or-other-impairment.

Nevertheless, some social security scholars view the use of age as more of a function of the social construction of disability and the inclusion of some factors related to realistic successful adjustment to new work and tasks, while generally excluding others such as the discriminatory perspectives of employers. From the standpoint of worthiness for exemption from the social obligation of work, older persons with disabilities are viewed more sympathetically as being closer in age to the retirement program's exemption from work, usually having toiled in the work force for a longer period of time than others. The significant political opposition engendered by an abandoned 2005 regulatory attempt to raise the grid's age categories five years reflects some indication that this sociopolitical consensus perseveres to the present day.[33]

13

The Twenty-First Century Labor Market for Low-Skill Work

The Warshawsky/Marchand proposal also relies in part on the belief that there must be bases for reducing the scope of the disability program in view of a more "modern and realistic consideration of physical effort needed to hold down jobs in today's economy given changes in the nature of work."[1] It points out that due to "mechanization and computerization" the "nature of work has evolved causing less reliance on physical labor."[2] The proposal does not elaborate further on how those labor market changes have expanded successful work adjustments among persons with adverse medical-vocational profiles that would otherwise meet SSDI/SSI disability criteria. It is undeniable that the labor market has changed since the grid and the updating of the last edition of the DOT. However, it is by no means clear that those changes have produced greater work adjustment capacity for persons with the disadvantaged and negatively synergistic mix of medical and vocational limitations who represent a large part of the population found disabled at the SSA's work adjustment assessment step 5.

The U.S. General Accounting Office (GAO) has found that, while certain advances in technology have made it easier for disabled individuals to participate in the labor force, the fast-paced nature of the nation's service-based economy has increased some of the physical and mental demands of many entry-level jobs:

> [T]he nature of work has changed in recent decades as the national economy has moved away from manufacturing-based jobs to service- and knowledge-based employment. . . . Although certain jobs in the service economy continue to be physically demanding—a cashier in a fast food restaurant might be expected to stand for most of his or her shift—other service and knowledge-based jobs can allow greater participation for persons with physical limitations. In addition, telecommuting and part-time

> work provide other options for persons with disabilities. However, some labor market trends—such as an increasing pace of change in office environments and the need for adaptability—can pose particular challenges for some persons, such as those with severe mental illness and learning disabilities. Moreover, other trends—such as downsizing and the growth in contingent workers—can limit job security and benefits, like health insurance, that most persons with disabilities require for participation in the labor force. Whether these changes make it easier or more difficult for a person with a disability to work appears to depend very much on the individual's impairment and other characteristics, according to experts.[3]

A frequently referenced study by Professors David Autor and David Dorn, who are labor economists, on transformation of the U.S. labor market from 1980 to 2005 due to the effects of skills-based technological changes, further elucidates these labor market trends.

Autor and Dorn document "job polarization" and a U-shaped curve of job growth with significant growth in the upper two skills quartiles, substantial decline in the middle quartiles, but also significant growth in the lowest quartile.[4] However, Autor and Dorn found that rise in the "lower tail" of the distribution was substantially accounted for by growth in "a single broad category" of the economy: service occupations that involve assisting or caring for others.[5] These occupations include "food service workers, security guards, janitors, gardeners, cleaners and home health aides, hairdressers and beauticians and recreation occupations."[6] These service occupations grew by 30 percent between 1980 and 2005 compared with a substantial decline "in all similarly low-educated occupation groups, which include production and craft[], operative and assembly[], and transportation, construction, mechanical, mining and farm occupations"[7] as well as in "clerical and administrative" assistance positions.[8]

Autor and Dorn explain that these growth and decline patterns in the low-skill labor market are driven by technological advances and automation: "[T]he adoption of computer substitutes for low-skill workers performing routine tasks—such as . . . repetitive production and monitoring activities, which are readily computerized because they follow precise, well-defined procedures."[9] However, automation of routine tasks neither substitutes for nor complements low-education service occupations that rely heavily on "manual" tasks such as physical dexterity, direct physical proximity, and flexible interpersonal communication.[10] The "physical and interpersonal activities" performed in these service occupations–such as "personal care, table-waiting, order-taking, housekeeping, [and] janitorial service—have proven expensive and cumbersome to computerize."[11]

These types of labor market trends suggest a more limited labor market for characteristically lower-skilled SSA disability claimants. Indeed, the grid's occupational bases only include occupations that are unskilled,[12] and these labor market trends suggest a contraction, rather than an expansion, of the grid's bases for work adjustment assessments. The shift in the low-skill labor market away from production, clerical, assembly, and the like and toward various service occupations signals a diminution of the exertional sedentary and light work occupational bases that support the tables that supply the decisional rules for most grid-based work adjustment denials. For example, current ORS data on food preparation and service-related occupations—likely less exertionally demanding types of service occupations than many of the other growing service occupations such as janitor, security guard, and health care aid—reflect exertional requirements beyond those required for sedentary or light work as defined in the SSA regulations. The mean time spent standing in these food service occupations is 97.4 percent of the workday (close to eight hours), and 100 percent of them have standing requirements in the ninetieth percentile.[13] This is well in excess of the six hours per day limit for light work and two hours for sedentary work. The mean lifting requirement is 28.36 pounds, and 44.8 percent of them require lifting from 25 to 50 pounds[14] which exceeds the 20-pound limit of light work and 10-pound lifting limit of sedentary work.

These labor market trends also suggest that the work adjustment occupational bases will be even further eroded in grid exception cases with nonexertional, mental restrictions. For example, in cases involving claimants with nonexertional psychiatric or cognitive impairments, the vocational experts in work adjustment assessments often identify unskilled occupations that involve "simple, routine, repetitive" tasks; limited personal interaction with others; a predictable and consistent pace of work and work demands; and the ability to pause or take breaks when needed.[15] Autor and Dorn have shown that automation has significantly replaced work involving routine, repetitive tasks throughout the labor market.[16] However, ORS data on the same food service occupations show that 79.2 percent of them require a varying job pace; 89 percent do not include the ability to pause work; 72.6 percent have personal contact with others and require at least basic people skills; 27.4 percent require more advanced people skills; and 69.6 percent require interaction with the general public.[17]

The trend toward more mentally and temperamentally demanding work in the twenty-first century's labor market as a consequence of automation is not confined to the United States. The Organization for Economic Cooperation and Development (OECD), an intergovernmental economic organization with thirty-seven member countries, including the United States, has reached similar conclusions about the labor market of its members. It stated:

> With manufacturing and other low-skill tasks in the services sector becoming increasingly automated, the need for routine cognitive and craft skills is declining, while the demand for information-processing skills and other high-level cognitive and interpersonal skills is growing. In addition to mastering occupation-specific skills, workers in the 21st century must also have a stock of information-processing skills, including literacy, numeracy and problem solving, and "generic" skills, such as interpersonal communication, self-management, and the ability to learn, to help them weather the uncertainties of a rapidly changing labour market.[18]

There are additional twenty-first-century labor market trends that have further reduced (or in the future will reduce) the unskilled labor market for SSA work adjustment assessments. One such trend is globalization and market outsourcing. Globalization has led to "outsourcing" of production where "low-skilled jobs are increasingly seen as being 'offshorable'—i.e. being relocated from high wage or high cost locations to low wage and low cost locations in less developed countries."[19] Another, more recently emerging, and perhaps anticipated future trend is the evolution of automation, computerization, and artificial intelligence to the development of functional industrial robots. While there has been little empirical study on the labor market impact of robots to date, the World Bank's 2019 World Development Report observed that "robots are taking over thousands of routine tasks and will eliminate many low-skill jobs in advanced economies and developing countries."[20]

Finally, a variety of structural changes in the low-skill, low-wage job market portend particularly greater obstacles for claimants of color, who are disproportionately represented among the claimant population due to, among other factors, the confluence of lesser health care treatment and health insurance consistency and quality, lesser education levels, and higher poverty. One study, which included employment testing for race discrimination in the low-wage labor force, revealed that "a black applicant has to search twice as long (or apply to twice as many jobs) as an equally qualified white applicant for access to these low-wage positions" with Latinx candidates in the midpoint between Black and White applicants.[21] It concluded that structural and compositional changes in the twenty-first-century low-wage economy, including the growth of the service sector and greater resulting opportunities for interpersonal preference based on biases—together with the rapid decline of unionization, rise in temporary or "gig" employment, and declining civil rights enforcement—"represent additional potential sources of disadvantage for minority low-wage workers."[22]

In summary, despite technological advances that have reduced the amount of strenuous physical exertion required in many occupations, a more comprehensive look at emerging labor market trends suggests that the current grid regulations (dating to 1978) have become additionally restrictive of eligibility. The grid now likely overpredicts the degree of work adjustment success (relative to work adjustments in the 1978 labor market) for many persons with various medical and vocational mixes of adversities in light of the reduction of jobs in the relevant unskilled occupational bases. This conclusion likely holds true for grid exception work adjustment assessments based on the DOT since they, too, overstate the degree to which the current economy can support labor market work adjustments, especially for claimants with mental impairments.[23]

14

The Disability Benefits Reform Debate

Warshawsky and Marchand have also argued that their proposal is necessitated by budgetary concerns around the depletion of the Social Security Trust Fund, the social undesirability of high and increasing disability benefits utilization or prevalence, the standard's lack of strictness and elasticity, excessively subjective and increasingly claimant-slanted ALJ decision-making, and fraud. These claims reflect a common thread in a variety of disability benefits "reform" proposals seeking benefit reductions and either substantive standard restrictions or removal of various procedural protections for claimants. Apart from the propriety of addressing budgetary concerns through the collateral and nontransparent device of standard revisions that disproportionately place the burden of budgetary reform on the most vocationally disadvantaged and socioeconomically challenged subgroups of claimants, the validity of these budgetary assertions is questionable.

The Disability Insurance Trust Fund's Solvency/Insolvency

The Social Security Act established so-called trust funds for the Old Age and Survivors' Insurance and Disability Insurance programs whereby taxes paid by workers and their employers are deposited when they exceed social security program costs.[1] However, demographic trends have been placing greater demands on these trust funds. These include: (1) the substantial increase in women in the labor market and first large generation of women who are insured for social security purposes; and (2) aging of the baby boom generation into older age groups and into the disability benefits programs' "sweet spot" of greater eligibility between age fifty to retirement age based on the grid's age categories and the negative progression and impact of degenerative impairments and greater vulnerability to illness. As a result of these trends, Congress and policy makers braced for the disability trust fund's depletion and resulting inability to pay 100 percent of benefits at the end of 2016.[2]

Congress, usually with bipartisan support, has often reallocated payroll taxes from one program to the other to balance the programs' finances; it has done so eleven times in the past, and Congress fully anticipated the need to reallocate again in 2016 when it approved rebalancing in 1994.[3] Reallocating a small share of the payroll tax from OASI to SSDI would have averted a 20 percent cut in SSDI benefits and made both the OASI and SSDI trust funds solvent until 2033.[4] In early 2015, however, the 114th Congress manufactured a showdown and referendum on the SSDI program by passing a resolution precluding trust fund reallocation without the adoption of measures mandating cost-saving "reform" of the SSDI program.[5] Accordingly, disability benefits reform was, at least initially, thrust into the crucible of the 2016 congressional session.

As the National Academy of Social Insurance described at the time:

> The DI shortfall does not come as a surprise. Social Security's actuaries long ago anticipated that the costs of both disability and retirement benefits would rise with the aging of the disproportionately large baby-boom generation (born 1946–1965). Boomers entered their high-disability-risk years (ages 50–66) starting in 1996. In 1995, the actuaries accurately projected that the DI trust fund would face a shortfall in 2016. The shortfall is manageable. In testimony before the Senate Finance Committee in July 2014, Social Security's Chief Actuary, Stephen C. Goss, noted that "many analysts have raised questions about the 'sustainability' of the recent period of rapid growth in the numbers of DI beneficiaries and the cost of their benefits." He added: "I am glad to report that this period of rapid growth (1) was foreseen, (2) can be explained, and (3) is now at its predicted end." The growth of the cost of benefits as a percent of GDP, from just under 0.4 percent in 1990 to nearly 0.9 percent in 2010, is "almost entirely explained by changes in the population and the economy," Goss testified.[6]

In late 2015, President Obama and Congress brokered a budget deal that authorized the requisite trust fund reallocation from OASI to SSDI in advance of the 2016 SSDI trust fund expiration date. The reallocation ensured the DI trust funds' solvency through 2022, included a few minor program integrity measures, and reauthorized demonstration project authority to encourage additional SSDI reform measures and experimentation.[7] The OASI trust fund was projected to pay full benefits to 2034.[8]

The DI trust fund has become significantly more solvent since 2016. The 2020 annual report of the board of trustees of the federal OASI and DI trust fund reported significantly greater solvency than earlier projected.[9] Based on 2020 projections, the fund can pay full (100 percent) benefits until 2065, which is thirteen years beyond the 2019 report's projections and thirty-three years longer than estimated in the 2018 report. After 2065, the DI fund would still be able to cover 92 percent of benefits without bolstering measures.[10] The regularly increasing DI trust fund solvency is attributable to several factors, including a 2.3 percent decrease in DI beneficiaries since FY 2019 and decreasing applications (which have been in decline since 2014).[11]

Disability Program Growth/Reduction and Prevalence/Diminution

Disability program prevalence and growth are often viewed not only as budgetary issues but also as social and perhaps even moral issues pertaining to how one should measure a society and its medical or spiritual health, with large and increasing numbers of persons deemed disabled from work. As described in the 2020 trustees report, the numbers of both DI beneficiaries and DI applications are on the decline: The chart below reflects the latest trend in DI applications and benefit awards over several years:

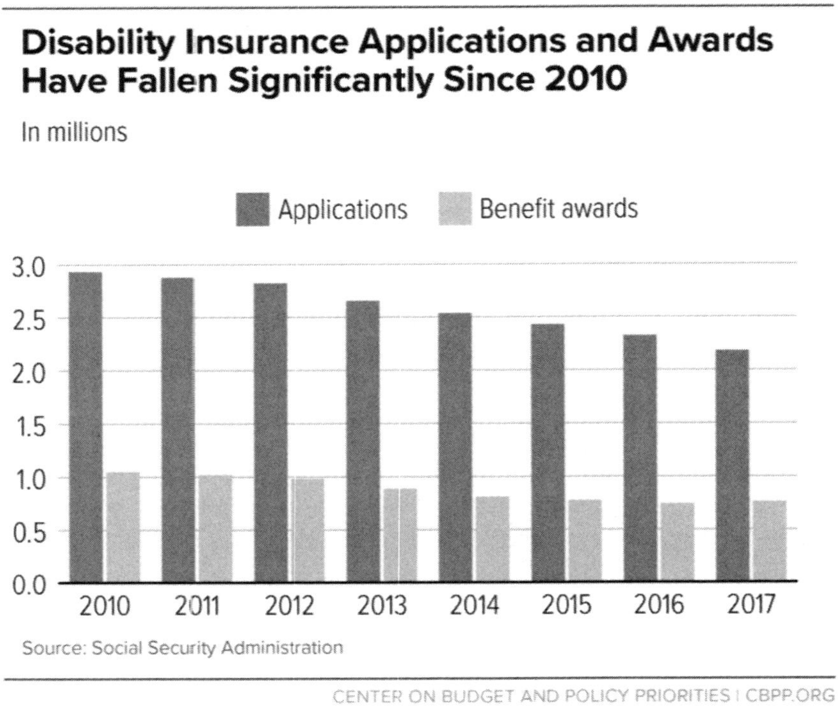

Figure 14.1. Chart from Center for Budget Policy Priorities (CBPP), Disability Insurance Applications and Awards Have Fallen Significantly Since 2010 (2018), www.cbpp.org/disability-insurance-applications-and-awards-have-fallen-significantly-since-2010.

Moreover, viewed as a question of the measure of American society's disability benefits program effort relative to comparable developed counties around the world, disability benefits prevalence is lower than the large majority of countries surveyed by the Organization for Economic Cooperation and Development as the United States falls into the bottom third of all countries:

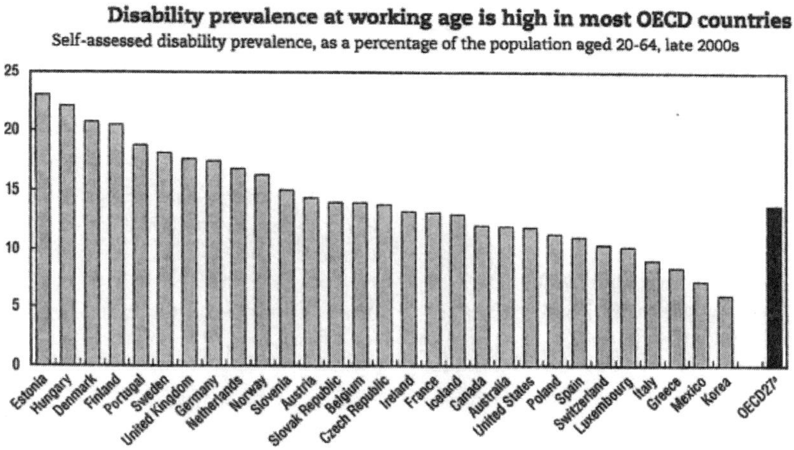

a) OECD27 is an unweighted average for 27 countries. Estonia and Slovenia are not included in the OECD average. See Annex 1.A1 on definitions and measurement of disability.

Definitions and sources: Chronic health problem for at least six months limiting daily activities from EU-SILC (Income, Social Inclusion and Living Conditions) 2007 (wave 4), except: Australia: profound/severe or moderate/mild core activity restriction, from SDAC (Survey of Disability and Carers) 2003; Canada: persons with health and activity limitation (from mild to very severe), from PALS (Participation and Activity Limitation Survey) 2006; Denmark, Norway: persons with a long-standing health problem or disability, from LFS (Labour Force Survey) 2005; Korea: persons registered to the local government with their type of disability and level of severity as assessed by a medical doctor, from National Survey on Persons with Disabilities 2005; Mexico: permanent or temporary disability, from ENESS (National Survey of Employment) 2004; Netherlands: suffering from a long-lasting complaint, illness or disability which impedes carrying out or obtaining a paid job (work disabled), from LFS 2006; Poland: persons declaring they are legally disabled, from LFS 2004; Switzerland: persons with reduced capacity due to a long-lasting health problem of more than a year, from LFS 2008; United Kingdom: persons with reduced capacity due to a long-lasting health problem of more than a year, from LFS 2006; United States: work-limiting physical or mental condition from SIPP (Survey of Income and Program Participation) 2008.

Figure 14.2. Chart from OECD, Sickness, Disability and Work, Breaking the Barriers, a Synthesis of Findings Across the Countries 22 (2010).

Program and Disability Standard Leniency/Strictness

The Warshawsky/Marchand proposal, as with the Reagan administration proposal and related proposals, would take a standard touted for its unusual stringency and make it even more restrictive. A unique, open letter by all then-existing eight former commissioners of the Social Security Administration, appointed by Republican and Democratic-administrations alike, touted the program's unusual strictness. The commissioners wrote in response to National Public Radio's "Unfit to Work" series, which they perceived as inaccurately sensationalizing perceived excesses in the program. This bipartisan group of commissioners responded:

> The statutory standard for approval is very strict, and was made even more so in 1996. To implement this strict standard, Social Security Administration (SSA) regulations, policies, and procedures require extensive documentation and medical evidence at all levels of the application process. Less than one third of initial DI and SSI applications are approved, and only about 40 percent of adult DI and SSI applicants receive benefits even after all levels of appeal.[12]

They also pointed out that "[d]isabled beneficiaries often report multiple impairments, and many have such poor health that they are terminally ill: about 1 in 5 male DI beneficiaries and 1 in 7 female DI beneficiaries die within 5 years of receiving benefits."[13]

Similarly, studies of the program have found that a significant percentage of claimants who obtain benefits die within two years of receiving benefits.[14] In one study, almost half of the disability recipients either died or reached the retirement age of sixty-five by the end of the study's six-year period.[15] Even the majority of those who are found ineligible for disability benefits remain out of the workforce.[16] Indeed, even some commentators who earlier joined calls for reconsideration of the Reagan administration's type of eligibility-restrictive, medical-only disability concept to reduce disability benefit program growth by eliminating vocational and labor market factors acknowledge that it would harm "deserving claimants."[17]

The Warshawsky/Marchand proposal also couples assertions of the program's leniency with the promise of ameliorating the "learned helplessness" associated with disability benefit receipt and the resulting "perception of powerlessness in the face of hardship" leading to "depression and inability to perform ordinary tasks."[18] This assertion implies that disability benefits claimants are either voluntarily choosing to leave the labor market or they need a more robust pep talk to labor through the confluence of their severe medical adversities and vocational challenges to attain alternative work for their own good. These types of assertions and generalizations are not new; Professor Mashaw has bluntly explained why they are unsupported:

> Although Charles Murray [in *Losing Ground* (1984)] and others have popularized the myth of the modestly impaired migrating out of the workforce in pursuit of ever-more-available disability benefits, serious social science has completely discredited that claim. . . . The availability and real value of disability benefits were decreasing during much of the period that work disability was increasing. Furthermore, it is difficult to imagine that a person who can continue to work will instead leave work to seek disability benefits that pay (on average) one-third of the mean wage, require a six month waiting period for application, a two-year waiting period for medical benefits, and provide any benefit to fewer than one-half of those who apply.[19]

Rather than hypothesizing harm from benefit receipt by medically infirm and often financially destitute claimants and their families, the bipartisan eight former SSA commissioners have focused on the hardship and harm to program beneficiaries whose benefits are wrongfully terminated or denied. In the commissioners' view, "[w]ithout Social Security or SSI, the alternatives for many beneficiaries are simply unthinkable."[20] The hardships include those associated with workers who are precluded from working and achieving a source of life support for all or most of the wage earner's and often a family's needs. These hardships are compounded by the absence of a meaningful alternative safety net that has diminished rapidly since the late 1990s.[21]

This is a circumstance made more apparent to many by the COVID-19 pandemic of 2020–21 as it cratered economies and shut down work around the country and the world. These consequences include home foreclosures and evictions, homelessness, family dissolutions, bankruptcies, hunger, malnutrition, greater illness from the absence of necessary treatment or medication due to lack of copays, deductibles, or ability to pay health care premiums or locate coverage, and sometimes even death.[22] The social costs of wrongful DI benefits denials can also include the social malaise and frustration generated from a perception that the social contract has failed and that a government insurance system, which most claimants have been compelled to pay into for decades on the promise of protection in the event of disability and the inability to make a work adjustment, has proven illusory.[23]

A common additional argument about the standard's purported leniency is that it has been amended recently in a manner that has liberalized its criteria and produced an explosion of claims and beneficiaries.[24] While the applicant and beneficiary downward trends shown above undermine the suggested causal link of recent standard amendments to previous program growth, the disability program's congressional and regulatory history also betrays this assertion. Virtually every amendment to the Social Security Act in the past half-century or so, including and subsequent to the Social Security Amendments of 1967 (with the exception of a few provisions of the 1984 Disability Benefits Reform Act)[25] and virtually every recent regulatory change,[26] have rendered the substantive disability standard more stringent. Benefits based on substance abuse and alcoholism, as well as benefits for most immigrants and for persons with outstanding felony warrants, have been eliminated; other impairments such as obesity and diabetes have been removed as separate listed disabilities; and medical standards for conditions such as HIV, mental/cognitive impairments, and other impairments have been made stricter.[27] Benefits have also been expressly restricted for claimants deemed capable of performing no gainful employment other than previously performed work that no longer even exists in significant numbers in the American economy and has been fully automated, such as elevator operator jobs.[28] Most recently, the agency has repealed regulations that had included inability to communicate in English as a consideration or eligibility category in the grid regulations.[29]

Several of these proposals also point to a perception of explosive growth due to the addition of program eligibility based on pain and mental impairments (or substantial liberalization of previous such standards) by the Disability Reform Act of 1984.[30] The proponents did not credit the previously known and predicted demographic trends identified by the trustees, all eight former SSA commissioners,[31] and SSA chief actuary Steve Goss.[32] Neither do these restrictive proposals, designed to reduce benefits eligibility, point to the specific statutory language with respect to mental or musculoskeletal impairments or pain and compare them to prior language to support their conclusions.

For example, Warshawsky and Marchand reasoned that "it is inherent in the nature of these impairments [musculoskeletal and mental] that they are more subjective to judge."[33] Professor Richard Pierce has equated musculoskeletal impairments to all "non-exertional restrictions" and the more universal symptom of pain, "which can neither be supported nor refuted based on application of objective diagnostic criteria."[34] Professor Richard Burkhauser has opined that the Disability Reform Act of 1984 first allowed for "mental illness and pain to be counted when assessing SSDI eligibility regardless of whether the person had a verifiable medical diagnosis."[35] He also suggests the SSA "has increasingly been tasked" with making work adjustment decisions based on these more subjective conditions.[36]

Social Security law and agency policy, and their history, do not support these assertions. Rather, the 1984 Disability Reform Act did not unleash a new series of elastic and subjective criteria for disability based on pain, mental disorders, or musculoskeletal conditions, in departure from prior law.[37] For more than a half-century since the 1967 amendments, the Act has required:

> [A] "physical or mental impairment" [which] is an impairment that results from anatomical, physiological, or psychological abnormalities which are *demonstrable by medically acceptable clinical and laboratory diagnostic techniques*. . . . An individual *shall not be considered to be under a disability* unless he furnishes such medical and other evidence of the existence thereof as the [SSA commissioner] may require.[38]

Long before the 1984 Disability Reform Act amendments, several U.S. Courts of Appeals had held that pain could be disabling under the Act.[39] Indeed, the Disability Reform Act's pain standard clarified the connection between subjective pain symptoms and the requirements of objective medical proof by adopting an interim standard (now permanent) establishing that

> pain or other symptoms shall not alone be conclusive evidence of disability . . . ; there must be medical signs and findings, established by medically acceptable clinical or laboratory diagnostic techniques, which show the existence of a medical impairment . . . which could reasonably be expected to produce the pain or other symptoms alleged and which, when considered with all evidence required to be furnished . . . , would lead to a conclusion that the [claimant] is under a disability.[40]

Congress, the agency, and the courts all perceived the Disability Reform Act's pain standard as essentially codifying both agency pain regulations and case law prior to 1984.[41] Moreover, the perception of subjective pain symptoms as overwhelmingly or largely connected to non-verifiable musculoskeletal impairments, in the SSA's residual functional capacity determinations used in work adjustment assessments, is also questionable. The necessary underlying, pain-producing, medically determinable musculoskeletal impairment can be established (or refuted) with accepted medical techniques and testing such as x-rays, magnetic resonance imaging, CT scans, nerve conduction studies, nuclear bone scans, myelography, and clinical examination.[42]

It is unclear why the functionally limiting effects and degree of pain from musculoskeletal impairments, such as degenerative spinal disease, would be deemed more difficult to measure and evaluate than that from rheumatic disorders such as lupus or fibromyalgia; neurological disorders or brain injury producing severe migraine headaches; hematological disorders such as sickle cell anemia producing sickle cell crises; or cardiac disorders producing pain from angina. In each case, clinical evaluation from medical professionals would be a major source of evidence informing this assessment. As to all of these types of pain-producing impairments, numerous studies, including a congressionally mandated Pain Commission report, have rejected the suggestion that faking or malingering cannot be sufficiently screened in the SSA adjudicative process; the Pain Commission report specifically found that "there is a clear consensus that malingering is not a significant problem [and] that it can be diagnosed by trained professionals, medical and other."[43]

Moreover, apart from temporal inaccuracy, the suggestion that a new disability standard authorizing consideration of pain in disability assessments for the first time only after 1984 is questionable on other grounds. The argument conjures nostalgia for an earlier, perhaps mythical, era in the disability benefit programs' history when claimants largely established eligibility with conditions that presumably produced no pain or in which pain was otherwise irrelevant to the claimants' disabling limitations. This categorical proposition is medically dubious and undermined by the failure to delineate which painless (or pain-irrelevant) yet functionally limiting medical conditions predominated in this earlier period.

However, to the extent claimants largely established eligibility without ever experiencing pain from their functionally limiting impairments in an earlier unspecified time period, it does not necessarily follow that a proportionate increase in documented severe pain among those more recently found disabled would reflect a loosening or liberalization of eligibility criteria or decision-making as opposed to a tightening to restrict claims by persons with pain-free conditions.[44]

Similarly, mental impairments had been included in the disability program from its inception. The 1958 handbook for disability evaluation prepared by the agency to guide state disability determinations, included guidance on "organic brain syndrome," "functional mental illnesses (psychoses, psychoneuroses, and personality disorders [including 'alcoholism and drug addiction'])," and "mental deficiency [based on 'intelligence tests']."[45] The Disability Reform Act provisions dealing with mental disability were a response to what the courts, including a rarely unanimous United States Supreme Court, described as an "illegal" "clandestine policy" pursued only in the period from 1978 to 1983 to deny benefits to claimants whose mental impairments did not meet the mental listing criteria at step 3 of the five-step sequential evaluation process without considering whether claimants' mental functional limitations precluded actual work performance at steps 4 and 5.[46] It is illegal and discriminatory to mandate a five-step process and inexplicably and secretly abolish potential eligibility in the last two steps only for persons with mental impairments.

It is true that Congress, through the 1984 Disability Reform Act, imposed a temporary moratorium on mental disability terminations and a requirement that the agency promulgate updated mental listings and eligibility criteria in part in response to the agency's temporary, secret, illegal policy.[47] Congress itself did not create new standards but directed the agency to promulgate "revised criteria . . . to realistically evaluate the ability of a mentally impaired individual to engage in substantial gainful activity in a competitive workplace environment."[48] However, it is not clear that the 1984 Act, coupled with the additional statutory and regulatory eligibility restrictions since its passage, have meaningfully expanded mental disability standards beyond the *lawful* requirements in effect prior to 1984. It is, of course, also true that the injunction against and abandonment of the SSA's secret, illegal restrictive approach to mental disability increased eligibility through the resumption of the lawful standards that had been in place prior to its imposition.

Since 1984, Congress and the agency have actually restricted mental impairment eligibility: In 1996, Congress removed substance abuse disorders from the listings of mental impairments and otherwise restricted eligibility where substance abuse is a material factor in a claimant's disability;[49] and in 2017, the agency promulgated regulations limiting listing-level disability due to borderline cognitive IQ-based impairments.[50] While there are also no definitive objective measurements of the precise degree and extent of mental impairments, psychiatrists, psychologists, and neuropsychologists routinely provide professional and clinical evaluations and severity assessments of patients diagnosed with cognitive, neuropsychological, or psychiatric illness. They employ professionally accepted clinical and diagnostic criteria in their assessments, and these professional assessments inform the disability determination.[51] Indeed, professional assessments of mental impairment severity are widely accepted as bases for determining a host of other legal determinations, often with somewhat more at stake, such as imposition of capital punishment, the need for civil commitment, competency for trial with substantial incarceration on the line, and other significant infringements on basic liberties.

In short, there are other reasons for the significant share of persons with mental and musculoskeletal disorders as their primary diagnosis among the ranks of the now-declining number of persons determined eligible for disability. The proportionate share of these impairment categories among the disability insurance beneficiary ranks "is consistent with global health trends."[52] The OECD reports that the leading causes of disability in its member countries around the world are musculoskeletal and mental impairments, with mental disability rising to 40–50 percent in some countries.[53] The global rise of mental impairments "is often attributed to increased awareness and reduced stigma of mental illness."[54] In the United States, the deinstitutionalization of persons with mental illness up through the 1980s also likely contributed to greater participation in the disability benefit programs.[55] Musculoskeletal disorders are more likely a function of the effects of aging and wear and tear on the spine and other degenerative impairments.[56]

Viewing the question of the American disability standard in the global context, the degree of disability required under the Social Security Act has been characterized as "extreme in comparison to that required in disability insurance programs in other countries."[57] The OECD has found the United States, along with a handful of other countries, as having "the most stringent eligibility criteria for a full disability benefit, including the most rigorous reference to all jobs in the labour market."[58] The OECD's compensation index—a multifactor calculus of factors measuring the generosity of disability benefit programs (such as the replacement rate of benefits compared to prior work earnings and degree of incapacity needed), places the United States second-to-last in the world behind only South Korea, as shown in the table below:[59]

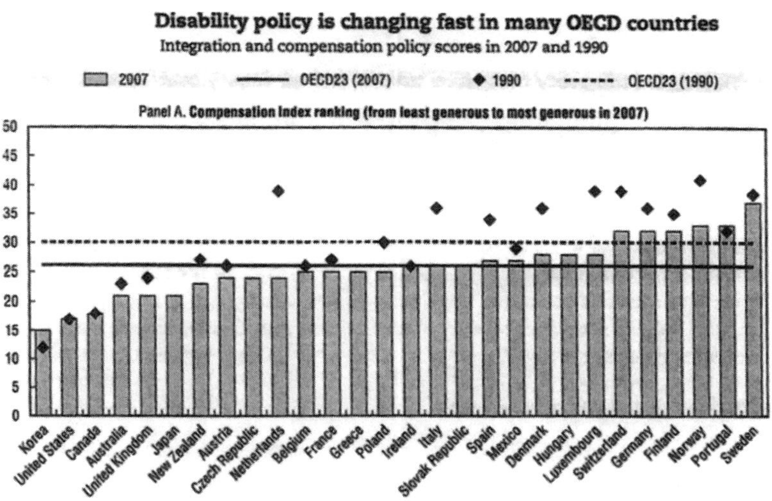

Figure 14.3. Chart from OECD, Sickness, Disability and Work, Breaking the Barriers, A Synthesis of Findings Across The Countries 87 (2010), Disability Policy Is Changing Fast in Many OECD Countries.

Similarly, American spending on disability benefit programs as a percentage of gross domestic product (GDP) is also near the bottom, as reflected below:

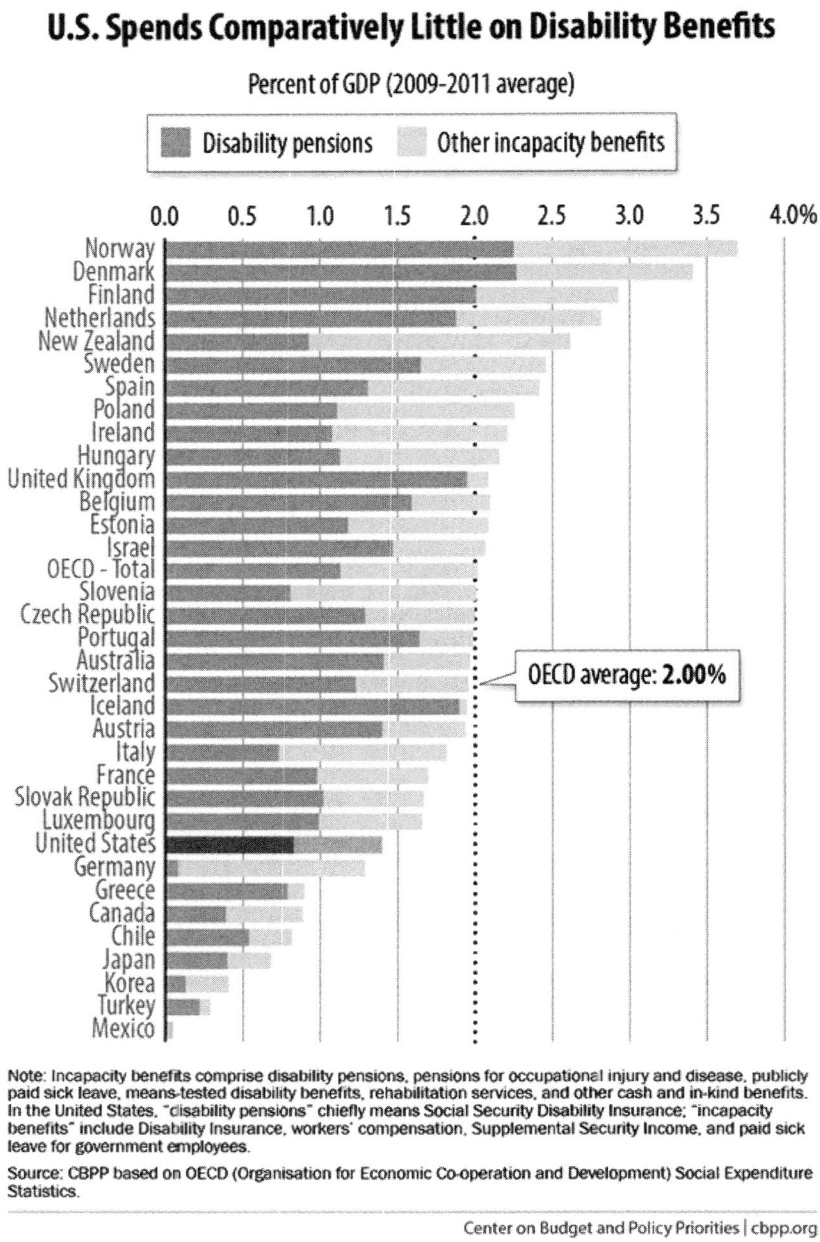

Figure 14.4. Chart from Center for Budget Policy Priorities (CBPP), U.S. Spends Comparatively Little on Disability Benefits (2016), www.cbpp.org/us-spends-comparatively-little-on-disability-benefits.

A further international measure of disability standard stringency is reflected in the rejection rate for disability applicants; the United States has the highest rejection rate in the world:

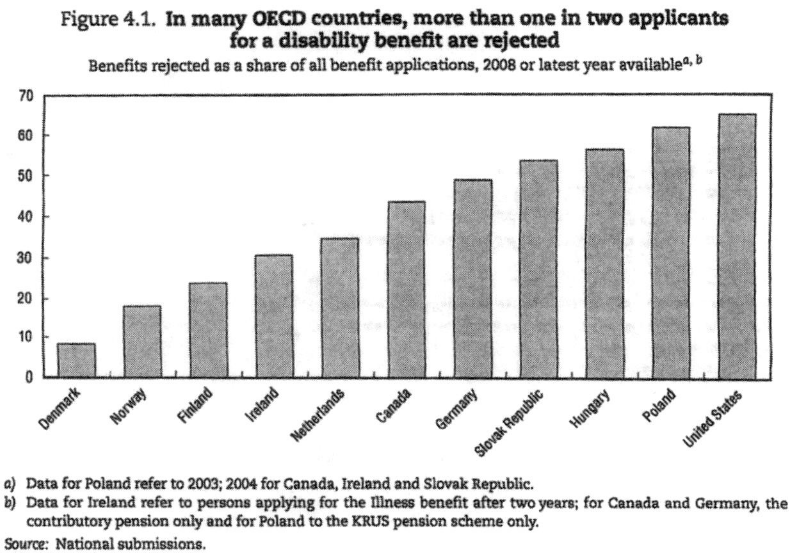

Figure 14.5. Chart from OECD, Sickness, Disability and Work, Breaking the Barriers, A Synthesis of Findings Across The Countries 113 (2010), In Many OECD Countries, More Than One in Two Applicants for a Disability Benefit Are Rejected.

Administrative Law Judge Impartiality/Bias

Warshawsky and Marchand[60] and Professor Pierce[61] have each asserted that ALJs are playing a significant and improper role in the growth of the disability benefit recipient population and that the current disability standard further facilitates biased and inaccurate ALJ decision-making. Warshawsky and Marchand claim that judicial impartiality has declined significantly, as evidenced by the high approval rate of benefit applications of approximately 70 percent.[62] They point to an outdated disability standard and grid regulations out of touch with the "actual labor market" as a factor in this growth of ALJ benefit approvals and in constraining proper ALJ decision-making by mandating consideration of improper vocational factors.[63] They also suggest placing fifteen-year term limits on ALJs and limits on ALJ decision-making to 500 cases per year, as well as quality reviews of the decisions of high-approval-rate ALJs, presumably with stricter limits on the number of their decisions.[64] Professor Pierce asserts that "most" of the increase in the number of disability recipients "is attributable to ALJ decisions." He ties the perceived high disability growth rate to increasingly subjective and claimant-favorable decision-making, facilitated by an increasingly subjective disability standard.[65] Pierce then proposes that, as a remedy, the entire ALJ corps, the ALJ hearing process, and the right to an oral hearing should be eliminated.[66]

Again, the data on ALJ disposition tells a different story. ALJ rates, like the decision-making in any judicial system, is subject to temporal and other variations. Over three decades, ALJ grant rates have been as high as 75.2 percent (in 1994).[67] The current ALJ approval rate is only

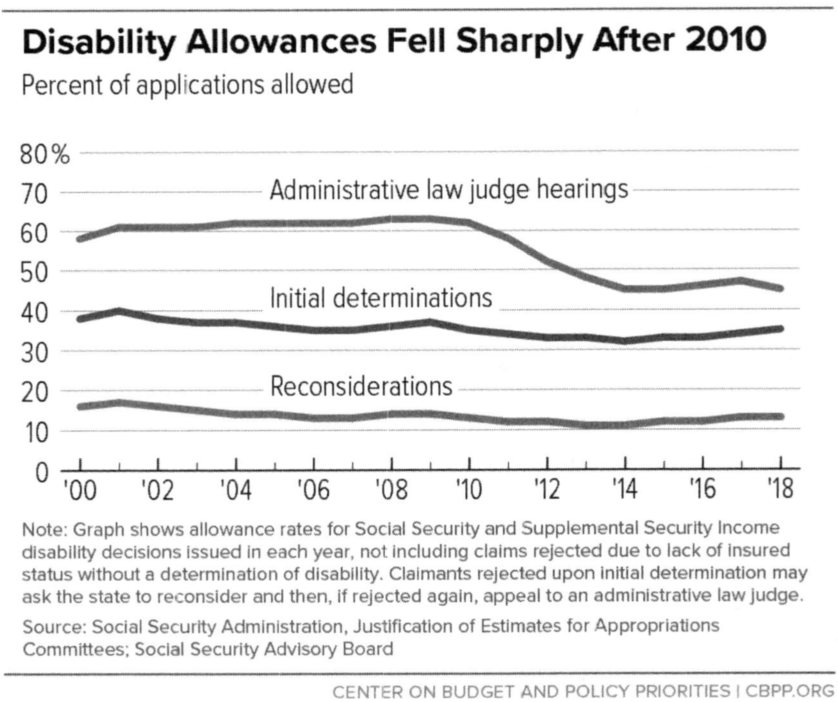

Figure 14.6. Chart from Center for Budget Policy Priorities (CBPP), Disability Allowances Fell Sharply After 2010 (2019), www.cbpp.org/disability-allowance-fell-sharply-after-2010.

45 percent based on the last full year of data (2019).[68] This means more than half of all claimants are turned down at their ALJ hearings. The chart above also reflects a downward trend in ALJ approvals, further undermining the Warshawsky/Marchand and Pierce proposals' assumptions.

The reality is that there is and has always been a bell curve of ALJ decision-making, with most ALJ rates clustered around the median (which is at or close to its lowest point in the program's history now).[69] There is still a group significantly above the median at more than 75 percent approval and a significant group below at 25 percent approval; both are relative "outliers."[70] As with much judicial and agency adjudicative decision-making, there are variations in outcomes. This problem of variation and perceived inconsistency in decision-making is by no means confined to SSA disability adjudication. It can be also found in criminal and capital sentencing[71] and asylum adjudication[72] among countless other areas of agency and formal judicial adjudication. Those variations are sometimes inexplicable and at their worst—and in the case of some outliers—the product of corruption or racial or invidious bias.

Proponents of more restrictive disability standards or disability hearing process reform often point to the outliers at the top of the bell curve of ALJ decision-making to support policy initiatives. The outliers also provide grist for high-profile media stories about fraud, waste, and abuse in the program, supplying further impetus for restrictive policy changes. For example, an account of a West Virginia ALJ who awarded benefits in 99 percent of the cases before him produced a media feeding frenzy about renegade and corrupt ALJs and the need to curtail the Social Security Administration's disability programs.[73] Professor Pierce's proposal also referenced this particular ALJ and incident.[74] That ALJ was eventually indicted and pled guilty to conspiracy and criminal fraud for accepting bribes amounting to $609,000 from a local attorney to rule favorably in the lawyer's cases, which the ALJ had managed to reassign to his own docket.[75] He was sentenced to four years in prison and $93 million in restitution.[76] One would like to view this case as an aberration.

In other cases, the decisions of a fairly restrictive ALJ in Pennsylvania were the subject of a class-action challenge alleging systemic racial discrimination and various other invidious biases in *Grant v. Commissioner, Social Sec. Admin*.[77] After many years of litigation, the developed record before the court, including testimony from an SSA hearing office colleague who referenced the ALJ as a "close friend," pointed out that the ALJ had a system where he found claimants noncredible and whom the ALJ labeled "no-goodniks."[78] The term "no-goodniks" included African Americans, Latinx, poor whites, the mentally impaired, and substance users, among others.[79] With respect to African American claimants, the ALJ used the N-word in his office on multiple occasions and had referenced a "Senator Bilbow who allegedly introduced a Bill to Congress calling for the return of all African Americans to Africa."[80] The court found on the evidence that this ALJ systematically "harbored biases which rendered him unable to fulfill his duty to decide cases fairly."[81] In *Pestrana v. Chater*,[82] another restrictive ALJ opined about the perceived laziness and lesser work ethic of Puerto Ricans and was castigated by the court with a recommendation for the SSA to pursue disciplinary action for "statements that can be characterized as racist."[83]

One would also like to view each of these cases as aberrations as well. However, unlike the situation of criminal bribery, conspiracy, and corruption of a single West Virginia ALJ leading to improper benefit approvals, the U.S. General Accounting Office has supplied documentation of larger-scale, systemic racial bias against African American and other persons of color in ALJ decision-making nationally, leading to improper benefit denials across the country. In 1992, the GAO studied the issue of disparities in agency decision-making and found unexplained differences in approval rates by race, with lower approval rates for African American claimants, at the ALJ level.[84] The GAO recommended "that the [SSA] Commissioner . . . investigate the reasons for the racial difference in allowance rates . . . and that the Commissioner act to correct and prevent any unwarranted disparities."[85] A decade later, the GAO reexamined the SSA's efforts to address ALJ racial bias and concluded that "[t]he steps SSA has taken over the last decade have not appreciably improved the agency's understanding of whether . . . racial bias exists in its disability decision-making process."[86] No further public action has been pursued by the agency on this issue.

The issue of outlier decision-making should garner more attention. It bears repeating that the grid was designed to provide some degree of greater consistency, efficiency, and accuracy of decision-making through the cabining of widely inconsistent discretionary decision-making prior to the grid's promulgation. Indeed, one of the ALJs who has written in support of a stricter disability standard, as well as the abolition of the mandatory grid, has pointed to the grid's rules and framework as an impediment to the more unrestrained and open-ended decision-making he would like to pursue.[87] This identified problem reinforces the grid's importance as a component of several needed steps to constrain problematic and exceedingly "outlier" ALJ decision-making when contrary to law.

The Pierce proposal's extreme remedy of abolishing the hearing process and removing the entire ALJ corps is unnecessary, illegal under current law,[88] and likely unconstitutional in part with respect to benefit terminations in the SSI disability program and the oral hearing rights in welfare programs stemming from *Goldberg v. Kelly* and its progeny.[89] The Warshawsky/Marchand proposal of focusing quality and quantity controls only on high-approval ALJs is also likely illegal and unconstitutional. A one-sided review program of high-approval ALJs, conducted by the agency that employs the ALJ, has a chilling effect on ALJ decision-making, sends an unmistakable message to ALJs to limit claimant-favorable decisions to avoid scrutiny, and treads on the claimant's due process right to an impartial decision maker.[90] However, to the extent a remedy is sought to reduce substantial overall decisional variation, and not merely the claimant-favorable variety, a review system predicated on significant deviation from the decisional norm in either direction sends no similar particular message and has been sustained against a facial challenge.[91]

Such a systematic, evenhanded outlier review program would continue to supply a considerably less drastic and more targeted alternative to the problem of substantial outlier deviance than would complete ALJ abolition. This remedy could also be applied to substantial outlier state agency adjudicators who decide a much greater proportion of cases than ALJs.[92] The reviews could include targeted investigation of the reasons for the substantial statistical deviations from the norm, supplementary education, and training. Where the substantial decisional disparities reflect a systematic pattern of disregard or indifference to governing law, basic facts, settled procedure,[93] or racial or invidious discrimination, discipline should be sought and corrective action pursued until remedied. In any event, none of these measures justify a tightening of the disability standard and/or elimination of the grid as proposed by

Warshawsky and Marchand; indeed, elimination of the grid would be counterproductive to the expressed desire to bring greater consistency to agency decision-making.

Finally, the problem of ALJ outlier denial rates, when potentially coupled with racial bias, should not be overlooked in an evenhanded evaluation of ALJ decision-making around the discretionary margins. When these patterns emerge, they will less likely be accompanied with the overt bigotry displayed in *Grant* and *Pestrana*. The Third Circuit Court of Appeals has explained that "extreme manifestations of discrimination are thankfully rare. . . . It has become easier to coat various forms of discrimination with the appearance of propriety, or to ascribe some other less odious intention to what is in reality discriminatory behavior. In other words, while discriminatory conduct persists, violators have learned not to leave the proverbial 'smoking gun' behind."[94] Racially disparate patterns in ALJ decision-making in areas such as assessing credibility and the evaluation of pain and subjective symptomology may also be a function of unconscious or implicit bias. Put simply, "explicit bias and overt discrimination are only part of the problem. Also important, and likely more pervasive, are questions surrounding implicit bias—attitudes or stereotypes that affect our understanding, decisionmaking, and behavior, without our even realizing it."[95] In other words, some ALJs may implicitly and less consciously harbor perceptions that Black and Brown claimants are less trustworthy or credible as was expressed in *Grant*, or less hardworking or diligent as was expressed in *Pestrana*, contributing to less-favorable hearing outcomes. Other factors such as greater interaction with the criminal justice system, racialized mass incarceration, and the "stigma of criminality" may also play a role in ALJs' perceptions of program-eligibility "worthiness" in adjudicating cases as it does in the low-wage employment context.[96]

Rather than leave the 1992 and 2002 GAO racial disparity studies unexamined and unresolved, the SSA should take steps to explore and mitigate racially disparate ALJ decision-making. For example, as in the low-wage employment context discussed above—in which Black applicants were found to face twice the difficulty obtaining callbacks for jobs than White applicants in controlled employment "tests" with similarly situated "testers" of different races[97]—the SSA should conduct similar controlled testing or audits of ALJ decision-making to ascertain further the extent and nature of racial disparities and where to prioritize pursuit of needed training and other corrective action.[98]

Fraud

Perceived widespread fraud in the program is also often cited as a reason to adopt a more stringent disability standard. Warshawsky and Marchand point out that "numerous cases of fraud recently discovered in New York City and Puerto Rico have shown that certain disability categories such as mental illness are more vulnerable to applicants gaming the system."[99] The Office of the Inspector General (OIG) referred to all three cases—New York, Puerto Rico, and West Virginia—as relatively sophisticated criminal conspiracies using the same lawyers/representatives and medical sources and fabricating similar evidence.[100] The New York conspiracy received much media attention because all the criminal conspirators seeking benefits also worked in law enforcement and public safety (police officers and firefighters)—some of whom continued to work off the books as security guards at a strip club, thereby also committing tax fraud.[101] All were apprehended, convicted, and are, have served, or will be serving time for these crimes.[102]

In none of the cases, however, did the OIG find that the laxity of disability standards contributed to the fraud. Indeed, if all of the particular applicants as well as their doctors, lawyers, witnesses, and other representatives are willing to risk imprisonment (and, in the cases of the latter, their professional licenses and careers) and conspire to commit criminal fraud by intentionally fabricating fraudulent medical evidence and suborning perjury in order to meet a particular eligibility standard, this criminally fabricated evidence can be adjusted to match any disability standard. Agencies such as the OIG and FBI must therefore pursue fraud enforcement mechanisms to thwart such coordinated criminal conspiracies, much as they would for sophisticated criminal conspiracies to commit bank fraud, tax fraud, government contracting fraud, and other federal fraud, all of which risk theft of far greater amounts than the relatively meager DI/SSI benefits.

The bipartisan group of eight former commissioners and a White House report on SSDI have identified a very low rate of fraud in the program.[103] The rate has been quantified as less than 1 percent of all cases.[104] This is a lower rate of fraud than many government spending and contracting programs and with much lower amounts at issue.[105] The SSA and OIG have also undertaken several measures to develop predictive tools and identify patterns for detection that would more rapidly uncover fraud in the aftermath of the New York, West Virginia, and Puerto Rico criminal fraud conspiracy prosecutions.[106]

15

Amendments to Simplify Work Adjustment Assessments by Expanding Eligibility

A European-Style Occupational Standard

The 1960s-era congressional bills that sought to add an occupational disability standard to the disability insurance program would have significantly expanded eligibility while simplifying the adjudicative process by eliminating the work adjustment assessment and all vocational and labor market considerations other than those pertaining to one's own principal occupation(s).[1] Under those proposals, claimants who demonstrated an inability to perform past relevant work would be deemed disabled.[2] In today's climate, such a proposal would confront a series of functional, conceptual, and political obstacles. First, it is likely inconsistent with the American ethos on job mobility assumptions outside of one's social or economic class.[3] With an occupational disability standard, persons unable to perform their past highly skilled, highly remunerative work would be excused from the social obligation of making adjustments to a wider range of less demanding, less esteemed, and less remunerative work than those whose past work was unskilled and more generic.[4]

Second, with the creation of the Supplemental Security Income program in 1972, claimants could establish entitlement to benefits without any past relevant work.[5] Thus, an occupational standard would either provide a much easier path to benefits for claimants without past work, or it would still require a work adjustment process for this category. For example, a large number of impaired seventeen-year-old minors who have never worked, but who have been previously found eligible for SSI benefits as children, would be presumptively eligible for adult benefits upon their eighteenth birthdays if their impairments remained severe and the SSI work adjustment step were eliminated by an occupational standard.[6] Such a proposal would undoubtedly confront significant political opposition.

Other proposals for loosening the strict eligibility standards or expanding benefits for other persons precluded from the workforce would also likely confront major political opposition. Professor Lance Liebman has long called for a more inclusive disability standard based on worker expectations and a private insurance model.[7] Under Liebman's approach, the standard "should cover all cases in which a medical cause leads to total unemployment, even if the claimant might be put to work by an ideal labor market."[8] He stated that

> [t]o visualize Social Security disability protection as a function of worker expectations is to see a way through the *Kerner* problem. If an individual bought private insurance against total medical disability and then became so sick that he could not do his former job, would he not expect to be paid—even if he could still perform some work but could not obtain a job? What point would insurance have, if not to pay when sickness leads to zero income? The insured might be less 'needy' because of his theoretical capacity to work, but the point of the insurance would surely be income continuation if labor could not produce cash. We would be outraged if the small print in a Mutual of Omaha policy denied payments to Mr. Kerner. Because the United States, in its Social Security program, has tried to be Mutual of Omaha, judicial interpretation of the statutory ambiguity should mirror adjudication of a claim against a private insurer.[9]

Professor Mark Weber has called for providing benefits for partial or temporary disability in a manner similar to the disability benefits programs in other countries and in other programs in the United States.[10] Weber urges a particular focus on reducing the severity of the disability standard with respect to desperately low income SSI applicants who can no longer obtain life support benefits from the U.S. safety net of residual welfare and general assistance programs, which have been discontinued or reduced since the 1990s.[11] Professor and Dean Matthew Diller has argued that social policy should recognize the reality that disability benefits programs now serve a residual sustenance or life support function for society's most employment-challenged individuals; this is problematic, he argues, because not all of the most employment-challenged individuals have a medical disability as defined in the Act.[12] Thus, according to Diller, the government should reconsider the universal guaranteed income and negative income tax proposals of the late 1960s and early 1970s, which would have provided a minimum subsistence benefit to all unemployed and low-income persons and have obviated the need for a disability benefit residual safety net.[13]

Without evaluating the merits of these proposals, only the Diller proposal would unquestionably simplify the disability programs' work adjustment adjudication process. As to Diller's call for a federal general welfare program, however, it bears recognition that the creation of new or significantly expanded permanent income support programs is still unlikely, notwithstanding the short-term and more universal income support measures (stimulus payments and extended and enhanced unemployment benefits) adopted during the 2020–21 COVID-19 pandemic and the rise of universal basic income experiments in various cities here and in countries around the world.[14] It is telling, however, that Republicans and Democrats alike have largely and consistently lauded the Personal Responsibility and Work Opportunity Reconciliation Act (PRWORA) of 1996 and the "end [of] welfare as we know it."[15] A more likely adoptable general or universal safety net proposal that would undoubtedly reduce the incidence of medically preventable, or treatable and avoidable disability, would be the enactment of universal health care—for which public support increased during the coronavirus pandemic.[16]

16

Proposals to Impose a "Welfare Reform" Mandatory Work Incentives Model

A variety of proposals have urged amending the disability benefits programs by adding stronger or mandatory work incentives and time limits and a "work first" model, such as those at the core of PRWORA's "welfare reform" initiatives.[1] Similar to PRWORA's treatment of the Temporary Assistance for Needy Families (TANF) program, this would presumably entail active supervision of claimants by agency and professional rehabilitation personnel, with the goal of maximizing return to the workforce and reducing the amount of benefits received. Apart from the highly questionable assertion of TANF's success—through time limits, mandatory work requirements, and work sanctions—in producing sustained employment, moving families out of deep poverty, and generally improving the quality of life of TANF-eligible caretakers and their families,[2] some commentators and public policy bodies have viewed the enactment of the Americans with Disabilities Act (ADA) of 1990[3] as reflecting a recognition of a shift in disability social policy away from income supports to a paramount focus on entering or returning to the workforce by surmounting obstacles to work.[4] The availability of cash assistance is perceived as an impediment to the ADA's work thrust.[5]

The proposed TANF-like mandatory "sink or swim"[6] approaches to work incentives for disabled claimants are misguided for several reasons. First, they are predicated on the assumption of claimants' largely voluntary withdrawal from the workforce. As Mashaw and others have explained, and as discussed above, the strictness of the disability standard already in place, coupled with the modesty of benefit awards relative to wages, debunks that assertion.[7]

Second, the ADA has not yet created significantly expanded employment opportunities for lower-skill workers with disabilities.[8] The opportunities the ADA may create are most likely to benefit persons with less medically and vocationally disadvantaged profiles than those found eligible for disability benefits.[9] Thus, it is more likely that such mandatory work measures would have a deleterious impact on recipients of disability benefits and would cause "unnecessary suffering, anxiety and turmoil" for a particularly vulnerable population.[10] Third, to the extent a mandatory work incentive model would require active supervision and discretionary management by vocational and rehabilitation professionals, the model would suffer from the greater unpredictability and inconsistency inherent in professional judgments and characteristic of the professional treatment model of benefactory agency administration.[11]

Finally, this approach to disability benefits would be expensive. While some persons advocated passage of the ADA as a way to reduce expenditures in the disability benefits programs, Professor Samuel Bagenstos has explained that more meaningful integration of disabled persons into the workforce, beyond the ADA's initial limited achievements, would require "massive ongoing public investments" in many other social welfare initiatives.[12] This, according to Bagenstos, follows from the fact that, "[f]or a large number of people with disabilities, it is not the discriminatory acts of particular employers but instead deep-rooted structural barriers—such as the lack of personal-assistance services, assistive technology, and accessible transportation and, above all, the current setup of our health insurance system—that keep them out of the workforce."[13] Without a fuller understanding of an alternative, work-supportive, social welfare safety net, and without the ability to finance such an alternative,[14] an analysis of such mandatory work and rehabilitation proposals is categorically premature.

Other PRWORA-type welfare reform–inspired disability reform proposals focus on mandating "work first" interventions with disability claimants while incentivizing employers to hire persons with disabilities seeking disability benefits. Professor Richard Burkhauser and labor economist (and president of the Federal Reserve Bank of San Francisco) Mary Daly propose following the Dutch disability reform model of imposing "experience rating" on employers paying into the SSDI system through payroll taxes.[15] The government would raise the payroll tax on employers whose workers "enroll in the system at above average rates and lower[] the SSDI payroll taxes on firms whose workers enroll at below average rates."[16] This would "more directly link the costs to the firm of one if its employees moving onto the SSDI program."[17]

Consequently, employers would "be more incentivized to make investments in accommodation and rehabilitation that could prolong the tenure of a worker with disability."[18] Burkhauser and Daly ground their proposal on lessons learned from PRWORA welfare reform, which "discouraged entry as much as it encouraged exit."[19] This, they argue, "suggests that a work first strategy, combined with work-based support, can be important for motivating individuals to move into the labor market."[20]

Critics of disability reform through experience rating and the Dutch model, such as Elaine Fultz, Kathy Ruffing, and Paul Van De Water, emphasize significant differences in the Dutch and American disability programs and relevant comparative social welfare safety nets and the disincentives for employment of persons with disability built into the system.[21] The Dutch have a far more lenient disability standard (which includes coverage for only partial disability) and devote a much higher proportion of GDP to disability benefit programs—twice that of the United States.[22] Thus, a greater percentage of Dutch disability recipients are less medically impaired and more likely to adjust to work.[23] At the same time, a Dutch "tradition of social partnership between the government, employer organizations and trade unions" created supportive conditions for this program's reliance on employers "to finance and implement rehabilitation," make on-the-job accommodations, and even "find a new job for workers for whom they can no longer offer comparable employment."[24] The Dutch safety net also includes various supports for workers with disabilities, such as two years of employer-paid sick leave at 70 percent of earnings and universal health coverage.[25]

Despite the numerous disabled worker–friendly conditions in the Netherlands not present in the United States, the results remain mixed at best. Elaine Fultz identified three problems the Dutch program produced: "(1) increased employer reluctance to hire workers with health problems; (2) increased unemployment of persons with disabilities; and (3) an increase in temporary employment coupled with higher rates of sickness and illness among these workers."[26] Even Burkhauser and Daly acknowledge that "critics are justified in arguing that, perversely, the net impact [of their proposal] could be a decrease in employment and an increase in the use of SSDI by working-age people with disabilities."[27] They also concede that "there is insufficient research to justify moving forward with experience rating nationally today"[28] or to implement "such a "major change in SSDI policy."[29]

A similar employer-centered proposal by David Autor and Mark Duggan calls for employers to purchase private disability insurance (PDI) with minimum contributions by employees, which would combine a mandatory rehabilitation– and work accommodation–focused screening and diversion process for most disability insurance claimants.[30] The limited number of claimants who fall into SSA's exceedingly narrow and stringent "compassionate allowance" criteria would not be diverted and would have immediate resort to the existing SSA disability eligibility process.[31] After a period of at least twenty-one months, resort to the SSA disability insurance process would be available for the other putative disability claimants who had been unsuccessful in the mandatory vocational rehabilitation and work-focused activities.[32] This PDI coverage would provide vocational assistance, workplace accommodation, and limited wage replacement to employees.[33]

Just as with the Burkhauser and Daly proposal, employers would have incentives to minimize disability applications because their costs (premiums) would increase based on higher disability rates.[34] This proposal would likely suffer the same deficiencies of the Burkhauser and Daly proposal based on the Dutch model.[35] The Autor/ Duggan PDI proposal has also garnered criticism as both unaffordable and potentially counterproductive for truly disabled persons.[36]

Miscellaneous Proposal

In 1994, the SSA prepared a "reengineering plan" proposal to change the substantive approach to the sequential evaluation process to simplify criteria and focus more broadly on functional capacity and baseline occupational demands. In part, this aspect of the plan was directed to the perceived inability to identify an appropriate methodology to measure such capacities. While touted as a proposal to streamline the fragmented, multistage state agency/SSA adjudication processes, it also included a proposal to alter the SSA's substantive eligibility criteria.[37] Thus, while primarily drawing attention for its call to eliminate the reconsideration and appeals council stages in the administrative process, the plan also recommended alterations of steps 2 through 5 in the substantive five-step sequential evaluation process.[38]

First, the step 2 medical severity threshold would be replaced with a requirement of demonstrating a medically determinable impairment.[39] Second, the step 3 listings would be replaced with an index of medical conditions that would obviate the need for highly technical test results and would "describe impairments so severely debilitating that [they] can be presumed to equal a loss of functional ability to perform [SGA] without assessing the individual's functional ability." Because functional equivalence is factored into the index, the current process for evaluating equivalence to a listing would be eliminated.[40] Finally, at steps 4 and 5 of the current sequential process, the RFC determination would be replaced with an individual assessment of functional capacity that would also consider the claimant's education.[41]

After such an assessment, "the individual's age will determine whether his or her functional ability is compared against the demands of the individual's previous work or against a 'baseline' of occupational demands."[42] "The baseline will describe a range of work related functions that represents work that exists in significant numbers in the national economy that does not require prior skills or formal job training."[43] Individuals nearing retirement age would be evaluated under an occupational approach to disability and would be found disabled if unable to perform the functional demands of prior work.[44] All other workers would be evaluated against the functional demands of the baseline work.[45] To accomplish this task, the proposal called for the development of "functional assessment instruments [that] will be designed to measure, as objectively as possible, an [individual's] abilities to perform a baseline of occupational demands that includes the principal dimensions of work and task performance, including primary physical, psychological and cognitive processes."[46] These instruments would also obviate the need for VE and medical expert testimony at disability hearings.[47]

Professor Diller pointed out that this "reengineering" proposal would "essentially end consideration of vocational factors such as age, education, and work experience in the disability determination process."[48] That is because "[i]t is difficult to see how any such baseline could be an accurate measurement of the ability of both older workers with few skills and little education and younger workers with significant skills or advanced education."[49] The proposal would also eliminate the labor market work adjustment assessment based on adjustment to specific identified work existing in significant numbers in the economy for claimants with various combinations of medical and vocational limitations. Diller also argued against an earlier draft of the reengineering proposal that would have tied the proposed "baseline" to "any reasonable accommodations that employers are expected to make under the Americans with Disabilities Act," and he identified obstacles to any such ADA-predictive assessment.[50] Because the reasonableness of any accommodation is employer-specific based on a determination of potential undue hardship from the accommodation, it cannot be determined outside of its specific context.[51]

A study undertaken to create these assessment instruments concluded that "no single instrument would fulfill SSA's vision."[52] A veteran administrative law judge writing about the proposal suggested that it was based on "social science fiction."[53] Within a relatively short period, the GAO urged the agency to prioritize the reengineering proposal's presumably time-saving process initiatives and discontinue work on the proposed substantive sequential evaluation criteria changes.[54] To date, no further work has been pursued on the latter.[55]

Conclusion

For sixty-five years, the Social Security Administration, courts, Congress, and millions of disabled workers have struggled to attain a greater understanding of how to answer an elusive question: Where are the jobs to which persons with severe medical and vocational challenges can adjust in the American labor market? The system created by the Congress and the SSA, as interpreted by the courts, for making the work adjustment assessments in disability benefit cases is large, complex, and in urgent need of updating and some repair. Many thousands of work adjustment assessments and resulting SSA decisions are made every year that are currently unsupportable.

Nevertheless, proposals calling for scrapping the current standard's work adjustment step and its labor market and vocational considerations, for either significantly more eligibility restrictive or less restrictive alternatives, rest on outdated and uninformed assumptions, are not politically or functionally realistic or feasible, or a combination of both. The initial exaggerated fears of a disability explosion and social security trust fund depletion have been revealed as overstated based on the decline in disability applications and recipients in accordance with long-predicted economic and demographic trends.

Similarly, the claims of widespread fraud, and allegations of claimant-slanted ALJ impartiality, as feeding such a disability explosion have been revealed as unfounded; ALJ general allowance rates have dropped close to all-time lows. However, racial bias in ALJ adjudication, as revealed by the GAO in its reports, remains an issue of concern and is suggestive of impartiality in the other direction. The GAO's call to investigate the disparities should be heeded and corrective action taken to uncover and reduce unexplained racially disparate ALJ decision-making, such as through testing for biased decision-making with use of bias testers and implementation of implicit bias training and other antidiscrimination decisional adjudicator training.

In addition, American labor market changes and trends over the past half-century, and the state of the twenty-first century's low-skills labor market, portend a more constricted economy and labor market for characteristically low-skilled, low-education disability benefits claimants than at any time in the disability programs' history. These trends include the substantial reduction of the manufacturing base and evolution from a goods-producing to a service-providing economy; globalization and outsourcing of many low-skill sectors; computerization, automation, artificial intelligence, robotics, and other technological changes reducing or eliminating the need for humans to perform simple routine, repetitive work; and an increasing need for greater degrees of worker skill, dexterity, flexibility, and human judgment. The vocational factors of age, education, and work experience remain highly relevant factors bearing on the ability to make successful work adjustments in the twenty-first century's low-skill labor market based on credible studies and, in some areas, Bureau of Labor Statistics ORS data evaluating the impact of these factors on job requirements and/or work adjustments.

The American disability standard remains one of the strictest in the world as measured based on domestic indicators and when compared to those of other developed countries. Disabled workers and claimants also face substantially restricted and readily diminishing safety-net alternatives, rendering the consequences of wrongful disability benefit denials as potentially damaging and far reaching as at any time in recent history. Under the circumstances, the agency and Congress should resist the temptation to which they have succumbed in the vast majority of statutory and regulatory changes adopted in the previous five-plus decades to make an already restrictive disability standard stricter and less inclusive.

Instead, the agency and all stakeholders should pursue a "mend it don't end it approach" to the current system and adopt a series of steps to improve the accuracy, consistency, fairness, and credibility of the current process in light of the above-identified system flaws. First, a new, realistic, comprehensive, and temporally accurate taxonomy linked to regularly collected occupational statistics must be completed. While the SSA and/or DOL have been working on such a new occupational taxonomy for more than two decades, work on this project, known as the Occupational Information System, needs to proceed with a greater sense of urgency. Without such an OIS, the entire system, as currently structured, collapses like a house of cards. After completing such a new system, the DOL and SSA should take steps to ensure its continued temporal reliability through a process of regular updating at least every five years. As described above, in conducting the work and data collection for the OIS, the agency would be well-advised to let the data shape needed policy changes, and not the other way around.

Second, the vocational expert program needs to be strengthened and steps for greater integrity and reliability pursued. SSA should adopt some type of certification process for VEs to demonstrate sufficient background and experience to offer informed expert opinions on the job market and relevant work adjustment and vocational facts. All VEs should be able and willing to effectively articulate sound and supportable methodologies for their vocational conclusions. While doctors and lawyers appearing in SSA disability proceedings are independently certified as capable for their respective crafts, there is no such process for VEs. Federal law requires that non-attorney representatives must possess a bachelor's degree or equivalent qualifications, pass a written examination administered by the SSA, secure professional liability insurance or equivalent, undergo a criminal background check, and regularly complete continuing education courses.[1] A similar system of certification should be developed for VEs.

In addition, SSA should insist on adherence to what the Supreme Court declared in *Biestek* as the "best practice" for VE testimony and is expressly required in the current SSA VE handbook: VEs must not only be prepared to explain cogently the methodology behind their work adjustments assessments and job incidence numbers but also make the underlying source material on which their assessments rest available at the hearing or through the hearing process. The ALJs must also provide meaningful opportunities for claimants to review and confront the VE testimony and source material. On judicial review, the courts should follow the lead of the Eleventh Circuit in *Goode* and Seventh Circuit in *Brace and Chavez* and insist on demonstration of articulable, supportable, and methodologically credible bases for VE work adjustment testimony in order for the agency to be found to have met its work adjustment burden under the substantial evidence standard of review for appeals of agency benefit decisions.

The grid and its adjudicative framework should be updated as well. The grid has represented a positive and important development toward improving consistency and fairness in disability benefits adjudications involving labor market assessments, notwithstanding its considerable empirical, temporal, and structural deficiencies. It is a major advancement over the pre-grid, entirely ad hoc approaches of agency adjudicators' intuition-based official notice and vocational experts' unguided suppositions. If employed properly, it also aids in reduction of biased or arbitrary ALJ and adjudicator decision-making by regularizing work adjustment criteria and supplying content to the meaning of the statutory requirement of identifying "work which exists in significant numbers" in the economy and how many such jobs are "significant."

As described above, it is conceivable that an updated grid and duly promulgated grid regulations might be expanded to cover a larger range of circumstances than the current exertional scope if empirically supported. Unlike the attempts to manufacture "mini-grids" on nonexertional limitations through subregulatory guidance in the SSRs, the agency should pursue any such efforts at "gridding" nonexertional limitations into its rules that presume successful work adjustments through transparent, participatory, and democratically accountable processes such as the notice and comment processes in the APA (5 U.S.C. §553 et seq.) utilized for agency regulations with full legal effect. This would avert the official notice doctrine and due process violation issues emerging through the use of non–APA promulgated subregulatory guidance and ALJ speculation.

However, because mental impairments are highly variable, it is less likely that mental limitations could be sufficiently quantified in a manner that comports with the grid's matrix of generalized work adjustment presumptions. The agency's past history counsels against removing mental limitations and other highly individualized and contextual nonexertional limitations from case-by-case assessments. There will always be "gaps in the grid" simply because humans are too complex and layered and the labor market is too fluid and varied to control for all outcomes. As a consequence, even with an updated and expanded grid, there will remain a need for residual work adjustment assessments in those cases and adherence to the statutory mandate recognized by the Supreme Court for appropriately individualized determinations in each case.[2]

However, such remaining "off the grid" assessments should still be informed by the grid's framework and by using, where needed, particularized vocational evidence on the extent of erosion of the grid's administratively noticed occupational bases attributable to these highly variable and individualized limitations. Use of the grid's framework in this manner ensures consistency and equity in adjudication. In short, a properly updated and potentially expanded grid, and use of the grid's adjudicatory framework, can still provide consistent and nonarbitrary bases to circumscribe the labor market work adjustment assessment in mental impairment and other nonexertional or "nongridable" cases and promote the principles of greater bureaucratic rationality that its proponents lauded. The SSA should provide training and assistance to all adjudicators to ensure consistent application of its own subregulatory guidance establishing how to make such "grid framework" assessments in cases falling into the grid's gaps.

Finally, because the disability standard and the meaning of disability for SSA program purposes are socially constructed, opinions on the role and obligations of society for addressing the needs of persons with medical and vocational challenges realistically left out of the labor market will vary widely in a diverse constitutional democracy. This book suggests practical solutions for many of the identified deficiencies in the current disability system's operations. But debates on the big picture—the proper disability standard and the best approach to securing justice under these circumstances—will never be fully resolved because there is no epistemic answer to these value-laden issues. It is my hope that this book can provide a contribution to this ongoing and likely long-continuing discussion along with suggestions for progress in the continuing work of this enormous and overburdened agency and the struggle for basic human needs and survival among the millions of disability claimants living on the margins.

ACKNOWLEDGMENTS

This book is based on two decades of research and writings by the author, further informed by three decades of clinical practice and firsthand observation of the operation of the social security disability programs' adjudicative system and the life circumstances and experiences of disability claimants attempting to navigate the SSA bureaucracy. Several ideas first introduced in Jon C. Dubin, *Torquemada Meets Kafka: The Misapplication of the Issue Exhaustion Doctrine to Inquisitorial Administrative Proceedings*, 97 COLUM. L. REV. 1289 (1997); Jon C. Dubin, *Overcoming Gridlock: Campbell after a Quarter-Century and Bureaucratically Rational Gap-Filling in Mass Justice Adjudication in the Social Security Administrations Disability Programs*, 62 ADMIN. L. REV. 937 (2010); Jon C. Dubin, *The Labor Market Side of Disability Benefits Policy and Law*, 20 S. CAL. REV. L. & SOC. JUST. 1 (2011); Jon C. Dubin and Robert E. Rains, *Scapegoating Social Security Disability Claimants (and The Judges Who Evaluate Them)*, 6 ADVANCE: J. AM. CONST. SOC. ISSUE GROUPS 109 (2012); and Jon C. Dubin, *A Modest, Albeit Heavily Tested Social Security Disability Reform Proposal: Streamlining the Adjudicative Process by Eliminating Reconsideration and Enhancing Initial Stage Development*, 23 GEO. J. OF POVERTY. L. & POL'Y 203 (2016), have been further developed, augmented, and updated in the course of this writing. I thank the referees selected by New York University Press for their thoughtful critiques and careful analysis of the book proposal and first draft of this manuscript; Vanderbilt Professor of Law *Emeritus* Frank Bloch and Fordham Dean and Professor of Law Matthew Diller, whose many related writings and ideas, as well as conversations with the author over many years, have contributed to this work; Penn State Dickinson Professor of Law *Emeritus* Robert E. Rains for his careful review of an earlier draft of this book and valuable comments; veteran social security attorneys Eric Schnaufer and Carolyn Kubitschek, who shared their deep insights and extraordinary expertise in social security disability litigation and agency adjudication in their review of drafts or sharing of ideas developed in the manuscript; my Rutgers Law School colleagues Professors David Noll, Alan Hyde, Bernard Bell, Randi Mandelbaum, and Carlos Ball for research suggestions, formulation of ideas through conversations in the manuscript's development, or advice on publication issues; and my research assistants, from Rutgers: Deanna Christian, Micauri Vargas, Christina Sabato, and Megyn MacMullen; and from my N.Y.U. Law School "Law of the Welfare State" seminar: J. Luke Pizzato. I also gratefully acknowledge support from the Rutgers Law School Summer Research Grant Fund, the Martini Research Fund, and the Simmons Research Fund for work on this book. Finally, I thank editors Clara Platter, Martin Coleman, and Veronica Knutson and the entire team at New York University Press for their work in bringing this manuscript to publication.

—JCD
Newark, New Jersey
January 2021

NOTES

INTRODUCTION

1 *See* Soc. Sec. Admin. NEVER Beneficiaries, Aged 60–89, 2015, Office of Ret. Policy, www.ssa.gov (noting that 97 percent of Americans will receive some form of social security benefit and discussing the characteristics of the 3 percent who never become beneficiaries); *see also* Richardson v. Perales, 402 U.S. 389, 399 (1971) ("The Social Security Act has been with us since 1935 . . . [, and it] affects nearly all of us.").

2 Elise Gould, *Social Security Kept 27 Million Out of Poverty in 2013*, Econ. Policy Inst. (Oct. 30, 2014), www.epi.org ("Social Security is, by far, the most effective anti-poverty program in the United States. Without Social Security, an additional 8.6 percent of Americans, or nearly 27 million, would fall below the SPM poverty threshold."); *see also* The Obama White House, Soc. Sec. Disability Ins.: A Lifeline For American Workers and Families (2015), https://obamawhitehouse.archives.gov (the SSDI program alone annually "keep[s] 3 million Americans out of poverty and lessens the degree of poverty for another 1.9 million Americans").

3 *See* 42 U.S.C. §§ 401–22 (2012) (setting out statutory authority for the social security Old Age, Survivors' and Disability Insurance (OASDI) programs).

4 *See* 42 U.S.C. §§ 1381–83 (2012) (setting out statutory authority for the Supplemental Security Income SSI program).

5 Paul R. Verkuil, *The Self Legitimating Bureaucracy*, 93 Yale L.J. 780, 781 (1983).

6 Jerry L. Mashaw, Charles L. Goetz, Frank I. Goodman, Warren F. Schwartz, Paul R. Verkuil & Milton Carrow, Soc. Sec. Hearings and Appeals: A Study of the Soc. Sec. Admin. Hearing System xi (1978) [hereinafter Mashaw, Hearings]; Heckler v. Campbell, 461 U.S. 458, 460 n.2 (1983).

7 Mashaw, Hearings, at xi; *see* Soc. Sec. Admin., Hearings and Appeals, www.ssa.gov (reporting the Office of the Chief Administrative Law Judge oversees more than 1,500 ALJs); U.S. Courts, Authorized Judgeships (1789–2019), www.uscourts.gov (reporting 860 Article III Authorized Judgeships in 2019).

8 *See* Charles H. Koch, Jr. & David A. Koplow, *The Fourth Bite at the Apple: A Study of the Operation and Utility of the Soc. Sec. Admin.'s Appeals Council*, 17 Fla. St. U. L. Rev. 199 (1990).

9 *See* SOC. SEC. ADMIN., FY 2021 Congressional Justification 156 (2020), www.ssa.gov; SOC. SEC. ADMIN., ANNUAL PERFORMANCE REPORT: FISCAL YEARS (FY) 2019–21, 44 (2019–21), www.ssa.gov (reporting 2.31 million completed claims for 2019 and targeting 2.35 million completed claims for 2020); OFFICE OF THE INSPECTOR GENERAL, AUDIT REPORT: OVERSIGHT OF ADMIN. LAW JUDGE DECISIONAL QUALITY App. C, fig. C-1 (2017), https://oig.ssa.gov; Soc. Sec. Admin., Hearings and Appeals, www.ssa.gov.

10 *See* JONAH GELBACH AND DAVID MARCUS, ADMIN. CONFERENCE OF THE U.S., A STUDY OF SOCIAL SECURITY LITIGATION IN THE FEDERAL COURTS 4 (2016).

11 UNITED STATES INST. OF MEDICINE, COMM. TO REVIEW THE SOC. SEC. ADMIN. DISABILITY DECISION PROCESS RESEARCH, THE DYNAMICS OF DISABILITY: MEASURING AND MONITORING DISABILITY FOR SOC. SEC. PROGRAMS 113–14 (Googloo S. Wonderlich, Dorothy P. Rice & Nicole L. Amado eds., 2002).

12 Bauer v. Astrue, 532 F.3d 606, 609 (7th Cir. 2008).

13 Social Security Amendments of 1967, Pub. L. No. 90–248, 81 Stat. 821 (1967) (codified at 42 U.S.C. § 423(d)(2)(A) (2006)).

14 *Id.*

15 I use the phrase "social obligation to work" while mindful that there are elements in society in a wealth or leisure class who elude comparable scrutiny as socially nonfunctional, undignified, or nonproductive when not employed. *See, e.g.*, Ezra Klein, *Mitt Romney Flashback: Stay-at-Home Moms Need to Learn the Dignity of Work*, WASHINGTON POST, April 15, 2012, www.washingtonpost.com (discussing the contradiction in then–presidential candidate Mitt Romney's assertion that low-income mothers need to leave the home and child-care duties and assume mandatory employment obligations in the labor market to have "the dignity of work," while defending his wife, Ann Romney, from charges that she had "not worked [a] day in her life" because her functioning as a stay-at-home mom and caring for the Romney children was real "work" and should be respected as such).

16 *See* Annual Statistical Report on the Social Security Disability Program 2018, Outcomes of Applications for Disability Benefits, Charts 66–65, www.ssa.gov (40.1 percent of denials and 50.1 percent of worker approvals in DI or concurrent DI/SSI claims were based on ability to adjust to other work determinations in 2017).

17 *See* Rules for Adjudicating Disability Claims in Which Vocational Factors Must Be Considered, 43 Fed. Reg. 55,349, 55,349 (Nov. 28, 1978).

18 Based on 2014 data, 31 percent of DI beneficiaries had mental impairments (4.1 percent cognitive mental impairments; 26.9 percent psychiatric and other mental impairments) and 57.4 percent of adult SSI beneficiaries had mental impairments (18.8 percent cognitive mental impairments; 38.6 percent psychiatric and other mental impairments); see *Social Security Advisory Board, Disability Chartbook* ch. 6, Chart 2 (January 24, 2017), www.ssab.gov.

1. THE DISABILITY CATEGORY AND THE CONGRESSIONAL IDEAL

1 *See* DEBORAH STONE, THE DISABLED STATE 29–89 (1984) [hereinafter STONE, THE DISABLED STATE]; Matthew Diller, *Entitlement and Exclusion: The Role of Disability in the Social Welfare System*, 44 UCLA L. REV. 361, 372 (1996) [hereinafter Diller, *Entitlement*].

2 Matthew Diller, *Dissonant Disability Policies: The Tensions Between the Americans with Disabilities Act and Federal Disability Benefit Programs*, 76 TEX. L. REV. 1003, 1014 (1998) [hereinafter Diller, *Dissonant Disability Policies*].

3 Social Security Act, ch. 531, 49 Stat. 620 (1935) (codified as amended in various scattered sections of 42 U.S.C. and 26 U.S.C. (2006)).

4 Frank S. Bloch, *Medical Proof, Social Policy, and Social Security's Medically Centered Definition of Disability*, 92 CORNELL. L. REV. 189, 190 (2007) [hereinafter Bloch, *Medical Proof*]; *see also id.* at 190 n.4 ("The core distinction between public assistance and social insurance is that eligibility for the latter is contingent on having contributed to the program through taxes paid on wages, while public assistance is a noncontributory program with eligibility contingent on financial need.").

5 Bloch, *Medical Proof*, at 190.

6 *See generally* R. KENT WEAVER, ENDING WELFARE AS WE KNOW IT (2000) (describing elimination of the AFDC welfare entitlement program through the Personal Responsibility and Work Opportunity Reconciliation Act of 1996) [hereinafter WEAVER, ENDING WELFARE].

7 *See* Matthew H. Hawes, *So No Damn Politician Can Ever Scrap It: The Constitutional Protection of Social Security Benefits*, 65 U. PITT L. REV. 865 (2004) (deriving title from President Franklin Roosevelt's quote regarding political implications of the social security program's contributory design).

8 *Id.*

9 Bloch, *Medical Proof*, at 190.

10 *See* Social Security Act Amendments of 1950, ch. 809, pt. 351, §§ 1401–1405, 64 Stat. 477, 555–58.

11 Bloch, *Medical Proof*, at 196–97.

12 *Id.*

13 *See* Lance Liebman, *The Definition of Disability in Social Security and Supplemental Security Income: Drawing the Bounds of Social Welfare Estates*, 89 HARV. L. REV. 833, 855–56 (1976) [hereinafter Liebman, *The Definition of Disability*].

14 *See* Diller, *Entitlement*, at 428–33.

15 *See* Liebman, *The Definition of Disability*, at 857–60.

16 *See id.*

17 *See id.*

18 *Id.*

19 Bloch, *Medical Proof*, at 196–97.

20 The original Social Security Act of 1935 created a three-person Social Security Board to run the new program. In 1946, Congress replaced the Social Security

Board (SSB) with the Social Security Administration, with a single commissioner as head of the SSA. Arthur J. Altmeyer, the incumbent chairman of the board, became the first commissioner of Social Security. *See generally*, U.S. Soc. Sec. Admin., SSA Organizational History, www.ssa.gov (explaining the origins of the SSA and how it was originally the SSB).

21 Diller, *Entitlement*, at 399–400.

22 *Id.* at 400.

23 *Id.*

24 *Id.*

25 *Id.*

26 *Id.*

27 *Id.* at 402–03.

28 *Id.*

29 *Id.* Indeed, the trend of significantly increasing applications for disability benefits in times of recession continues, although data reflects that award rates also decline in these periods. *See* Kathy Ruffing, Center on Budget and Policy Priorities, *Disability Benefits Are Hard to Get—Even in Recessions* (Sept. 3, 2013), www.offthechartsblog.org; *see generally* Diller, *Dissonant Disability Policies*, *supra* note 19, at 1078 (suggesting applications rise in recessions because disabled persons are among the first to be laid off or terminated in times of recession and are more likely to apply for benefits as opposed to seeking to beat the odds and find appropriate, retainable employment during such economic downturns).

30 Stone, The Disabled State, at 88.

31 *See* Social Security Act Amendments of 1954, Pub. L. No. 83-761, § 106(a), 68 Stat. 1052, 1079–80. Congress defined "disability" under the disability freeze program as "inability to engage in any substantial gainful activity by reason of any medically determinable physical or mental impairment which can be expected to result in death or be of long continued or indefinite duration." *Id.*

32 Bloch, *Medical Proof*, at 97 n.52.

33 Liebman, *The Definition of Disability*, at 840.

34 Bloch, *Medical Proof*, at 197; Diller, *Entitlement*, at 416.

35 *See* Inst. of Med., Improving the Social Security Disability Decision Process 71 (John D. Stobo, Michael McGeary & David K. Barnes eds., 2007). These guidelines are the precursors to the SSA's present-day listings of medical impairments, which provide a presumptive but not exclusive basis for demonstrating disability under the SSA's disability benefit programs at step 3 of the SSA's five-step sequential evaluation process. *Id.*; Diller, *Entitlement*, at 416.

36 *See* Jennifer L. Erkulwater, Disability Rights and the American Social Safety Net 36 (2006) [hereinafter Erkulwater, Disability Rights]. The disability insurance bill actually passed the Senate by a two-vote margin, but since all assumed that then–Vice President Richard Nixon would vote against it and would have cast the decisive tiebreaking vote, one change in the vote would have doomed the legislation. *See* Edward D. Berkowitz,

ROBERT BALL AND THE POLITICS OF SOCIAL SECURITY 99 (2003). Indeed, President Dwight Eisenhower opposed the legislation but declined to veto it in an election year. *See* ROBERT DALLEK, LONE STAR RISING: LYNDON JOHNSON AND HIS TIMES, 1908–1960, at 95–96 (1991). Many attribute the bill's narrow success in the face of such significant opposition to the considerable legislative skill of Lyndon Johnson who, as Senate Majority Leader with only a one-vote majority, managed to navigate the legislation to a positive vote on the Senate floor despite its defeat in committee. *See id.*

37 Bloch, *Medical Proof*, at 197.

38 Diller, *Entitlement*, at 415–16.

39 Amendments to Title II of the Social Security Act of 1956, Pub L. No. 84-880, § 103, 70 Stat. 807, 815 (1956) (codified at 42 U.S.C. § 423(c)(2)).

40 Social Security Amendments of 1954, Pub. L. No. 83–761, §216(b), 68 Stat. 1080 (codified at 42 U.S.C. § 416(i)(1)).

41 H.R. REP. NO. 84–1189, at 5 (1955).

42 *See* STONE, THE DISABLED STATE, at 125.

43 In a Senate debate on the standard, Senator George argued: "A [s]econd requirement which the individual must meet is that he must be so disabled that he is 'unable to engage in any substantial gainful activity.' I ask you Senators to note this requirement very carefully . . . This is a very conservative requirement." 102 Cong. Rec. 15107 (July 27, 1956).

44 *See* STONE, THE DISABLED STATE, at 125; *see also* EDWARD D. BERKOWITZ, DISABLED POLICY: AMERICA'S PROGRAMS FOR THE HANDICAPPED: A TWENTIETH CENTURY FUND REPORT 75–76 (1989) [hereinafter BERKOWITZ, DISABLED POLICY].

45 STONE, THE DISABLED STATE, at 125. Between 1960 and 1965, Congress expanded the initial eligibility criteria by removing the age fifty or older requirement and by changing "the definition of 'permanent disability' from a condition with a 'long, continued and indefinite duration' to one 'expected to continue for at least 12 months.'" *Id.* at 78. Congress also eventually eliminated the mandatory rehabilitation provisions and reduced the waiting period to five months. *See* FRANK S. BLOCH, BLOCH ON SOCIAL SECURITY § 1:4 (2020) [hereinafter BLOCH, BLOCH ON SOCIAL SECURITY] (available at Westlaw database "BLOCHSS"). *See* 42 U.S.C. § 423(e); Social Security Amendments of 1954, Pub. L. No. 83–761, §216(b), 68 Stat. 1080 (codified at 42 U.S.C. § 416(i)(1)). Congress has also tightened the disability standard and contracted eligibility in a variety of ways.

46 Diller, *Entitlement*, at 416. In addition, to enhance the program's political popularity, Congress delegated primary responsibility for disability determinations to state disability agencies acting under uniform federal criteria, thereby also creating state jobs and state agencies as part of the program. *See* BERKOWITZ, DISABLED POLICY, at 77–78. Thus, initial and reconsidered determinations for benefits are handled by the state agencies, and administrative hearings and administrative appeals are handled by components of the SSA. *See* 42 U.S.C. §

421(a). *See generally* Bowen v. New York, 476 U.S. 467, 472 (1986) (describing the four-stage administrative process and the division of state and federal responsibility). Further, Congress developed a separate trust fund for disability insurance so as not to endanger the social security survivors' and retirement trust fund through the new program. *See* BERKOWITZ, DISABLED POLICY, at 77–78.

47 ERKULWATER, DISABILITY RIGHTS, at 35.

48 STONE, THE DISABLED STATE, at 80 (citation omitted).

49 *Id.* at 80–82. To underscore this point, one representative referenced a poll of cardiac specialists after President Eisenhower's heart attack in 1955 in which 114 specialists believed him capable of continuing to serve as president, while 92 believed he could not. *Id.* at 82.

50 *See id.*

51 *See id.*

52 ERKULWATER, DISABILITY RIGHTS, at 35.

53 102 CONG. REC. 13,038 (1956) (statement of Sen. Walter George).

54 *See* Diller, *Entitlement*, at 419.

55 *See* Flemming v. Booker, 283 F.2d 321, 324 (5th Cir. 1960) (citing internal SSA guidelines establishing presumption that earnings of $1,200 per year amounted to substantial gainful activity to conclude that earnings under $1,000 per year for work performed between 1956 and 1960 was not SGA). Current agency rules establish a presumption that work performed in 2021 that does not produce earnings of at least $1,310 per month is not SGA. *See* U.S. SOC. SEC. ADMIN., SUBSTANTIAL GAINFUL ACTIVITY, www.ssa.gov; *see generally* 20 C.F.R. §§ 404.1574, 416.974 (2021) (guidelines for evaluating substantial gainful activity).

56 The Social Security Council is a "catch-all label for the six-decade succession of (mostly) citizen groups appointed by the secretary of HEW[/HHS], Senate Finance Committee, and, in one case, the president to deliberate questions of Social Security policy and recommend changes, often enacted into law." *See* James Edward Gibson III, The Last Council: Social Security Policymaking as Coalitional Consensus and the 1994–96 Advisory Council as Institutional Turning Point 2 (July 5, 2007), http://scholar.lib.vt.edu (unpublished Ph.D. dissertation, Virginia Polytechnic Institute and State University); *see also* Social Security Independence and Program Improvements Act of 1994, Pub L. No. 103-296, § 103, 108 Stat. 1464, 1467 (replacing the Social Security Council with the Social Security Advisory Board in 1994 when Congress established the SSA as an independent agency).

57 *Old Age, Survivors, and Disability Insurance: Hearing on H.R. 2893 Before the H. Comm. on Ways and Means*, 81st Cong. 1560 (1949) (statement of Sumner H. Slichter, Professor of Economics, Harvard University).

58 *See* Diller, *Entitlement*, at 417–19 & n.189.

59 SUBCOMMITTEE ON THE ADMINISTRATION OF SOCIAL SECURITY LAWS FOR THE USE OF THE COMMITTEE ON WAYS AND MEANS, DISABILITY INSURANCE FACT BOOK 21 (1959).

60 *Id.*

61 *Id.* at 32–33.

62 The first congressional oversight committee report studying the disability insurance program acknowledged the complications involved in creating specific criteria for nonmedical factors but insisted that such criteria were required:

> The subcommittee recognizes the difficulty of developing and enunciating specific criteria for the weight to be given nonmedical factors in the evaluation of disability and the extreme sensitivity of this area. But the subcommittee believes that the time has come, if it is not well overdue, to make a determined effort to develop and refine these criteria and make them available to the evaluators and to the public in the form of published regulations.

SUBCOMM. ON THE ADMIN. OF THE SOC. SEC. LAWS, 86TH CONG., 2D SESS., ADMIN. OF SOC. SEC. DISABILITY INS.: PRELIMINARY REP. TO THE HOUSE COMM. ON WAYS & MEANS 18 (Comm. Print 1960) (emphasis omitted).

63 *See* 20 C.F.R. § 404.1502 (1961). Previous regulations promulgated in 1957 provided simply that "[i]n determining whether an individual's impairment makes him unable to engage in [substantial gainful activity] . . . consideration is also given to such other factors as the individual's education, training and work experience." 20 C.F.R. § 404.1501(b) (1957).

64 *See* 20 C.F.R. § 404.1502(c) (1961).

65 ROBERT G. DIXON, JR., SOCIAL SECURITY DISABILITY AND MASS JUSTICE: A PROBLEM IN WELFARE ADJUDICATION 54–57 (1973) [hereinafter DIXON, SOCIAL SECURITY].

2. THE JUDICIAL GLOSS

1 *See* 20 C.F.R. § 404.1502(b) (1961).

2 *See* DIXON, SOCIAL SECURITY, at 58–59; *see also* Robert G. Dixon, Jr., *The Welfare State and Mass Justice: A Warning from the Social Security Disability Program*, 1972 DUKE L.J. 681, 706–08 (1972) [hereinafter Dixon, *Welfare State*]; *see also* OASI Disability Insurance Letter No. III-3 (Sept. 20, 1963), *reprinted in* STAFF OF THE HOUSE COMM. ON WAYS & MEANS, 93D CONG., DISABILITY INSURANCE PROGRAM 51–54 (Comm. Print 1974) [hereinafter COMMITTEE STAFF REPORT].

3 Kerner v. Flemming, 283 F.2d 916 (2d Cir. 1960).

4 *Id.* at 918–19.

5 *See id.*

6 *Id.* at 921.

7 *Id.*

8 *Id.* at 921–22 (*citing* §§ 216(i)(1), 223(c)(2) of the Social Security Act, 42 U.S.C. §§ 416(i), 423(c)(2) (2006), and § 7(c) of the Administrative Procedure Act, 5 U.S.C. § 1006 (2006)).

9 *Id.* at 922.

10 Landon H. Rowland, *Judicial Review of Disability Determinations*, 52 Geo. L.J. 42, 79, 84 (1963); *see also* Note, *Soc. Sec. Disability Benefits: Three Current Problems*, 52 Minn. L. Rev. 165, 179 (1967) [hereinafter *Three Current Problems*] ("The [Social Disability] Act's legislative history provides support for several strong arguments against the shift in the burden of proof [onto the Secretary] and the imposition of the area availability requirement."); *see also* Note, *Social Security. Disability Determinations: The Burden of Proof on Appeal*, 63 Mich. L. Rev 1465, 1472 (1965) [hereinafter *Burden of Proof*] (stating that post-*Kerner* shifting of burden to secretary to prove actual employment opportunities to which claimant can make work adjustment is inconsistent with legislative history of the Act).

11 King v. Gardner, 391 F.2d 401, 405–10, 409 n.7 (5th Cir. 1967) (Wisdom, J., dissenting).

12 Stoliaroff v. Ribicoff, 198 F. Supp. 587, 591 (N.D.N.Y. 1961).

13 *Id.*

14 *See, e.g.*, Parfenuk v. Flemming, 182 F. Supp. 532, 536 (D. Mass. 1960) (stating that there must be evidence of "other kinds of work which are available and for which the claimant is suited"); *see also* Butler v. Flemming, 288 F.2d 591, 595 (5th Cir. 1961) ("[I]f there was any work for which this clamant was able to perform, the record fails to disclose it.").

15 *See, e.g.*, Cyrus v. Celebrezze, 341 F.2d 192, 196 (4th Cir. 1965) (setting aside SSA decisions despite vocational expert testimony that claimant could make adjustment to other jobs because there was "no proof of specific job openings or vacancies which would have been available to the claimant"); Hodgson v. Celebrezze, 312 F.2d 260, 263 (3d Cir. 1963) (reversing determination of nondisability based on agency finding that the claimant could make a work adjustment to elevator operator work and finding that "there has been no attempt to show that this occupation is one in which jobs are open to someone like Hodgson").

16 *See, e.g.*, Massey v. Celebrezze, 345 F.2d 146, 157–58 (6th Cir. 1965) ("[P]roof of available job opportunities must be supported by evidence that such job opportunities are available in the general area in which the applicant lives."); Hall v. Celebrezze, 314 F.2d 686, 689 (6th Cir. 1963) ("We cannot believe that the Secretary is suggesting that if employment opportunities for a disabled person are not available in the state where he has lived for practically all of his life that he should pull up stakes and move to some far off place where such opportunities might be better."). The local job market cases presented particular problems in the Appalachia regions of the Fourth and Sixth Circuits, where it was harder to disentangle depressed and limited labor market conditions from medical or other vocational bases to make work adjustment determinations involving workers medically precluded from previous work in the coal industry. *See* James M. Haviland & Michael B. Glumb, *The Disability Insurance Benefits Program and Low Income Claimants in Appalachia*, 73 W. Va. L. Rev. 109, 129–30 (1971); Robert M. Viles, *The Social Security Administration Versus the Lawyers . . . And Poor People Too, Part I*, 39 Miss. L.J. 371, 402–03 (1968).

17 *See, e.g.*, Sayer v. Gardner, 380 F.2d 940, 951–52 (6th Cir. 1967) ("[W]here the hiring practices of employers, based on health insurance, workmen's compensation premiums, and liability insurance, preclude the hiring of an employee because of his physical impairment, he must, under the statute, be considered disabled."); Kirby v. Gardner, 369 F.2d 302, 305 (10th Cir. 1967) (same).

18 *See, e.g.*, Boyd v. Gardner, 377 F.2d 718, 722–25 & nn. 7, 9 (4th Cir. 1967) (noting impropriety of looking to four-state regional labor market to determine potential work adjustment for claimant in depressed Appalachian mountain county in Virginia, as well as failure to consider employment practices of employers there and "economic realities" for securing jobs for disabled persons in claimant's locality); *Cyrus*, 341 F.2d at 196 (setting aside SSA decision despite vocational expert testimony that claimant could make adjustment to jobs in shoe industry since there was "no proof of specific job openings or vacancies which would have been available to the claimant" and no indication of whether vocational expert checked whether the only shoe industry employers "in the vicinity of [claimant's] home" actually "employed persons for those jobs" or whether these employers' hiring practices would support hiring persons with claimant's impairments).

19 *See* Viles, at 397–98 (collecting cases). Even before *Kerner*, some courts had identified the injustice of imposing a burden on claimants to prove the broad negative proposition that they were unable to adjust to every conceivable job in the U.S. labor market. *See, e.g.*, Scales v. Flemming, 183 F. Supp. 710, 714 (D. Mass. 1959) ("Claimants were usually poor. Rarely did they have lawyers. Efforts to show the state of the labor market would be expensive.").

20 *See* Social Security Administration, Social Security History, www.ssa.gov.

21 Mashaw, Hearings, at 142; *see id.* at xv–xvii (noting that Mashaw served as project director for this study).

22 Foundations of Forensic Vocational Rehabilitation 312 (Richard H. Robinson ed., 2014). By 2010, the agency had contracts with approximately 1,300 vocational experts. *Id.*

23 *See* Stone, The Disabled State, at 86.

24 Mathews v. Eldridge, 424 U.S. 319, 343–44 (1976).

25 *See* Henry J. Friendly, *Some Kind of Hearing*, 123 U. Pa. L. Rev. 1267, 1285 (1975) ("Why do we not have the good sense in such cases to use something like the English medical appeals tribunal, two of whose members are private physicians, and avoid the calling of experts altogether?").

3. THE CONGRESSIONAL RESPONSE

1 Compare Social Security Ruling (SSR) 63–11c (acquiescing in *Kerner*) with SSR 66-23 (nonacquiescing in *Cyrus* and *Massey*) and SSR 67-14c (nonacquiescing in *Hodgson*). These latter rulings were the SSA's first nonacquiescence rulings. *See* Carolyn A. Kubitschek, *Social Security Administration Nonacquiescence: The Need for Legislative Curbs on Agency Discretion*, 50 U. Pitt. L. Rev. 399, 402 n.15 (1989). "Nonacquiescence is the agency's policy of not following precedent set

by a court of appeals decision in the circuit which established the precedent, and instead disregarding that decision except for the individual claimant named in the decision." CAROLYN A. KUBITSCHEK & JON C. DUBIN, SOCIAL SECURITY DISABILITY LAW & PROCEDURE IN FEDERAL COURT § 1:21 (2021 ed.). The Supreme Court has still not passed on the constitutional validity of nonacquiescence and consistency with separation of powers and equal protection principles. *See id.* at § 1:23.

2 H.R. 805, 89th Cong. (1st Sess. 1965); *accord* H.R. 911, 89th Cong.(1st Sess. 1965); *see generally Burden of Proof*, at 1473 n.46 (describing these bills); *see also* H.R. 18008, 89th Cong. (2d Sess. 1966) (providing eligibility for claimants at least age fifty-five whose impairments prevent performance of substantial gainful activity "requiring skills or abilities comparable to those of any gainful activity in which [they have] previously engaged with some regularity and over a substantial period of time"); *Three Current Problems*, at 180–81 n.103 (describing H.R. 18008 and its failure to secure passage because it was "introduced too late in the session to get adequate consideration").

3 *See* NATIONAL ACADEMY OF SCIENCES, INSTITUTE OF MEDICINE, PAIN AND DISABILITY: CLINICAL, BEHAVIORAL AND PUBLIC POLICY PERSPECTIVES 33 (Martin Osterweis ed. 1987) [hereinafter "NAS, PAIN AND DISABILITY"] (contrasting Germany's disability program with the SSA's programs and noting that the former "defines disability as an inability to earn a fixed amount of money (much higher than the American amount) by doing one's previous job or any other job that corresponds to one's education and capabilities and that does not entail a significant decline in social status"); *id.* at 33 (describing the Netherlands' disability program as inability "to earn what similarly trained healthy people earn in the same community by working at the place where the person last worked or in a similar place"); *see also* STONE, THE DISABLED STATE, at 58–66 (describing the German disability program's history and the cultural influences behind its largely occupational disability approach); *see generally* Frank S. Bloch & Rienk Prins, *Work Incapacity and Reintegration: Theory and Design of a Cross-National Study*, 50 INT'L SOC. SEC. REV. 3, 10 (1997) (describing the stricter American SSA disability standard compared with disability programs in Sweden, Israel, and the Netherlands and noting that, in the latter, "eligibility is measured in relation to work normally done").

4 The Social Security Act's separate standard for benefits based on blindness for claimants age fifty-five and older looks to whether a claimant's condition precludes "substantial gainful activity requiring skills and abilities comparable to those of any gainful activity in which he has previously engaged with some regularity and over a substantial period of time." 42 U.S.C. § 423(d)(1)(B) (2006); *see also* STONE, THE DISABLED STATE, at 27, 173 (describing the social construction of the "legal blindness" category and the social reasons for preferential treatment over other disabilities in social policy "even though everyone knows

that it is quite possible for blind people to work"); BLOCH, BLOCH ON SOCIAL SECURITY, § 2:2 (describing "significantly more liberal" SSA standards for blindness as opposed to other disabilities); Diller, *Entitlement*, at 373 n.28 (describing history and preferential treatment of aid to the blind over aid to the disabled in means-based social welfare system).

5 *See* DIXON, SOCIAL SECURITY, at 55–56, 139 (describing occupational standard for "'worn out' manual laborer syndrome"). The SSA has long employed a narrow occupational labor market work adjustment standard for the category of claimants with only marginal education who performed arduous, unskilled labor for thirty-five years or more. *See* 20 C.F.R. §§ 404.1565(a), 416.965(a) (2021). Although the original regulations provided that such claimants would be found disabled only if unable to perform light work, internal agency guidelines essentially provided for a disability finding even if claimants with this profile could perform a wide variety of other work. *See* DIXON, SOCIAL SECURITY, at 55–56, 139 (describing the administrative test derived from interpretation of the predecessor regulation (20 C.F.R. § 404.1502(c)(1961)) to this profile that is "designed to take account of the reality that such workers are not willing to go very far from their established homes or to accept retraining for sedentary jobs, even though theoretically they have sufficient residual capacity to perform some kind of gainful employment that exists in significant numbers"). In 1978, the SSA modified its regulations to more clearly provide for presumptive occupational disability for claimants with this profile. *See* 43 Fed. Reg. 55352, 55362 (Nov. 28, 1978).

6 Social Security Amendments of 1967, Pub. L. No. 90–248, 81 Stat. 821 (codified at 42 U.S.C. § 423(d)(2)(A)); *see* S. REP. NO. 90–744, at 46–69 (1967), *reprinted in* 1967 U.S.C.C.A.N. 2834, 2880–83.

7 Viles, at 400 n.88 (citing H.R. 5700).

8 *Id.* (citing H.R. 12080).

9 *Id.*

10 *Id.*; 113 CONG. REC. 33113 (1967).

11 *Id.* at 33, 115.

12 *Id.*; Leftwich v. Gardner, 377 F.2d 287 (4th Cir. 1967).

13 *Id.*

14 *Id.* at 33,119.

15 Viles, at 400 n.88; CONF. REP. NO. 1030, 90th Cong., 1st Sess., § 109 (1967), reprinted in 1967 U.S.C.C.A.N. 3179, 3197–98.

16 *Id.*

17 Viles, at 401.

18 *Id.*

19 *See* H.R. REP. NO. 90–544, at 29 (1967).

20 *Id.* at 30; Viles, at 402.

21 *See* Viles, at 402.

22 The agency's first regulations implementing the 1967 Amendments incorporated this statutory language, as does the current version. Compare 20 C.F.R. § 404.1502(b) (1969) with 20 C.F.R. §§ 404.1566(a)–(c), 416.966(a)–(c) (2021).

23 The most significant substantive amendments to the SSA's disability benefits programs since 1967 (other than the previously discussed creation of the SSI disability program in 1972) were the Social Security Disability Benefits Reform Act of 1984, Pub. L. No. 98–460, 98 Stat. 1794 (codified at various subsections of 42 U.S.C. §§ 423, 1382 (2006)) (establishing a substantive medical improvement standard for evaluating whether to terminate benefits; requiring that the combined or cumulative effects of a claimant's impairments and limitations be considered throughout the disability evaluation process including in the determination of threshold medical severity; providing an interim standard for evaluation of pain and subjective symptomology; directing the SSA to rewrite its mental impairment criteria; and extending an administratively imposed moratorium on mental disability benefit terminations until the new criteria were in place); Contract with America Advancement Act of 1996, Pub. L. No. 104–121, § 105, 110 Stat. 847 (codified at 42 U.S.C. §§ 423(d)(2)(C), 1382c(a)(3)(J) (2006)) (precluding persons from receiving benefits "if alcoholism or drug addiction would . . . be a contributing factor material to the [SSA commissioner's] determination that the individual is disabled"); and the Personal Responsibility and Work Opportunity and Reconciliation Act of 1996, Pub. L. No. 104–193, § 402, 110 Stat. 2105 (1996) (codified at various subsections of 42 U.S.C. §§ 423(a)(1)(C), (d)(2)(A), 1382(e)(B), 1382(e)(4)(A) (2006)) (imposing sweeping restrictions on noncitizen eligibility; narrowing eligibility for children's SSI disability; and removing from SSI eligibility persons fleeing prosecution, custody, or confinement for a felony); *see also* Social Security Protection Act of 2004, Pub. L. No. 108–203, §203, 118 Stat. 493 (2004) (extending fleeing felon prohibitions to the disability insurance program); *see generally* BLOCH, BLOCH ON SOCIAL SECURITY, at §§ 1.8, 1.9 (describing statutory amendments affecting the disability programs from 1984 to present); L. SCOTT MULLER, BRETT O'HARA & JOHN R. KEARNEY, SOC. SEC. ADMIN., TRENDS IN THE SOC. SEC. AND SUPPLEMENTAL SEC. INCOME DISABILITY PROGRAMS 79–80 (2006), www.ssa.gov (describing all amendments to the Act from 1970 to 2003).

24 *See* Report of the 1971 Advisory Council on Social Security, H.R. DOC. NO. 92–80, at 29–30 (Apr. 5, 1971); Reports of the Quadrennial Advisory Council on Social Security, H.R. DOC. NO. 94–75, at 38–40 (Mar. 10, 1975).

25 *See* SUBCOMM. ON SOC. SEC. OF HOUSE COMM. ON WAYS & MEANS, 97TH CONG., 1ST SESS., REAGAN ADMINISTRATION DISABILITY PROPOSALS 3–13 (Comm. Print 1981); see John J. Capowski, *Accuracy and Consistency in Categorical Decision-making: A Study of Social Security's Medical–Vocational Guidelines—Two Birds with One Stone or Pigeon-Holing Claimants?*, 42 MD. L. REV. 329, 373–74 and n. 195 (1983) [hereinafter Capowski, *Categorical Decision-making*] (describing the proposal).

26 *See* Capowski, *Categorical Decision-making*, at 373 n.195.

27 *See* chapter 10 and Part 5 of this book, discussing this "*Modernizing SSDI*" proposal of former SSA deputy commissioner Marc J. Warshawsky, joined by Ross Marchand.

28 *See* H.R. Rep. No. 90–544, at 28–29 (1967).

29 Social Security Act Amendments of 1967, Pub. L. No. 90–248, 81 Stat. 821, § 158(b) (codified at 42 U.S.C. § 423(d)(4)–(5)(2006)).

30 *See, e.g.*, Meneses v. Sec'y of Health, Educ. & Welfare, 442 F.2d 803, 807 (D.C. Cir. 1971).

31 *Id.* at 807–809 ("[T]he 1967 Amendments lighten the burden of what the Government must show, but claimant's showing of inability to return to former work does shift to the government a burden of coming forward.").

32 *See also* Johnson v. Heckler, 769 F.2d 1202, 1210 (7th Cir. 1985), *vacated on other grounds sub nom.*, Bowen v. Johnson, 482 U.S. 922 (1987); *see also* 20 C.F.R. § 416.920(g)(1) (2021) (describing how the work adjustment inquiry is triggered in SSI cases through demonstration of either the absence of past relevant work or an inability to perform past relevant work).

33 *See Johnson*, 769 F.2d at 1210 (collecting cases adopting this burden-shifting formulation from all twelve circuits).

34 *See* Bowen v. Yuckert, 482 U.S. 137, 146 n.5 (1987).

35 *See* 20 C.F.R §§ 404.1512(g), 404.1560(c)(2), 416.912(g), 416.960(c)(2) (2021).

36 68 Fed. Reg. 55,153, 55,155 (Aug. 23, 2003) (quoting *Yuckert*, 482 U.S. at 146 n.5).

4. THE OFFICIAL NOTICE/ADMINISTRATIVE NOTICE DOCTRINE

1 *See, e.g.*, *Meneses*, 442 F.2d at 809 (noting that the SSA had the burden on the other jobs issue, that "[n]o evidence whatever was adduced by the Secretary, neither testimony of a vocational expert such as he often provides, nor deposition or interrogatories," and that even "[a]ssuming that it is common knowledge that there are jobs available in the national economy for high school graduates with radio technology credits, *we do not think it is subject to judicial notice*, and the record is devoid of evidence on whether or to what extent there are *significant numbers* of jobs in the national economy which could be filled by a person with [claimant's] limited training and [medical condition]") (emphasis added); *see* Garrett v. Richardson, 471 F.2d 598, 603–04 (8th Cir. 1972) ("[I]t would be beyond the realm of reason to further require a claimant . . . to produce a vocational counselor to testify that there are no jobs in the national economy which he can perform. The burden of producing such a person must rest with the hearing examiner and in the absence of substantial evidence from other sources bearing directly on the issue of [SGA], the testimony of the vocational counselor is essential."); *see also* Taylor v. Weinberger, 512 F.2d 664, 669 and n.9 (4th Cir. 1975) (holding, in light of the shifting burden of proof to the agency, that internal agency guidelines put hearing officers on notice that to proceed with the hearing "without specific evidence of alternate employability, as might be given by a vocational expert, is to invite reversal").

2 *See* MASHAW, HEARINGS, at 76.

3 Walter Gellhorn, *Official Notice in Administrative Adjudication*, 20 TEX. L. REV. 131, 137 (1941). Courts and commentators use the phrases "administrative notice" and "official notice" interchangeably in this context.

4 CHARLES H. KOCH, JR., ADMINISTRATIVE LAW AND PRACTICE § 5.55, at 212 (2d ed. 2010).

5 The enactment of the Administrative Procedure Act of 1946 was an important development in the expansion of the administrative state after the New Deal. The APA classified different types of agency decision-making and established procedural rules to govern that decision-making. By establishing rules for regulating agency action, "the APA preserved individual rights as against the abuse of administrative power and made such action more authoritative and acceptable to the public." Roni A. Elias, *The Legislative History of the Administrative Procedure Act*, 27 FORDHAM ENVTL. L. REV. 207, 207–08 (2016).

6 301 U.S. 292, 299–307 (1937).

7 *Id.* at 301.

8 *Id.*

9 *Id.* at 302.

10 *Id.* at 302–03.

11 *Id.* at 301–02 (citations omitted).

12 *See, e.g.*, Sykes v. Apfel, 228 F.3d 259, 272–73 (3d Cir. 2000) (interpreting and applying *Ohio Bell* in an SSA case on official notice of labor market work adjustment issues); Union Elec. Co. v. FERC, 890 F.2d 1193, 1202 (D.C. Cir. 1989) (interpreting and applying *Ohio Bell* to FERC case); *see also* Sayers v. Gardner, 380 F.2d 940, 954–55 (6th Cir. 1967) (applying *Ohio Bell* to place substantive and procedural limits on use of official notice doctrine in SSA case); Ross v. Gardner, 365 F.2d 554, 557–58 (6th Cir. 1966) (same).

13 Rule 201(b) of the Federal Rules of Evidence provides: "A judicially noticed fact must be one not subject to reasonable dispute in that it is either (1) generally known within the territorial jurisdiction of the trial court or (2) capable of accurate and ready determination by resort to sources whose accuracy cannot reasonably be questioned." FED. R. EVID. 201(b). The Advisory Committee notes to this rule emphasize that "caution" should be taken in the use of judicial notice based on a "tradition of circumspection" and judgment based on experience that the taking of evidence, subject to established safeguards, is the best way to resolve disputes of adjudicative facts. *See* Rules of Evidence for United States Courts and Magistrates, 56 F.R.D. 183, 204–05 (1973).

14 *See* Ernest Gellhorn, *Rules of Evidence and Official Notice in Formal Administrative Hearings*, 1971 DUKE L.J. 1, 46 (1971) (noting the academic debate over different approaches to categorize noticeable facts).

15 *Id.* (quoting FINAL REPORT OF THE ATTORNEY GENERAL'S COMMITTEE ON ADMINISTRATIVE PROCEDURE, S. DOC. NO. 77-8, at 72 (1941)).

16 *Union Elec. Co.*, 890 F.2d at 1202–03 (quoting ADMINISTRATIVE PROCEDURE IN GOVERNMENT AGENCIES: REPORT OF THE COMMITTEE ON ADMINISTRATIVE PROCEDURE APPOINTED BY THE ATTORNEY GENERAL 71 (1941)); TOM C. CLARK, U.S. DEP'T OF JUSTICE, ATTORNEY GENERAL'S MANUAL ON THE ADMINISTRATIVE PROCEDURE 79–80 (1947). The U.S. Department of Labor has its own express administrative notice regulation, which provides that noticeable facts must not be subject to "reasonable dispute" because they are either:

(1) Generally known within the local area,

(2) Capable of accurate and ready determination by resort to sources whose accuracy cannot reasonably be questioned, or

(3) Derived from a not reasonably questioned scientific, medical or other technical process, technique, principle, or explanatory theory within the administrative agency's specialized field of knowledge.

29 C.F.R. § 18.201(b) (2021).

17 *See* Kenneth Culp Davis, *An Approach to Problems of Evidence in the Administrative Process*, 55 HARV. L. REV. 364, 402–16 (1942) (distinguishing between adjudicative and legislative facts through analyzing the judicial treatment of the facts and their uses); Kenneth Culp Davis, *Official Notice*, 62 HARV. L. REV. 537, 549–66 (1949) (applying the legislative-adjudicative fact distinction with particular focus on the official notice doctrine).

18 Davis, *Official Notice*, at 549.

19 *Id.*

20 *Id.*

21 *See* KENNETH CULP DAVIS, ADMINISTRATIVE LAW TEXT § 15.03, at 300–01 (3d ed. 1972).

22 *See id.* § 15.09, at 314; Ernest Gellhorn, at 47. The Federal Rules of Evidence (Rule 201) adopt Kenneth Davis's distinction between legislative and adjudicative facts for the application of the judicial notice doctrine in court proceedings. The advisory notes point out that the rules pertain only to judicial notice of adjudicative facts and that there is no rule restricting judicial notice of legislative facts. Rules of Evidence for United States Courts and Magistrates, 56 F.R.D. 183, 201–06 (1973). This omission has drawn scholarly criticism, including from Kenneth Davis:

> [A] rule that parties should never have any rights with respect to judicial notice of legislative facts probably should not "govern." If a case turns on specific legislative facts which are doubtful, a party should have opportunity to show that the noticed facts are false. In an extreme case, denial of such an opportunity might even deny due process.
>
> A rule to govern judicial notice of legislative facts can be formulated . . . [:] (a) a court may notice legislative facts if it believes them, whether or not they are subject to reasonable dispute, (b) unless the facts are too obvious to state, the court should state or summarize them, and it should indicate

> their source whenever a source is identifiable, [and] (c) the court should grant a party's reasonable request for opportunity to challenge the noticed facts, exercising discretion as to whether written presentations suffice in the circumstances or whether oral argument or submission of evidence subject to cross-examination should be allowed.

DAVIS, ADMINISTRATIVE LAW TEXT, at § 15.07; *see also* Peggy C. Davis, *"There is a Book Out There . . .": An Analysis of Judicial Absorption of Legislative Facts*, 100 HARV. L. REV. 1539, 1542 (1987) (detailing "the deeply problematic nature of permissive legislative factfinding" and advocating "a more constrained method by which judges may take notice of legislative facts").

23 Ernest Gellhorn, at 47; *see also* DAVIS, at § 15.09, p. 314.

24 Ernest Gellhorn, at 47.

25 Administrative Procedure Act, 5 U.S.C. § 556(e) (2006) (formerly codified at 5 U.S.C. §1006(d)). Although the SSA had for some years taken the position that it need not hold hearings pursuant to the APA, in 2001 "the SSA Commissioner issued a written statement in which he confirmed the applicability of the APA to SSA adjudications." Robin J. Arzt, *Recommendations for a New Independent Adjudication Agency to Make the Final Administrative Adjudications of Social Security Benefits Claims*, 23 J. NAT'L ASS'N. ADMIN. L. JUDGES 267, 319 (2003) (citing a letter from Kenneth S. Apfel, SSA Commissioner, to Judge Ronald G. Bernoski, President, Association of Administrative Law Judges on January 9, 2001):

> Adjudications pursuant to the Social Security Act, . . . also are adjudications pursuant to the APA because (1) the SSA is an "agency" within the definition in Section 2(a) of the APA, and (2) a Social Security Act hearing is a proceeding that is an "adjudication" within the definition in Section 2(a) of the APA.

Id. at 320 (citations omitted); *see also* Robin J. Arzt, *Adjudications by Administrative Law Judges Pursuant to the Social Security Act Are Adjudications Pursuant to the Administrative Procedure Act*, 22 J. NAT'L ASS'N. ADMIN. L. JUDGES 279, 298 (2002) ("[I]n 1976, Congress expressly ended what it described as the confusion regarding the applicability of the APA to the Social Security Act by enacting Public Law Number 94–202 . . . which 'clearly placed all social security cases . . . under the APA.'") (emphasis omitted). For further discussion of some of the "complex history" of the SSA and the APA, including the Supreme Court's avoidance of the issue in *Richardson v. Perales*, see Jon C. Dubin, *Torquemada Meets Kafka: The Misapplication of the Issue Exhaustion Doctrine to Inquisitorial Administrative Proceedings*, 97 COLUM. L. REV. 1289, 1306 & n.86 (1997). Apart from the APA, the Social Security Act also contains a requirement that its hearing decisions be "bas[ed] on evidence adduced at the hearing" that has relevance for the application of the official notice doctrine. *See* 42 U.S.C. § 405(b)(1). Indeed, the Supreme Court has more broadly imposed an "evidence adduced at the hearing" requirement in administrative hearings as a component of procedural due process, in reliance on *Ohio Bell*.

See Goldberg v. Kelly, 397 U.S. 254, 271 (1970) (citing *Ohio Bell*). Thus, officially noticed facts may not be deemed to have been "adduced at the hearing" unless they are preceded by appropriate notice and the opportunity to confront such facts at the hearing. *Cf. id.* at 271–72 (finding that procedural due process at welfare benefits hearings also requires adequate notice and the opportunity to confront the evidence).

26 *See* FED. R. EVID. 201.

27 *See* City of Erie v. Pap's A.M., 529 U.S. 277, 297–98 (2000) (accepting noticed City Council findings regarding the harmful effects of nude dancing on a part of the City and observing that "it is well established that, as long as a party has an opportunity to respond, an administrative agency may take official notice of such 'legislative facts' within its special knowledge.").

28 Ernest Gellhorn, at 49. Louis Jaffe has offered a similar critique of Davis's position, noting that, while Davis "has a healthy distrust of categories, [h]e has here succumbed . . . to their lure." Louis L. Jaffe, *Administrative Procedure Re-Examined: The Benjamin Report*, 56 HARV. L. REV. 704, 719 (1943). To Jaffe, "where facts bear closely and crucially on the issue, and are prima facie debatable, they should be developed in an evidentiary fashion" with the opportunity for rebuttal, and "[s]uch facts will not necessarily be 'adjudicative' in Mr. Davis' sense." *Id.*

29 Ernest Gellhorn, at 48; *see also* Ohio Bell Tel. Co. v. Pub. Util. Comm'n of Ohio, 301 U.S. 292, 301–02 (1937) (noting that the critical effect of official notice is to relieve one of the parties of the burden of proving facts with the "usual forms of evidence").

30 Ernest Gellhorn, at 48.

31 *See, e.g.*, Meneses v. Sec'y of Health, Educ. & Welfare, 442 F.2d 803, 809 (D.C. Cir. 1971).

32 *See, e.g.*, Hall v. Sec'y of Health, Educ. & Welfare, 602 F.2d 1372, 1376–77 (9th Cir. 1979); Hephner v. Mathews, 574 F.2d 359, 362 (6th Cir. 1978) (same).

33 *See, e.g.*, Parker v. Harris, 626 F.2d 225, 233–34 (2d Cir. 1980).

34 Wilson v. Califano, 617 F.2d 1050, 1053–54 (4th Cir. 1980); *see also* Ross v. Gardner, 365 F.2d 554, 557–58 (6th Cir. 1966) (determining that administrative notice is improper when it is based on a hearing officer's notice and interpretation of medical texts and treatises that are beyond his competence and are not on matters of common knowledge).

35 *See, e.g.*, Fruge v. Harris, 631 F.2d 1244, 1247 (5th Cir. 1980) ("It is permissible for an ALJ to take administrative notice . . . that certain jobs are light and sedentary and exist in the national economy. . . . [But] the claimant must be aware of the 'administrative noticing' and given an opportunity to controvert the facts noticed. No mention of the ALJ's administrative noticing of any fact appears in the record. . . . [Thus, a]ctual evidence of these facts was required."); *see also* Banks v. Schweiker, 654 F.2d 637, 640–42 (9th Cir. 1981) (holding that, although mass justice efficiency considerations should permit SSA ALJs to take administrative notice whenever convenient and useful, the ALJ's inadequate communication of

intent to take administrative notice and lack of sufficient opportunity to rebut necessitates a new hearing).

36 *See* Office of the Chief Administrative Law Judge, CJB-09-03, Prohibition on Use of "Generic" Vocational Expert Interrogatories by Administrative Notice (2009), https://secure.ssa.gov/apps10/public/reference.nsf/links/05262009025802PM.

37 This is the *Heckler v. Campbell* decision; the "grid" regulations are discussed in chapter 6.

38 *Id.* (citing Heckler v. Campbell, 461 U.S. 458, 467, 470 (1983)).

39 *Id.*

40 *See, e.g.*, Breaux v. Finch, 421 F.2d 687, 689–90 (5th Cir. 1970) (claiming that, since claimant "is perfectly capable of engaging in an infinite variety of jobs which can be classified as light work," "it was quite proper for the Secretary to take administrative notice" that such light work exists in the national economy that claimant could perform); *see also* McLamore v. Weinberger, 538 F.2d 572, 574–75 (4th Cir. 1976) (finding that administrative notice was proper as "within the common knowledge and experience of ordinary men" and that a twenty-six-year-old semi-skilled high-school graduate who could perform light and sedentary work with only a "minor injury" "can engage in a number of light manual and semi-skilled jobs").

41 *See, e.g.*, Rinaldi v. Ribicoff, 305 F.2d 548, 550 (2d Cir. 1962) (finding that "even a cursory examination" of an officially noticed Department of Labor study of 214 jobs in which workers with back impairments, such as the claimant, were found employed demonstrates that "an extremely wide range of employment opportunities was available to him"); *see also* McDaniel v. Celebrezze, 331 F.2d 426, 428–30 (4th Cir. 1964) (ruling that "official notice of recognized publications [e.g., DOT, medical texts] is not, in itself, grounds for reversing the decision of the Secretary" when the APA § 7(d) rebuttal rights provision has been met; the opportunity of counsel to "challenge and contradict" posthearing official notice of these publications by the SSA Appeals Council is sufficient).

42 Mashaw, Hearings, at 80–82 (explaining and distinguishing *Meneses*, 442 F.2d at 803, on that basis).

43 *Id.*

44 *Id. See* U.S. Dep't of Labor, Dictionary of Occupational Titles (DOT) (3d ed. 1965). The DOT is "a catalogue of the occupational titles used in the U.S. economy" and was intended to provide "reliable descriptions of the type of work performed in each occupation." Nat'l Research Council, Work, Jobs, and Occupations: A Critical Review of the Dictionary of Occupational Titles 1 (1980) [hereinafter Critical Review]. It was created to assist employment offices and the U.S. Employment Service, which were established in Depression era of the 1930s, to properly classify and place job-seekers. *Id.* Employment Service officials believed that a "dictionary was of great practical importance because getting qualified workers into appropri-

ate jobs is a task that can be most adequately performed when the transition is based upon a thorough knowledge of both worker and job." *Id.* at 1–2. The DOT's first edition was published in 1939. *Id.* at 1. The DOL produced a fourth edition of the DOT in 1977 and a revised fourth edition in 1991. U.S. DEP'T OF LABOR, DICTIONARY OF OCCUPATIONAL TITLES (DOT): REVISED FOURTH EDITION (4TH ED. 1991) [hereinafter DOT REVISED 4TH ED.]. It has not produced an update since 1991. The DOL has long produced a companion publication to the DOT "in response to the special needs of public and private organizations for more detailed data than that contained [in the DOT]." U.S. DEP'T OF LABOR, SELECTED CHARACTERISTICS OF OCCUPATIONS DEFINED IN THE REVISED DICTIONARY OF OCCUPATIONAL TITLES v (1993) [hereinafter SCODOT]. Earlier versions of SCODOT, linked to earlier versions of the DOT, were published in 1966, 1968, and 1981. *See id.*

45 The "grid" regulations are discussed in detail in Part 3 of this book.

46 *See* 20 C.F.R. § 404.1509(c) (1979) (current version at 20 C.F.R. § 404.1566(d) (2021)).

47 For example, while an ALJ can take notice that light work or certain common occupations exist in the economy as a matter of common knowledge, using the DOT or otherwise, it does not follow that the ALJ can also notice a claimant's ability to perform or adapt to any given occupation in view of the claimant's unique medical and vocational restrictions. *See* O'Banner v. Sec'y of Health, Educ. & Welfare, 587 F.2d 321, 323 (6th Cir. 1978) (taking administrative notice that light work exists is permissible, but "there [must] be something more than mere intuition or conjecture" that the claimant has the capacity and qualifications to perform specific jobs). Indeed, an internal SSA memorandum supplied to Congress explained that while "administrative notice" of job incidence is permissible under the APA and agency rulings, the agency "must first respond to the issue of what type of work this claimant can do. This requires the use of live testimony by a vocational expert." STAFF OF H. COMM. ON WAYS & MEANS, 93D CONG., COMM. STAFF REPORT ON DISABILITY INSURANCE PROGRAM 100 (Comm. Print 1974).

48 20 C.F.R. § 404.1563(a) (1981).

49 65 Fed. Reg. 17,994, 17,995 (Apr. 6, 2000) (referencing 20 C.F.R. § 404.1563(a) (2000)). The 2000 revisions were not intended to alter the concepts of adaptability or adjustment to other work. They were directed to supersede court decisions that conflated adaptability considerations of workers approaching retirement age and lacking "highly marketable" skills with "employability" considerations pertaining to such workers that had been written out of the Act through the 1967 Amendments. *See id.* at 17,995; *cf.* Preslar v. Sec'y HHS, 14 F.3d 1107, 1112 (6th Cir. 1994) ("Implicit in the regulations and the judiciary's attempts to interpret 'highly marketable' is the notion that such skills, which are sufficiently coveted by employers and sufficiently specialized or unique so as to offset the disadvantage of advancing age, should normally enable the claimant to obtain employment."). The revisions also deleted reference to a "highly marketable skills" requirement for finding adaptability for such older workers. *See* 65 Fed. Reg. at 17,995.

50 43 Fed. Reg. 55,349, 55,359 (Nov. 28, 1978) (emphasis added).

51 Dixon, Social Security, at 61.

52 *See, e.g.*, Miki Malul, *Older Workers' Employment in Dynamic Technology Changes*, 38 J. of Socio-Econ. 809, 809 (2009).

53 *See, e.g.*, Jacob J. Sosnoff & Karl M. Newell, *Age-Related Loss of Adaptability to Fast Time Scales in Motor Variability*, 63B J. of Gerontology 344, 344 (2008). These issues are discussed in more detail in chapter 11.

54 *See* 20 C.F.R. § 404.1563(d) (2021); 20 C.F.R. pt. 404, subpt. P, app. 2, §§ 201.02, 202.02 (2021). Before the grid's adoption in 1978, the agency lacked any publicly available, promulgated guidance on how it evaluates age and adaptability in a broad range of cases.

55 *See* Dixon, Social Security, at 55–56.

56 *See* 20 C.F.R. § 404.1565(a) (2021). Matthew Diller has also described this rule as more of a socially constructed reward for past effort as opposed to an empirically supported factual proposition on the inability of such claimants to adapt to medium or lighter work. *See* Diller, at 419 & n.197. He stated:

> It is difficult to see how an individual of similar age, with the same level of education but a shorter work history, or a history of work that is demanding but not deemed "arduous," would be more employable than an individual who meets the terms of the rule. Moreover, in its current form the rule departs from the general framework the SSA has developed for evaluating vocational factors in that it is based on length of work history rather than age. Thus, an individual who left school in order to work could satisfy the 35-year requirement in his or her early fifties—an age at which the SSA [in the grid] generally considers an individual to retain some ability to adapt to new work. Cf. . . . rule 202.10 (finding of nondisability for individual approaching advanced age, with limited education and history of unskilled work, who can perform light work).

Id.

57 John Capowski has argued that the grid regulations' failure to account more fully for claimants' "set" and a broader adjustment concept beyond the crude and narrow adaptability generalizations in their age regulations, although contributing to consistency because of the subjectivity of the set concept, "seriously undermines" the grid regulations' worth in accurately assessing disability. *See* Capowski, *Categorical Decision-making*, at 351–53 (1983). Matthew Diller has characterized the SSA's somewhat ambiguous use of the age factor as more of a socially constructed "moral judgment that claimants who are likely to have worked for a long time" and are close to retirement "should be rewarded" with an easier path to benefits than other claimants, rather than an empirically justified consideration relevant to either job performance or adaptability. Diller, *Entitlement*, at 424. He pointed out that any health effects of age on medical processes (i.e., healing, progressive degenerative changes) already "would be encompassed in any medical assessment of the claimant's physical and mental capacity to work." *Id.* at 423. Diller also observed that "the SSA rationalized the treatment of age as a vocational factor in terms of the impact of age on adaptability to new work situation. However, it also "acknowledged that none of the studies of the impact of age on employment differentiated between employer preferences and actual loss of vocational capacity." *Id.* (citing 43 Fed. Reg. at 55,354). Despite the lack of clear empirical support or data, the agency, through the age regulations, still endeavored to "ascertain a point where it would be realistic to ascribe vocational limitations based on chronological age." 43 Fed. Reg. at 55,353. As Deborah Stone put it: "Essentially, the agency conceded that it had no idea how age is related to specific vocational abilities, and then it proceeded to formulate such a relationship." Stone, The Disabled State, at 166; *cf.* Capowski, *Categorical Decision-making*, at 353 (noting that, notwithstanding the SSA's admission of lack of supporting data and the resulting potential inaccuracies, there is a certain "rough justice" in the regulations' recognition of "the effects of the aging process" and the "proposition that aging affects adaptability"). Perhaps in recognition of this tenuous empirical foundation, the age regulations have always eschewed applying the age categories "mechanically in a borderline situation." *See* 20 C.F.R. §§ 404.1563(b); 416.963(b) (2021). Consistent with Diller's "moral judgment" thesis and undoubtedly reflecting the agency's perception of changing mores, assumptions, and expectations about older workers' responsibilities in the labor market, the agency commenced a rulemaking in 2005 to increase the chronological age cutoffs at which nonadaptability presumptions are conclusive to tighten eligibility standards for older recipients. *See* 70 Fed. Reg. 67,101, 67,101 (Nov. 4, 2005). Perhaps recognizing that this sociopolitical judgment may have been premature, the agency later withdrew the proposed rule. *See* 74 Fed. Reg. 21,563, 21,563 (May 8, 2009).

58 These provisions from the 1967 Social Security Amendments are discussed in chapter 3.

59 Fields v. Bowen, 805 F.2d 1168, 1171 (5th Cir. 1986) (citations omitted).

60 *See* David F. Traver, Social Security Disability Advocate's Handbook § 20-8 (2009); *See, e.g.*, Chavez v. Berryhill, 895 F.3d 962, 965 (7th Cir. 2018) ("Beyond being outdated, the DOT's other significant limitation is that it describes only job duties and requirements, without also reporting an estimate of how many of those positions exist in the national economy. To determine the number of jobs, a VE must consult another resource."); Gieseke v. Colvin, 770 F.3d 1186, 1189 (8th Cir. 2014) ("The DOT provides 'generic job descriptions that offer the approximate maximum requirements for each position,' not the number of jobs that exist in each category."); Brault v. Comm'r, Soc. Sec. Admin, 663 F.3d 443, 446 (2d Cir. 2014) ("The DOT, however, just *defines* jobs. It does not report how many such jobs are available in the economy.") (emphasis in original). *But cf.* White v. Harris, 605 F.2d 867, 869 (5th Cir. 1979) (suggesting without explanation that the "much-used" DOT can be officially noticed both for job detail and

job availability purposes). Some of the other government documents listed in the SSA's administrative notice regulations, such as miscellaneous job surveys, might supply relevant job incidence data. However, these other sources are also not without significant shortcomings. For a detailed deconstruction of these other documentary sources and analysis of their methodological deficiencies for SSA work adjustment evaluation purposes, *see* TRAVER, at ch. 15. *See also* chapter 5 below, which discusses problems with matching occupational titles from the DOT to Bureau of Labor Statistics, Standard Occupational Classification–based job numbers data.

61 Even put in the context of Davis's formalistic adjudicative-legislative fact binary, while job incidence might be legislative in nature, performability and usually adaptability are adjudicative. *See* 2 KENNETH CULP DAVIS AND RICHARD J. PIERCE, JR., ADMINISTRATIVE LAW TREATISE 163–64 (3D ED. 1994). Moreover, incidence is meaningless without first answering the performability and adaptability inquiries to discern the types of jobs about which incidence evidence should be sought. All three inquiries are central in work adjustment disability cases. If disputed, they arguably command evidentiary proof even under Davis's official notice paradigm in cases where the legislative grid rules are not dispositive. The Eleventh Circuit, in express reliance on Davis's binary, has gone one step further and crafted a unique restriction on the use of the legislative grid rules notwithstanding *Campbell*. It has determined that the issue of adaptability based on age is an adjudicative fact not ever properly subject to legislative determination, even by regulation, and must therefore be considered on a case-by-case basis despite the grid. *See* Broz v. Schweiker, 677 F.2d 1351, 1357–61 (11th Cir. 1982), *vacated in light of* Heckler v. Campbell, 461 U.S. 952 (1983). This court has since eased the SSA's burden on this factor by permitting the agency "to rely in the first instance on the age grids, but, if [claimants] introduce[] evidence that [their] ability to adapt is more limited than that presumed by the grids for [their age], the [agency] must prove [claimants'] ability to adapt by other evidence." Reeves v. Heckler, 734 F.2d 519, 525–26 (11th Cir. 1984).

62 Ernest Gellhorn, at 48.

63 *Id.* (citing cases).

64 Torres v. Schweiker, 682 F.2d 109, 111–12 (3d Cir. 1982).

65 *Id.*; *see also* Garrett v. Richardson, 471 F.2d 598, 604 (8th Cir. 1972); Thomas v. Celebrezze, 331 F.2d 541, 546 (4th Cir. 1964); Kerner v. Flemming, 283 F.2d 916, 922 (2d Cir. 1960); Scales v. Flemming, 183 F. Supp. 710, 714 (D. Mass. 1959).

66 *See* 68 Fed. Reg. 55,153, 55,155 (Aug. 23, 2003) (quoting Yuckert, 482 U.S. at 146 n.5).

67 *See generally* Lisa Brodoff, *Lifting Burdens: Proof, Social Justice, and Public Assistance Administrative Hearings*, 32 N.Y.U. REV. L. & SOC. CHANGE 131, 137 (2008) (arguing more broadly that the policies that inform evidentiary burden allocation—"efficiency, access to information, fairness and risk allocation"—all point toward placing a heightened burden on government in administrative hearings where critical social welfare needs are at stake).

5. VOCATIONAL EXPERT EVIDENCE AND THE VOCATIONAL EXPERT PROGRAM

1 As the Seventh Circuit described:

> Social Security officials introduced the vocational expert in 1962 after *Kerner v. Flemming* concluded that concrete evidence, rather than *a priori* reasoning by the hearing examiner, was essential. The agency initially responded by citing published studies and reports . . . ; when appellate courts concluded that these were too general to resolve specific claims, the agency turned to vocational experts who could apply their knowledge to each claimant's circumstances.

Banks v. Gonzales, 453 F.3d 449, 454 (7th Cir. 2006) (citation omitted); *see also* SOC. SEC. ADMIN., HISTORY OF SSA DURING THE JOHNSON ADMINISTRATION 1963–68, OPERATING METHODS, VOCATIONAL EXPERT PROGRAM (2010), www.ssa.gov (noting that, in response to criticism that SSA reliance on evidence of jobs from government and industrial surveys was too "theoretical" or "speculative," the SSA "decided to employ vocational experts at administrative hearings, at which time these expert witnesses would address their testimony to the claimant's particular and highly individual situation in an effort to satisfy the *Kerner* criteria"); Taylor v. Weinberger, 512 F.2d 664, 669 n.9 (4th Cir. 1975) (stating that, in light of the shifting burden of proof to the agency, internal agency guidelines put hearing officers on notice that to proceed with the hearing "without specific evidence of alternate employability, as might be given by a vocational expert, is to invite reversal") (citing SOC. SEC. ADMIN., BUREAU OF HEARINGS AND APPEALS HANDBOOK, Part I, § 87, SECTION 1-87-10 (1967).

2 *See* KUBITSCHEK & DUBIN, at § 3:101 (2021).

3 There is no agency guidance on the statutory phrase "region where the claimant resides." At least one circuit has found that VEs "almost always confine their testimony to . . . jobs that exist in the applicant's state or an even smaller area." Barrett v. Barnhart, 368 F.3d 691, 692 (7th Cir. 2004). Sometimes, VEs also include national job incidence figures, but rarely are those figures stated in terms of "several [specific and varied] regions of the country" as required under the alternative method of demonstrating a significant number of jobs under the 1967 amendments to the Act codified at 42 U.S.C. § 423(d)(2)(A) (2006). The failure to so delineate the specific regions from which national job figures derive is thus statutorily insufficient to satisfy the agency's burden. *See, e.g.*, Britton v. Berryhill, No. 4:17-CV-1956 DDN, 2018 WL 4332062, *6 (E.D. Mo., Sept. 11, 2018) ("The VE's testimony improperly provided only a sum total of jobs nationwide and no regional data. While the statute and regulations do not maximize plaintiff's

convenience in actually finding a job, they will not permit an abstract total of jobs nationwide without some regional reference."); Bragg v. Sullivan, No. 91-CV-1522, 1992 WL 278202, at *5 (N.D. Ohio, Aug. 6, 1992) (VE testimony establishing 58,000 national jobs is insufficient to satisfy SSA's work adjustment burden, as specific regions were not identified).

4 ALJs have an affirmative obligation to inquire about the consistency between VE testimony and the DOT regarding the requirements of specified jobs and to reconcile any conflicts between these two sources of jobs characteristics information. *See* SSR 00-4p. *See generally* KUBITSCHEK & DUBIN, at § 3:104 (describing case law variances in interpreting the extent of ALJ duties to reconcile VE and DOT conflicts under SSR 00-4p).

5 *See* TRAVER, at 20–28 (stating that the VEs "cannot possibly cite the DOT as the basis for their *job numbers* when the DOT contains no information of any type indicating *how many* jobs exist for each job or occupational category") (emphasis in original).

6 Mashaw has suggested that ALJs' approaches to VEs vary from treating them as "useless" and manipulating them through questioning to provide evidentiary cover to confirm the ALJ's predisposition, to timidly asking "an open-ended question that permits the [VE], in effect, to decide the case." JERRY L. MASHAW, BUREAUCRATIC JUSTICE: MANAGING SOCIAL SECURITY DISABILITY CLAIMS 189 (1983) [hereinafter MASHAW, BUREAUCRATIC JUSTICE]. In either situation, the credited VE testimony is decisive. *See* Ken Matheny, *Social Security Disability and the Older Worker: A Proposal for Reform*, 10 GEO. J. ON POVERTY L. & POL'Y 37, 46 (2003) (SSA appeals council appeals officer observed that "vocational expert testimony will [often] violate our notions of common sense and seem divorced from how we perceive the real world, but, nonetheless, SSA adjudicators and the federal courts will defer to those opinions even when they border on the ludicrous").

7 *See* MASHAW, HEARINGS, at 78–79.

8 Alan Goldhammer, *The Effect of New Vocational Regulations on Social Security and Supplemental Security Income Disability Claims*, 32 ADMIN. L. REV. 501, 508 (1980).

9 *Id.*

10 *Id.* The "adaptation by necessity" principle is similar to another maxim, widely rejected by the courts, of "pain management by necessity"—that much pain can be disregarded because people find ways to cope with even extreme pain, if necessary, to survive. The courts have recognized that at a certain (albeit difficult to quantify) point it is reasonable for society to excuse workers from enduring further pain, suffering, or substantial discomfort in the job market. In a series of early cases shortly after the Act's passage, courts rejected Judge Learned Hand's "now famous aphorism" in a case under the War Risk Insurance Act that "'[a] man may have to endure discomfort or pain and not be totally disabled; much of the best work of life goes on under such disabilities.'" Page v. Celebrezze, 311 F.2d 757, 762 (5th Cir. 1963) (*quoting* Theberge v. United States, 87 F.2d 697, 698 (2d Cir.

1937) ("[I]f the insurance had been against suffering, it would have read so.")). In *Page*, the Fifth Circuit observed:

> This notion that pain must be endured, that pain, no matter how severe or overpowering, is not disabling unless it will "substantially aggravate" a condition is "contrary to the standard announced in" cases from this and other Circuits since "the purpose of much social security legislation" including this Act, "is to ameliorate some of these rigors that life imposes."

Id.; *see also* COMM. ON PAIN, DISABILITY & CHRONIC ILLNESS BEHAVIOR, INSTITUTE OF MEDICINE, PAIN AND DISABILITY: CLINICAL, BEHAVIORAL, AND PUB. POL'Y PERSPECTIVES 11 (Marian Osterweis et al. eds., 1987) ("Pain is inherently subjective; there are no thoroughly reliable ways to measure it; and the correlation between the severity of pain and the level of dysfunction is imperfect."); *see generally* Jon C. Dubin, *Poverty, Pain, and Precedent: The Fifth Circuit's Social Security Jurisprudence*, 25 ST. MARY'S L.J. 81, 111–16 (1993) (describing pain standards).

11 *See* Ray v. Sec'y of Health, Educ. & Welfare, 465 F. Supp. 832, 837–38 (E.D. Mich. 1978) (noting the court's inability to "unearth[any] other case . . . giv[ing] substance to the phrase 'significant numbers'").

12 *See, e.g.*, Graves v. Sec'y of Health, Educ. & Welfare, 473 F.2d 807, 809 & n.5 (6th Cir. 1973) (ruling that 750 to 1,000 jobs is not a significant number); *Ray*, 465 F. Supp. at 838 (finding that "jobs which comprise only about .00013 of the work force in the plaintiff's region [200 jobs] do not exist in significant numbers," and "[w]hen jobs are this scarce, they exist 'only in a very limited number' as described in the Conference Report [to the 1967 Amendments]").

13 Hall v. Bowen, 837 F.2d 272, 275 (6th Cir. 1988) (emphasis added).

14 *Compare* Sally S. v. Berryhill, No.18-cv-460, 2019 WL 3335033, at *11 (N.D. Ind., July 23, 2019) (120,350 jobs are not significant); West v. Chater, No. C-1-95-739, 1997 WL 764507, at *2–3 (S.D. Ohio Aug. 21, 1997) (45,000 national jobs is insufficient); Walker v. Shalala, No. H-93-2507, 1994 WL 171209, at *2 (S.D. Tex. Jan. 6, 1994) (1,800 jobs in the claimant's region is insufficient), *and* Bragg v. Sullivan, No. 91-CV-1522, 1992 WL 278202, at *5 (N.D. Ohio Aug. 6, 1992) (58,000 national jobs is insufficient (specific regions not specified)), *with* Gutierrez v. Commissioner of Social Security, 740 F.3d 519, 528 (9th Cir. 2014) (25,000 national jobs is a significant number of jobs but its a "close call"); Weiler v. Apfel, 179 F.3d 1107,1110–11 (8th Cir. 1999) (32,000 national jobs is sufficient), and Allen v. Bowen, 816 F.2d 600, 602 (11th Cir. 1987) (174 jobs in the claimant's region is sufficient). *See generally* Petition for Writ of Certiorari, Pekrul v. Barnhart (No. 05-1020), 2006 WL 341276 (Feb. 8, 2006) (petitioning for certiorari to resolve asserted split in the circuits between competing ad hoc "substantial numbers" approaches and collecting cases); KUBITSCHEK & DUBIN, at § 3:105 (collecting "significant numbers" cases); Andrew T. Palestini, *Jobs Which Exist in Significant Numbers—How Many, How Far from Home*, 4 O.H.A. L.J. 7 (1994) [hereinafter Palestini, *Jobs Which Exist*] (same).

15 Sally S. v. Berryhill, 2019 WL 3335033, at *11 (N.D. Ind., July 23, 2019).

16 *See* OFFICE OF HEARINGS AND APPEALS, SOC. SEC. ADMIN., HALLEX I-2-1-30, PROFESSIONAL QUALIFICATIONS OF HEALTH CARE PROFESSIONALS (2005); see also Nathaniel O. Hubley, *The Untouchables: Why a Vocational Expert's Testimony in Social Security Disability Hearings Cannot Be Touched*, 43 VAL. U. L. REV. 353, 368 n.56 (2008) [hereinafter Hubley, *The Untouchables*] (quoting THOMAS E. BUSH, SOCIAL SECURITY DISABILITY PRACTICE § 340 (2006)) ("The experience, knowledge, ability, understanding of the [VE] role, and the prejudices of individual [VEs] vary much more widely than do the comparable skills and experience of medical experts.").

17 MASHAW, BUREAUCRATIC JUSTICE, at 165; *see also* S. NORMAN FEINGOLD, THE VOCATIONAL EXPERT IN THE SOCIAL SECURITY DISABILITY PROGRAM: A GUIDE FOR THE PRACTITIONER 54 (1969) (listing titles of a cross-section of VEs that included "professors of psychology, education, and rehabilitation counseling; directors of private counseling and employment agencies; assistant dean of students; director of institutional research and counseling in a college; [and] consultant in counseling in a public school system").

18 SSA VOCATIONAL EXPERT'S HANDBOOK 8–9 (June 2020), www.ssa.gov

19 *See* In re: Volker, 164 B.R. 308, 309 (W.D. Wisc. 1993) (summarizing and applying to evidentiary decision-making this famous Hans Christian Anderson fable about the touting of beautiful, invisible, and magical clothing made for the Emperor which was really nonexistent).

20 279 F.3d at 446.

21 *See* 42 U.S.C. § 406(e).

22 BARBARA SAMUELS, SOCIAL SECURITY DISABILITY CLAIMS: PRACTICE AND PROCEDURE, § 27:61 (2d ed. 2020).

23 *See* Rennaker v. Saul, 820 Fed. Appx. 474, 479 (7th Cir. 2020) ("Although the VE pointed to his own education, research, training and experience in job placement and vocational rehabilitation to explain the *kind* of work Rennaker could perform the VE did not tie this background to his estimate of nationwide job numbers . . . [or] bring any aspect of his experience to bear on those job numbers.") (emphasis in original).

24 *See* Cynthia M. v. Saul, No.19-CV-01612-JMS-DLP, at 17 (S.D. Ind., Jan. 10, 2020) (noting that SSA regulations recognize "a direct relationship" between age and employment, finding that the ALJ failed to properly consider the claimant's age in determining her ability to make a work adjustment, and that there was "no indication that the VE specifically considered [the claimant's] advanced age when providing job examples and figures in response to the ALJ's hypothetical.").

25 Hendrix ex. rel. G.P. v. Evenflo Co., 609 F.3d 1183, 1201 (11th Cir. 2010).

26 FED. R. EVID. 702 advisory committee notes to 2000 amendments (quoting Daubert v. Merrell Dow Pharm., Inc., 43 F.3d 1311, 1319 (9th Cir. 1995)).

27 Herrmann v. Colvin, 772 F.3d 1110, 1113–14 (7th Cir. 2014); *see also* Holtz v. Astrue, No. 07-C-314-C, 2007 WL 53237, at *5 (W.D. Wis., Nov. 8, 2007) ("All [the VE] cited was her experience, but that experience does not explain her math.").

28 *See generally* KUBITSCHEK & DUBIN, at §3:104 (referencing the adoption and interpretation of Social Security Ruling 00-4p).

29 The Supreme Court granted certiorari and vacated and remanded an earlier Eleventh Circuit decision "for further consideration in light of [the Eleventh Circuit's] opinion in Washington v. Commissioner of Social Security, 906 F.3d 1353 (C.A.11 2018)." Baker v. Berryhill, 139 S. Ct. 1257, 1257–58 (2019). The decision the Supreme Court vacated and remanded was decided before *Washington* and had relied on earlier Eleventh Circuit case law, prior to the SSA's change of policy in SSR 00-4p and holding that "the VE's testimony 'trumps' the DOT 'whenever the two conflict.'" Baker v. Commissioner of Social Security, 729 Fed. Appx. 870, 872 (11th Cir. 2018), *cert. granted, judgment vacated*, 139 S. Ct. 1257 (2019).

30 Washington v. Commissioner of Social Security, 906 F.3d 1353, 1362 (11th Cir. 2018); *see also* Lockwood v. Commissioner of Social Security Administration, 914 F.3d 87, 93 (2d Cir. 2019) ("the Commissioner's duty 'to identify and resolve apparent conflicts between [the DOT] and [VE] testimony . . . is not fulfilled simply by taking the [VE] at his word that his testimony comports with the [DOT] when the record reveals an apparent conflict'") (citing *Washington*, at *id.*).

31 Washington v. Commissioner of Social Security, 906 F.3d 1353, 1361–1362 (11th Cir. 2018).

32 RICHARD A. POSNER, DIVERGENT PATHS: THE ACADEMY AND THE JUDICIARY 136 (2016).

33 FED. R. EVID. 702 ("If scientific, technical, or other specialized knowledge will assist the trier of fact to understand the evidence or to determine a fact in issue, a witness qualified as an expert by knowledge, skill, experience, training, or education, may testify thereto in the form of an opinion or otherwise, if (1) the testimony is based upon sufficient facts or data, (2) the testimony is the product of reliable principles and methods, and (3) the witness has applied the principles and methods reliably to the facts of the case.").

34 509 U.S. 579, 592–93 (1993) (holding that a court's evaluation of proposed expert testimony must entail "a preliminary assessment of whether the reasoning or methodology underlying the testimony is scientifically valid and of whether that reasoning or methodology properly can be applied to the facts in issue"); *see also* Kumho Tire Co. v. Carmichael, 526 U.S. 137, 141 (1999) (extending *Daubert* to all expert testimony, not just testimony based on novel scientific methods).

35 *See* 42 U.S.C. § 405(b)(1) (2006) (stating that the Federal Rules of Evidence's admissibility rules do not apply in SSA proceedings); Richardson v. Perales, 402 U.S. 389, 400 (1971) (same); *see also* 5 U.S.C. § 556(d) (2006) (providing more generally under the APA that, in administrative hearings, "[a]ny oral or documentary evidence may be received, but the agency as a matter of policy shall provide for the exclusion of irrelevant, immaterial, or unduly repetitious evidence").

36 *See* 42 U.S.C. § 405(g) (2006); *cf.* 5 U.S.C. § 706(2)(E) (2006) (APA substantial evidence standard).

37 279 F.3d 441, 446 (7th Cir. 2002); *see also* Hubley, *The Untouchables*, 399–405 (proposing that the SSA's adopt a ruling that clarifies the application of *Daubert* and Rule 702 to VE testimony in SSA hearings). *See generally* D. Hiep Truong, Daubert *and Judicial Review: How Does an Administrative Agency Distinguish Valid Science from Junk Science?*, 33 AKRON L. REV. 365, 389 (2000) (arguing for the application of *Daubert* and Rule 702 to administrative proceedings).

38 Letter from Dixie Somers, Assistant Commissioner, Office of Occupational Statistics and Employment Projects, Bureau of Labor Statistics, U.S. Department of Labor, to David B. Lowry, dated November 26, 2007 ("The DOT is no longer in use by the Bureau of Labor Statistics, and we do regard it as obsolete since much of the information contained in the most recent version is based on research conducted at least two decades ago.") (on file with the author); Goode v. Commissioner of Social Security, 966 F.3d 1277, 1281 (11th Cir. 2020) ("Although the DOT is outdated—some would say obsolete—it remains one of the vocational expert's primary tools.").

39 *See Chavez*, 895 F.3d at 965.

40 ROBINSON, FOUNDATIONS, at 223; SOC. SEC. ADMIN., OCCUPATIONAL INFORMATION DEVELOPMENT ADVISORY PANEL: CONTENT MODEL AND CLASSIFICATION RECOMMENDATIONS FOR THE SOC. SEC. ADMIN. OCCUPATIONAL INFORMATION SYSTEM (2009), www.ssa.gov; EXEC. OFFICE OF THE PRESIDENT, STANDARD OCCUPATIONAL CLASSIFICATION MANUAL 5 (2018), www.bls.gov

41 *See* National Crosswalk Service Center Special Report DOT Occupations By SOC (May 12, 2009), www.soc.dot.sas.

42 The Seventh Circuit has been the most outspoken court of appeals in its criticism of VE work adjustment assessments in SSA disability cases. *See, e.g.*, Alaura v. Colvin, 797 F.3d 503, 508 (7th Cir. 2015) (referencing VE methodology as "preposterous" and leading to job numbers that "seem [] likely therefore, to be a fabrication.").

43 895 F.3d 962 (7th Cir. 2018).

44 *Id.* at 965–66 (emphasis added); citing Mary Barros-Bailey and Sylvia Karman, *Occupational and Labor Market Information*, in ROBINSON, FOUNDATIONS, at 203, 221–25, 232–33.

45 *See* National Crosswalk Service Center Special Report DOT Occupations By SOC (May 12, 2009), www.soc.dot.sas; *Chavez*, 965 F.3d at 966.

46 U.S. Department of Labor, Bureau of Labor Statistics, Occupational Employment Statistics, Occupational Employment and Wages, May, 2019, 35–2014 Cooks, Restaurants, www.bls.gov.

47 *Chavez*, 865 F.3d at 966–70.

48 *Id.* at 970.

49 *See* 20 C.F.R. §§ 404.1565(a), 416.965(a) (2021).

50 DOT REVISED 4TH ED., DOT Code # 706-684-010.

51 *Id.*

52 These issues are discussed in more detail in chapter 12.

53 Mark Trapani and Deborah Harkin, Social Security Administration, Occupational and Medical-Vocational Claims Review Study, Final Results (May 2011) (on file with author). The ten (really 11 with one tie) occupations are:

1. Addresser (9.5% of work adjustment denials)
2. Cleaner, Housekeeper (5.7%)
3. Photocopying, Machine Operator (5.3%)
4. Collator Operator (3/7%)
5. Surveillance-System Monitor (3.7%)
6. Table Worker (3.4%)
7. Packager, Hand (2.7%)
8. Lens-Block Gauger (2.6%)
9. Counter Clerk (2.3%)
10. Assembler, Small Products II (2.2%) (tie with) Call-Out Operator (2.2%).

54 DOT REVISED 4TH ED., at # 209.587-010.

55 *Id.*

56 *See, e.g.*, Dan Wolstein, *Surveillance System Monitors in the Workforce*, 19 J. OF FORENSIC VOCATIONAL ANALYSIS 49 (Winter 2016).

57 *See* 41 Social Security Forum 17 (January 2019), https://nosscr.org (39 percent of claimants in FY 2018 lacked attorney representation); *see also* Sims v. Apfel, 530 U.S. 103, 112 (2000) ("[A] large portion of Social Security claimants either have no representation at all or are represented by non-attorneys.").

58 *See, e.g.*, Alvarez v. Bowen, 706 F.Supp. 49, 53–54 (S.D.N.Y. 1989) (pro se claimant at hearing is prejudiced by inability to cross-examine a VE); *see also* Sears v. Bowen, 840 F.2d 394, 402 (7th Cir. 1988) (presumption of "best case" representation when the claimant has attorney representation at the hearing "does not necessarily hold true when the claimant is represented by a nonlawyer").

59 I have reached this conclusion anecdotally based on multiple decades of law school clinical practice supervising law students in SSID and SSDI hearings and from many conversations and conferences with SSA representatives as well as seasoned attorneys for social security claimants.

60 *Id.*

61 Donahue v. Barnhart, 279 F.3d 441, 446 (7th Cir. 2002)

62 McKinnie v. Barnhart, 368 F.3d 907, 911 (7th Cir. 2003) (citation and quotations omitted) (finding that an ALJ may not condition order to VE to supply basis for opinion upon claimant's payment of VE's fees for additional work).

63 Donahue v. Barnhart, 279 F.3d 441, 446 (7th Cir. 2002) ("When no one questions the vocational expert's foundation or reasoning, an ALJ is entitled to accept the vocational expert's conclusion.").

64 *See* Rennaker v. Saul, 820 Fed. Appx. 474, 478 (7th Cir. 2020); *cf.* Fernandez v. Schweiker, 650 F.2d 5, 8–9 (2d Cir. 1981) (finding that pro se claimants should not be deemed to have waived the right to subpoena and cross-examine consultant doctors who provided hearsay medical reports (or, presumably, have waived the right

to argue that the hearsay reports cannot alone amount to substantial evidence if the subpoenas were denied) per *Richardson v. Perales*, as the ALJ's heightened duty to develop the record on behalf of a pro se claimant should have "at the least" required informing claimant of the subpoena rights). *See generally*, KUBITSCHEK & DUBIN, at § 6:8 (discussing and collecting cases on the ALJs heightened duty to develop the record in cases where claimants lacked attorney representation at their hearings).

65 *Rennaker*, 820 Fed. Appx. at 478–79.

66 *Id.* at 109–12.

67 *Sims*, 530 U.S at 107.

68 *See* Bradshaw v. Berryhill, 372 F. Supp. 3d 349, 353–363 (E.D.N.C. 2019); *see id.* at 357–58 ("SSA's regulations provide a mechanism for a claimant to raise issues before the Appeals Counsel that they did not raise to the ALJ. 20 C.F.R. § 404.970(b). This suggests that the SSA does not consider there to be an issue-exhaustion requirement at the ALJ level for all types of issues.").

69 *Compare* Cirko v. Comm'r of Soc. Sec., 948 F.3d 148, 156–59 (3d Cir. 2020) (holding that ALJ issue exhaustion does not apply to preclude judicial challenges to the constitutionality of the ALJ's appointment where the issue was not raised before the ALJ at the hearing, in a case handled by an attorney at the hearing) *with* Shaibi v. Berryhill, 883 F.3d 1102, 1108–1110 (9th Cir. 2018) (holding that the claimant's attorney's failure to raise the accuracy or reliability of VE testimony during the ALJ hearing stage precludes challenge to the VE methodology on judicial review in federal court). The Supreme Court has granted certiorari in two cases raising the issue of whether the failure to raise or exhaust at the hearing stage, an Appointments Clause challenge to the ALJ, precludes asserting this argument on judicial review based on prudential issue exhaustion principles. Carr v. Saul, No. 19-1442, 2020 WL 6551771 (Nov. 9, 2020), and Davis v. Saul, No. 20-105, 2020 WL 6551772 (Nov. 9, 2020). For analysis of the arguments against application of prudential or common law ALJ issue exhaustion in SSA cases from a group of 56 law professors from 40 law schools, *see* Brief for Amici Curiae Social Security, Government Benefit Program and Administrative Law Professors and Scholars, in Nos. 19-1442, 20-106, Carr & Davis v. Saul (Dec. 31, 2020).

70 Bayliss v. Barnhart, 427 F.3d 1211, 1217–18 (9th Cir. 2005); *see* Brault v. Social Sec. Admin., Comm'r, 683 F.3d 443, 449–50 (2d Cir. 2012).

71 Bayliss, at *id.*; *see* Brault at *id.*

72 McIntrye v. Colvin, 758 F.3d 146, 152 (2d Cir. 2014).

73 Biestek v. Berryhill, 138 S.Ct. 2677 (2018).

74 Biestek v. Berryhill, 139 S.Ct. 1148, 1152–53 (2019).

75 *Id.* at 1153.

76 *Id.*

77 *Id.*

78 *Id.*

79 Biestek v. Berryhill, 880 F.3d 778, 790 (6th Cir. 2018).

80 *Id.* at 790–91.

81 Biestek v. Berryhill, No. 17–1184, Brief for the Petitioner i (August 27, 2018).

82 Biestek v. Berryhill, No. 17–1184, Brief for the Respondent in Opposition I (May 14, 2018).

83 *Id.* at 17–18 (quoting SSA VOCATIONAL EXPERT HANDBOOK (2017), at 37).

84 *See* Biestek v. Berryhill, 139 S.Ct. at 1155.

85 *Id.*

86 *Id.* at 1154 n.1, 1157.

87 *Id.* at 1155.

88 *Id.* at 1155, n.2

89 *Id.* at 1155–56

90 *Id.* at 1157.

91 *Id.* at 1156.

92 *Id.*

93 The SSA issued an even newer version of its VE Handbook in June 2020, which continues to require that the VE "explain" and "furnish any sources" relied upon in the hearing testimony. SSA Vocational Expert Handbook 3, 19, 28 (June 2020); see also id. at 37 ("You should have available, at the hearing, any vocational resource materials that you are likely to rely upon and should be able to thoroughly explain what resource materials you used and how you arrived at your opinions.").

94 20 C.F.R.§404.953(a) (2021) (emphasis added).

95 *Id.* at 1162–63 (Opinion of Gorsuch, J., joined by Ginsburg, J., dissenting) (citing [Walter] Gellhorn, *Official Notice in Administrative Adjudication*, 20 TEXAS L. REV. 131, 145 (1941)).

96 *See* 5 U.S.C. §556 (e). The official/administrative notice doctrine is discussed in detail in chapter 4.

97 *Id.* at 1162 (Opinion of Gorsuch, J., joined by Ginsburg, J., dissenting).

98 *Id.* at 1160.

99 *Id.* at 1558 (Opinion of Sotomayor, J., dissenting).

100 Some courts of appeal have also issued a few post-*Biestek* decisions declining to compel VEs to reveal their methodology, for various process reasons, and otherwise accepted questionable VE testimony. *See, e.g.*, Ford v. Saul, 950 F.3d 1141,1158–60 (9th Cir. 2020) (lauding the "inherent reliability" of VE testimony); Krell v. Saul, 931 F.3d 582 (7th Cir. 2019); *cf. See* Richard J. Pierce, *Has the Supreme Court Endorsed the Use of Junk Science in the Administrative State?*, THE REGULATORY REVIEW (Apr. 29, 2019) (questioning whether the Supreme Court majority's *Biestek* opinion will lead to greater reliance on unreliable methodology and data and other "junk science" in SSA cases involving vocational expert assessments and in administrative agency adjudication more broadly).

101 966 F.3d 1277 (11th Cir. 2020).

102 *Id.* at 1284–85.

103 *Id.* at 1283 (quoting *Biestek*, 139 S. Ct. at 1162, Gorsuch, J., joined by Ginsburg, J., dissenting) ("Some courts have . . . conflated the substantial evidence standard—a

substantive standard governing what's needed to sustain a judgment as a matter of law—with procedural rules governing the admission of evidence. These courts have mistakenly suggested that, because the Federal Rules of Evidence don't apply in Social Security proceedings, anything an expert says will suffice to meet the agency's burden of proof.").

104 *Goode*, 966 F.3d at 1283.

105 *See id.* at 1282 (quoting KUBITCHEK & DUBIN, at §3:106 ("One is hard-pressed to understand how vocational expert testimony lacking even minimal methodological support, when questioned, meets the 'substantiality' threshold, particularly at step five of the proceedings where the burden of demonstrating the claimant's ability to make a work adjustment to a significant number of jobs in the economy . . . has shifted from the claimant to the agency.")).

106 *Id.* at 1281 (citing *Chavez*, 895 F.3d at 965).

107 *Id.* at 1283 (citing *Chavez*, 895 F.3d at 965–66).

108 *Id.*

109 *Id.* at 1282–84.

110 *Goode*, 966 F.3d at 1282 (quoting *Chavez*, 895 F.3d at 968).

111 Brace v. Saul, 970 F.3d 818 (7th Cir. 2020).

112 *Id.* at 822 (quoting *Chavez*, 895 F.3d at 969–70).

113 *Id.* (citing *Biestek*, 139 S. Ct. at 1155).

114 *Id.* at 822–23.

115 *Id.* at 822.

116 *Id.*

117 *Id.*

118 *Id.* at 823 (citing *Chavez*, 895 F.3d at 964; emphasis in original).

119 *Id.* (citing *Chavez*, 895 F.3d at 970).

6. "GRIDDING" THE LABOR MARKET WORK ADJUSTMENT ASSESSMENT

1 *See* MASHAW, HEARINGS, at 80–82.

2 *Id.* at 82.

3 *Id.* at 25; *see also* Heckler v. Campbell, 461 U.S. 458, 466 n.10 (1983) (describing congressional calls for SSA rulemaking on nonmedical disability factors from 1954 to 1977).

4 Santise v. Schweiker, 676 F.2d 925, 930 n.14 (3d Cir. 1982) (quoting MASHAW, HEARINGS, at (24–27)).

5 COMMITTEE STAFF REPORT, at 6. Shortly thereafter, the agency concluded that it should promulgate regulations that would include the internal criteria that the state disability agencies had been instructed to apply. *See* SUBCOMM. ON SOC. SEC. OF THE HOUSE COMM. ON WAYS & MEANS, 94TH CONG., RECENT STUDIES RELEVANT TO THE DISABILITY HEARINGS AND APPEALS CRISIS 46 (1975) [hereinafter APPEALS CRISIS]; *see also* Edward Yourman, *Report on a Study of Social Security Beneficiary Hearings, Appeals and Judicial Review*, *reprinted in* APPEALS CRISIS, at 167 (The agency "hope[s] to be able to meet the vocational evaluation problem by a regulatory provision that would describe the classes of residual functions which are commonly encountered in adjudication and indicating for each whether work 'exists in significant numbers . . . in several regions of the country' which an unskilled person in the class could perform"). On a few occasions, the chairman of the Subcommittee on Social Security of the House Ways and Means Committee introduced legislation that would have required the agency to promulgate medical-vocational regulations. *See, e.g.*, H.R. REP. NO. 94–1745 (1976) (Conf. Rep.); H.R. REP. NO. 95–8076 (1977). This legislation was not enacted because the Department promulgated the grid regulations. *See* SUBCOMM. ON SOC. SEC. OF THE HOUSE COMM. ON WAYS & MEANS, 95TH CONG., PROPOSED DISABILITY INSURANCE AMENDMENTS OF 1978 (1978) (recommending that no change be made in the Act's disability definition pending a determination of the operation of the new ["grid"] regulations); *see also* Heckler v. Campbell, 461 U.S. 458, 466 n.10 (1983) (detailing congressional advocacy for more comprehensive SSA rulemaking on work adjustment issues from 1954 to 1977).

6 *Campbell*, 461 U.S. at 466; *see also* 42 U.S.C. § 405(a) (2006).

7 *See* Rules for Adjudicating Disability Claims in Which Vocational Factors Must Be Considered, 43 Fed. Reg. 55,349 (Nov. 28, 1978) (to be codified at 20 C.F.R. § 404).

8 Hogan v. Schweiker, 532 F.Supp. 639, 643 n.4 (D. Colo. 1982). The grid can be viewed as one grid with multiple parts or tables or in plural form as "grids."

9 While most courts, ALJs, and claimants' attorneys viewed the grid as a substantial departure from previous agency practice, the agency's comments on the grid when promulgated reflected its belief that the grid was based on "long-standing" internal practices. *Compare* 43 Fed. Reg. 55,349, 55,349 (Nov. 28, 1978) *with* Capowski, *Categorical Decision-making*, at 346–47 n.90 (discussing his Freedom of Information Act request for state agency guidance upon which the grid regulations were based and his conclusion that the suggested basis was not written "with the clarity that characterizes the [grid]" nor is it clear how widely and consistently such internal policies were applied).

10 *See* JERRY L. MASHAW, BUREAUCRATIC JUSTICE: MANAGING SOCIAL SECURITY DISABILITY CLAIMS 117 (1983) [hereinafter MASHAW, BUREAUCRATIC JUSTICE] ("From the perspective of an administration concerned with systemic rationality, these [grid] regulations have much to commend them.").

11 *Id.* at 21–46. Mashaw's conception of bureaucratic rationality also called for the complete elimination of the SSA hearing and judicial review processes. *See* MASHAW, BUREAUCRATIC JUSTICE, at 198, 201–02. Extended examination and critique of Mashaw's provocative thesis is well-tread territory and is not the subject of this book. For such examination, see Barry Boyer, *From Discretionary to Bureaucratic Justice*, 82 MICH. L. REV. 971, 971 (1984) (reviewing MASHAW, BUREAUCRATIC JUSTICE); Robert Kagan, *Inside Administrative Law*, 84 COLUM. L. REV. 816, 831–32 (1984) (reviewing MASHAW, BUREAUCRATIC

JUSTICE); Lance Liebman & Richard B. Stewart, *Bureaucratic Vision*, 96 HARV L. REV. 1952, 1954 (1983) (reviewing MASHAW, BUREAUCRATIC JUSTICE); Deborah Maranville, *Book Review*, 69 MINN. L. REV. 325, 345–47 (1984) (reviewing MASHAW, BUREAUCRATIC JUSTICE); Paul R. Verkuil, *The Self Legitimating Bureaucracy*, 93 YALE L.J. 780, 780 (1983) (reviewing MASHAW, BUREAUCRATIC JUSTICE). For the purposes of this writing, it is sufficient to observe that nearly forty years have elapsed since Mashaw's recommendations but the SSA's adjudicative process has persevered in virtually unchanged form.

12 Heckler v. Campbell, 461 U.S. 458, 467 (1983) (citations omitted).

13 *Id.* at 467. Moreover, the Court reasoned that claimants could still introduce evidence at their individual hearings to demonstrate that their circumstances did not fit into an unfavorable grid category. *Id.*

14 *Id.* at 469–70. In rejecting an earlier challenge to the grid's validity in the First Circuit, Judge (now Justice) Breyer explained:

> The Agency stated at the time the Grid was adopted that it was based upon "administrative notice" of conditions in the national labor market. That does not make the Grid an instance of "administrative notice." Rather, the Grid is a set of rules, promulgated pursuant to informal "notice and comment" rulemaking procedures, 5 U.S.C. §553. The terms of 5 U.S.C. §556(e) do not literally apply to informal rulemaking, see 5 U.S.C. §556(c), and thus do not automatically require a disability claimant to be given the chance at his adjudicatory claims hearing to contest the "facts" underlying the Grid.

Sherwin v. Sec'y of HHS, 685 F.2d 1, 4 (1st Cir. 1982).

15 In Campbell, the Court largely sidestepped the applicability of the Due Process Clause to the alleged violation of the right to notice and the opportunity to rebut administratively noticed facts by construing the Second Circuit's opinion and the Plaintiff's lower court briefs as not properly raising the issue. *See* 461 U.S. at 468–69 & nn.12–13. Viewed as a procedural due process issue, a challenge to the denial of notice and the right to challenge presumptions contained in the grid rules before their application in an individual case would fall within the legislative action/legislative fact exception to the procedural due process right to be heard. *See* Minn. Bd. for Cmty. Colls. v. Knight, 465 U.S. 271, 283, 285 (1984) ("The Constitution does not grant to members of the public generally a right to be heard by public bodies making decisions of policy."); United States v. Fla. E. Coast Ry. Co., 410 U.S. 224, 245–46 (1973) (explaining that "there [is] no across-the-board constitutional right to oral argument in every administrative proceeding regardless of its nature"); *compare* Bimetallic Inv. Co. v. State Bd. of Equalization, 239 U.S. 441, 445–46 (1915) (stating that there is no due process right to be heard where a large number of persons is affected in a similar manner through generally applicable legislative enactment) *with* Londoner v. City & Cnty. of Denver, 210 U.S. 373, 385 (1908) (affirming a right to be heard where a small number of persons is affected in an exceptional and particularized manner by governmental enactment). *See generally* 2 KENNETH CULP DAVIS & RICHARD J. PIERCE, JR.,

ADMINISTRATIVE LAW TREATISE §10.6 (3d ed. 1994) (suggesting that the grid reflects a legislative promulgation of broad general rules applicable to the public at large based on general legislative facts about the labor market, not adjudicative or particularized facts about individual claimants to which procedural due process would apply).

16 *Campbell*, 461 U.S. at 470.

17 *See id.* (concluding that the accuracy of the administratively noticed facts had already been "tested fairly during rulemaking").

18 *Id.* at 470 n.14.

19 *Id.* at 468. To the extent the majority's reference to the "record" and its relationship to the grid's substantive validity under the arbitrary and capricious standard implied a focus on the sufficiency of the grid's rulemaking record and underlying labor market data, that issue was not raised at any point in the litigation or discussed or analyzed in any of the lower court opinions. *See* Brief for Petitioner Richard S. Schweiker at 12, Heckler v. Campbell, 461 U.S. 458 (1983) (No. 81–1983) ("Neither the Court of Appeals nor respondent has challenged the accuracy of the job data underlying the regulations and tables.").

20 Bloch, *Medically Centered*, at 211; *see also* 20 C.F.R. § 404.1520 (2021) (describing each of the steps in the process). In 1980, as a part of a project titled "Operation Common Sense," the agency rewrote and reorganized the sequential evaluation and grid regulations in an effort to make them simpler and briefer. *See* 45 Fed. Reg. 55,566, 55,566 (Aug. 20, 1980). *See generally* Elizabeth S. Ferguson, Note, *Untangling "Operation Common Sense": Reopening and Review of Social Security Administration Disability Claims*, 87 MICH. L. REV. 1946 (1989) (describing a perceived shortcoming in the agency's clarification effort).

21 *See* 20 C.F.R. § 404.1571 (2021), SSA Program Operations Manual System DI 10501.015, https://secure.ssa.gov (describing current (2021) earning levels and levels in prior years at which SGA is presumed).

22 20 C.F.R. § 404.1520(c) (2021). The SSA defines "basic work activities" as "the abilities and aptitudes necessary to do most jobs." *Id.* at § 404.1521(b). Examples of these include:

> (1) Physical functions such as walking, standing, sitting, lifting, pushing, pulling, reaching, carrying, or handling; (2) Capacities for seeing, hearing, and speaking; (3) Understanding, carrying out, and remembering simple instructions; (4) Use of judgment; (5) Responding appropriately to supervision, co-workers and usual work situations; and (6) Dealing with changes in a routine work setting. *Id.*

23 *See, e.g.*, Dixon v. Shalala, 54 F.3d 1019, 1024–25 (2d Cir. 1995) (describing *de minimis* "slightness" step 2 standard, noting that five members of the Supreme Court in *Bowen v. Yuckert*, 482 U.S. 137 (1987), found that application of a greater-than-slightness standard would be unlawful and sustaining classwide invalidation of the SSA's systematic application of a greater-than-slightness step 2 threshold in the state of New York); KUBITSCHEK & DUBIN, at §§ 3:14–15 (collecting cases); *see also* Social Security Ruling 85-28.

24 *See* Bailey v. Sullivan, 885 F.2d 52, 60 (3d Cir. 1989); Social Security Ruling 85-28. *See generally* Dixon v. Heckler, 589 F. Supp. 1494, 1508 (S.D.N.Y. 1984) (explaining how step 2 should not be interpreted to prevent the SSA from finding a severe impairment from the combined effects of impairments "[i]n much the same way, a mathematician might prove that because two does not equal four, two plus two never equals four").

25 The listings are contained in Listing of Impairments, 20 C.F.R. pt. 404, subpt. P, app. 1 (2021).

26 The creation of the original administrative schedule of automatically disabling impairments is discussed in chapter 1.

27 *See* MASHAW, BUREAUCRATIC JUSTICE, at 165 (recounting conversations with SSA consulting physicians who made rhetorical observations that the listings "are so strict *live* patients don't have those symptoms.").

28 *See* COMM. ON IMPROVING THE DISABILITY PROCESS, INST. OF MED., IMPROVING THE SOCIAL SECURITY DISABILITY DECISION PROCESS 71 (John D. Stobo et al. eds., 2007) ("From the beginning, the guides were conceived as a way to quickly identify allowance cases without performing a comprehensive analysis of an individual's capacity to work."); Revised Medical Criteria for Determination of Disability, Musculoskeletal System and Related Criteria, 66 Fed. Reg. 58,010, 58,027 (Nov. 19, 2001) ("The Act does not, in fact, make any provision for the listings at all. The listings are an administrative convenience established by regulation to identify obviously disabled individuals."). While listing-level severity has been set at a high level because it is a "screen in" device that seeks to minimize "false positives," there may be claimants who are found disabled at step 3 who would be determined ineligible at steps 4 or 5. INST. OF MED., at 93; *see, e.g.*, Ambers v. Heckler, 736 F.2d 1467, 1470 (11th Cir. 1984) ("Consideration of the fact that [the claimant] could return to her past work is not a relevant inquiry once she met the Listing.").

29 Bloch, *Medical Proof*, 92 CORNELL L. REV. at 213.

30 *See* 20 C.F.R. § 404.1545(a) (2021) (addressing residual functional capacity). For the same reasons discussed herein about medical science's inability to objectively link impairment findings with ability to work or with the degree of pain and subjective symptomatology, the RFC assessment is similarly vulnerable to critique. In responding to questions about physicians' and adjudicators' abilities to determine claimants' abilities to function at "exertional levels," SSA's Commissioner Cardwell explained that while "considering the 'state of the art,' there is simply no satisfactory way to relate the effect of disease or injury to an individual's ability to work. However, since its inception, the [program], in making disability determinations, has included an assessment of an individual's residual functional capacity." STONE, THE DISABLED STATE, at 166. Deborah Stone characterized Cardwell's RFC response as saying it is "impossible to specify but we do it anyway." *Id.*

31 *See* 20 C.F.R. §§ 404.1567, 404.1569a(b) (2021). For example, sedentary work involves, in an eight-hour work day, sitting for up to six hours, standing and walking for up to two hours, and lifting up to ten pounds occasionally. Light work involves standing and walking for up to six hours and lifting up to twenty pounds with pushing and pulling of arm and leg controls while seated; medium work is light work with lifting up to fifty pounds; heavy and very heavy work involves lifting up to or more than one hundred pounds, respectively. *See id.* § 404.1567; SSR 96-8p, 61 Fed. Reg. 34,474, 34,475–77 (July 2, 1996); Social Security Ruling 83-10. Claimants deemed capable of performing one category are also considered capable of performing all less strenuous categories of work. Thus, a claimant capable of light work is deemed capable of also performing sedentary work. *See* Medical Vocational Guidelines, 20 C.F.R. pt. 404, subpt. P, app. 2, § 204.00 (2021). There are no grid tables based on exertional capacity for heavy or very heavy work because the agency presumes claimants whose only limitations are exertional and are capable of such a wide range of employment can make work adjustments regardless of vocational adversities. *See id.* The agency evaluates medical evidence of limitations caused by medically determinable impairments in making RFC assessments. *Id.* § 404.1545(a). The claimant's RFC is also based on the consideration of the claimant's "symptoms (such as pain), signs, and laboratory findings together with other evidence . . . obtain[ed]." *Id.* at pt. 404, subpt. P, app. 2, § 200.00(c).

32 Exertional and Nonexertional Limitations, 20 C.F.R. § 404.1569a(a) (2021).

33 *See id.* § 404.1569a(c)(i)–(iv).

34 SSR 96-8p, 61. Fed. Reg. 34,474, 34,475 (July 2, 1996).

35 To be "relevant," past work must (1) have been performed within the last fifteen years; (2) have lasted long enough to be learned; and (3) have constituted SGA. 20 C.F.R. § 404.1565(a) (2021).

36 *See* 20 C.F.R. §§ 404.1565(a), 416.965(a) (2021).

37 SSR 82-61, 1982 WL 31387 (1982). Because the DOT is often used at step 4, particularly with respect to the second "as generally performed" PRW prong, its limitations and deficiencies described herein are applicable to various step 4 labor market determinations as well.

38 *See* 20 C.F.R. §§ 404.1520(a)(4)(iv),(v), (e)–(g); 416. 920(a)(4)(iv),(v), (e)–(g) (2021).

39 *Id.*

40 *See* 20 C.F.R. §§ 404.1520(a)(4)(iv),(v), (e)–(g); 416. 920(a)(4)(iv),(v), (e)–(g) (2021).

41 *See id.* pt. 404, subpt. P, app 2, § 200.00(b), (e) (2021).

42 *See* Social Security Ruling 83-5a.

43 *See* 20 C.F.R. § 404.1563(c)–(e) (2021) (discussing age as a vocational factor); *see* ch. 4, note 57 (discussing potential rebuttal of the age presumptions generally and in "borderline" situations). Younger individuals are further subdivided into two categories (forty-five to forty-nine and eighteen to forty-four) in Table I used for claimants with an RFC for sedentary work. Claimants in the forty-five

to forty-nine younger individual subcategory limited to sedentary work who are either illiterate or unable to communicate in English, and are either unskilled or have no work experience, are deemed unable to make a work adjustment to a significant number of jobs. *See id.* pt. 404, subpt. P, app. 2, tbl.1, § 201.17 (2021). There are no other categories for younger individuals on any of the three tables where inability to make a work adjustment is presumed. *See id.* at tbls.1–3. In 2005, in an effort to tighten eligibility standards for older claimants, the agency commenced a rulemaking to increase the chronological age cutoffs in the grid at which nonadaptability presumptions are conclusive. *See* 70 Fed. Reg. 67,101 (Nov. 4, 2005). However, after receiving many negative comments, the agency withdrew that proposed rule. *See* 74 Fed. Reg. 21,563 (May 8, 2009).

44 *Id.* § 404.1564 (2021).

45 *See* Social Security Ruling 20-1p. (The year in which a Social Security Ruling was issued is identified by the first number; thus SSR 20-1p was issued in 2020.) Social Security Rulings "represent precedent final opinions and orders and statements of policy and interpretations" adopted by the SSA and "are binding on all components of the Social Security Administration." 20 C.F.R. § 402.35(b)(1) (2021). *See* Heckler v. Edwards, 465 U.S. 870, 873 n.3 (1984) ("'Rulings do not have the force and effect of the law or regulations but are to be relied upon as precedents in determining other cases where the facts are basically the same. A ruling may be superseded, modified, or revoked by later legislation, regulations, court decisions or rulings.'") (citations omitted).

46 *Id.*

47 *Id.*

48 *Id.*

49 *See* 85 Fed. Reg. 10586, 10587 (February 25, 2020).

50 *Id.*

51 The top-ten most identified occupations by VEs is discussed in chapter 5 and note 53.

52 20 C.F.R. § 404.1565(a) (2021). Unskilled work needs little or no judgment to do simple duties that can be learned on the job in a short period of time (thirty days or less); semiskilled work may require alertness and close attention to watching machine processes, inspecting, testing or looking for irregularities, or tending equipment or property; skilled work requires use of judgment to determine the operations to be performed in order to obtain the proper form, quality, or quantity of material to be produced and may require dealing with people, facts, or figures or abstract ideas at a high level of complexity; transferability of skills is only a consideration when prior work was either skilled or semiskilled and is most probably found among jobs in which the same or a lesser degree of skill is required, the same or similar tools and machines are used, and the same or similar raw materials, products, processes, or services are involved. *See id.* § 404.1568(d)(1)–(4); Social Security Ruling 83-10, at 27–28; Social Security Ruling 83-11; Social Security Ruling 82-41; *see also* Draegert v. Barnhart, 311 F.3d 468, 474–75 (2d Cir. 2002). The grid only takes notice of unskilled jobs, and transferable skills may not

be transferred to unskilled work. *See* Social Security Ruling 82-41, at 849. Thus, if a claimant would be deemed unable to make a work adjustment under the grid without considering transferable skills, such a claimant can only be found not disabled if demonstrated that such claimant's transferable skills permit a work adjustment to a meaningfully enhanced occupational base as a result of those skills. *See* TRAVER, at § 1712, ch.18. While agency guidance does not mandate the presence of a vocational expert to evaluate the presence and potential vocational impact of transferable skills at hearings, the ALJ's application of administrative notice of these issues, consistent with proper official notice principles, would present substantial challenges. *See* KUBITSCHEK & DUBIN, at § 3:94 (listing situations when vocational expert testimony may be needed including "where the issue is whether the claimant has transferable skills or whether those skills transfer to a significant range of skilled work within the claimant's RFC."); *cf.* Kathleen Pickering, *Note, Social Security Disability Determinations: The Use and Abuse of the Grid System*, 58 N.Y.U. L. REV. 575, 597–98, 617 (1983) (suggesting the grid should be invalidated as arbitrary and capricious if interpreted, in cases with transferable skills findings, to permit direct application of grid rules to deny benefits to claimants deemed otherwise unable to make work adjustments under the grid if lacking such transferable skills, since the grid rules only take notice of unskilled work). Chapter 4 discusses the use and misuse of the official notice/administrative doctrine.

53 Social Security Ruling 83-11; *see* 20 C.F.R., pt. 404, app 2 § 200.00(a) (2021).

54 Social Security Ruling 83-10 (emphases added).

55 *See* 20 C.F.R. pt. 404, subpt. P, app. 2, §§ 201.00–203.00 (2021).

56 *See id.*

57 *See id.* § 200.00(b).

58 U.S. PUBLISHING, OCCUPATIONAL EMPLOYMENT QUARTERLY II 3.1, FOURTH QUARTER 2018. (OEQII3.1) 3 (Jan. 2019). This is probably something of an over count since the OEQII's data does not disaggregate part-time jobs from these figures and, while based on government data, contains estimates. *See* TRAVER, at § 15.10.3. In making its estimates, the U.S. Publishing Company relies on the "equal distribution method" criticized in *Chavez* (discussed in chapter 5) to extrapolate the skill and strength requirements (i.e., unskilled, semiskilled, or skilled; sedentary, light, or medium) from the broader SOC groupings and census codes based on their requirements in the DOT occupations encompassed within the broader code. *See* Letter from Don Vander Vegt, Publisher, U.S. Publishing Company, dated February 28, 2002, responding to Letter from Robert C. Angermeier, seeking explanation of U.S. Publishing Company methodology in its quarterly employment statistics publications, dated February 22, 2002 (on file with the author). Nevertheless, vocational experts often rely on the OEQII to support their labor market work adjustment assessments. *See* TRAVER, at § 1510.3.1.

59 *See* note 58, chapter 6 above; see also chapter 5 (discussing methodological deficiencies of the "equal distribution" method of VE job number estimates).

60 *See* Medical–Vocational Guidelines, 20 C.F.R., pt. 404, subpt. P, app 2, § 202.04 (2021) (listing RFC decisions for light work).
61 *Id.* § 203.14

7. GAPS IN THE GRID

1 Defrancesco v. Bowen, 867 F.2d 1040, 1045 (7th Cir. 1989).
2 *See id.*
3 The relevance of transferable skills is also discussed in chapter 6, note 58.
4 Medical–Vocational Guidelines, 20 C.F.R. pt. 404, subpt. P, app. 2, § 200.00(e) (2021) (emphasis added); *see id.* § 200.00(d).
5 Social Security Ruling 83-14 (emphases added).
6 See chapter 5 for discussion of the "ad hoc" or "common sense" adjudicative assessment approach to the question of what quantum of jobs constitutes "work which exists in significant numbers" under the Act.
7 Social Security Ruling 83-12 (emphasis added). Admittedly, for the likely relatively small number of cases where occupational base erosion analyses supply evidence that places claimants not significantly closer to one or the other, but firmly "in the middle" of two ranges of grid exertional category bases with differing work adjustment conclusions, a degree of ad hoc judgment with the potential for inconsistency cannot be fully avoided. I have assumed this is a relatively infrequent phenomena because I am unaware of a single reported case since the relevant SSRs' adoptions nearly forty years ago involving such a firmly middle grid range erosion finding.
8 20 C.F.R. pt. 404, subpt. P, app. 2, § 200.00(e) (2021); Social Security Ruling 85-15.
9 20 C.F.R. pt. 404, subpt. P, app. 2, § 200.00(d) (2021); Social Security Ruling 83-12.
10 20 C.F.R. pt. 404, subpt. P, app. 2, § 200.00(h)(1) (2021); Social Security Ruling 96-9p, 60 Fed. Reg. 34,478, 34,479–80 (July 2, 1996). Because there is no "subsedentary" grid table and occupational base, the grid framework job base erosion analysis is somewhat different for this grid exception. This approach evaluates the extent of erosion of the unskilled sedentary job base, using as guidance a variety of adjudicative examples that permit erosion presumptions. *See* 20 C.F.R. pt. 404, app. 2 § 200.00(h)(3) (2021). *See generally* TRAVER, at ch.12, § 1719 (describing the grid framework approach for younger claimants with subsedentary RFCs). The grid regulations acknowledge that "sedentary work represents a significantly restricted range of work." 20 C.F.R. pt. 404, subpt. P, app. 2, § 201.00(b) (2021). For examples of grid framework erosion analyses for all of these grid exceptions, see TRAVER at chs. 12 & 17. For the grid framework erosion approach in the situation where claimants have transferable skills, see *id.* at ch. 18.
11 The first published explication of the grid framework job base erosion approach to determining the ability to adjust to "work which exists in significant numbers" in grid exception cases appeared in an earlier version of the Social Security Disability Advocate's Handbook written by the former administrative law judge Ralph Wilborn. *See generally* RALPH WILBORN, WILBORN'S SOCIAL SECU-

RITY DISABILITY ADVOCATE'S HANDBOOK: THE SEQUENTIAL EVALUATION OF DISABILITY (2002). Because of adjudicators' difficulties in reaching consensus on a phrase as open-ended and ambiguous as work "which exists in significant numbers," Wilborn labeled the quest to discern the meaning of this phrase as analogous to the search for the "Holy Grail." *See generally* RALPH WILBORN, *In Search of the Holy Grail: A Definition of 'Work Which Exists In Significant Numbers,'* in WILBORN'S SOCIAL SECURITY DISABILITY HANDBOOK: THE SEQUENTIAL EVALUATION OF DISABILITY (2002). He stated:

> Studying federal court Social Security disability case law teaches that for claimants' representatives, agency adjudicators and federal court judges alike, comprehending the intricacies of the step-five "disability" determination process is much like piercing together a complex jigsaw whose patterns are so ill-defined that it often is only through a series of epiphanies that one piece is fitted to another. However like the complex jigsaw puzzle, once all the pieces of the process are fitted together, its solution may seem surprisingly obvious.

Id. at 1. After pointing out that there is no black-letter definition of this critical statutory phrase, Wilborn concluded as follows: "There is, however, a 'conceptual' definition. The statutory term of art, '*work which exists in significant numbers,*' is defined, conceptually, in" the grids, and the "SSA's Social Security Rulings . . . provide the key for determining *when, in terms of the* [grid], work exists in '*significant numbers.*'" *Id.* (emphases in original). Experienced social security practitioners have reported to the author that ALJ Wilborn was one of the few ALJs who regularly granted benefits in grid exception cases based on a determination that the claimant could not adjust to a "significant number" of jobs in reliance on the grid framework occupational base erosion approach derived from the Social Security Rulings and the grid's job base numbers.

12 876 F.2d 683 (9th Cir. 1989).

13 *Id.* at 688–89.

14 *Id.* at 689.

15 *Id.* Actually, the court, while properly recognizing that the work adjustment inquiry must be determined with reference to the grid job base figures, misinterpreted the facts and the VE's testimony and ultimately used the wrong figures. The VE had testified that the nonexertional limitations would erode the job base to a point below the job base in the grid category under which the claimant would be disabled when he reached age fifty-five. *Id.* That is the light work grid rule and job base. *See* Medical–Vocational Guidelines, 20 C.F.R. pt. 404, subpt. P, app. 2, rule 202.06 (2021). However, the claimant was only fifty-two at the time and therefore would be disabled under the sedentary grid rule and job base. *Swenson*, 876 F.2d at 689; *see* 20 C.F.R. pt. 404, app. 2, tbl.1, rule 201.14 (2021). Thus, the claimant's remaining job base at age fifty-two fell between the grid job base under which he would be found disabled (sedentary) and the grid job base under which he would be found not disabled (light). Pursuant to SSRs 83–14 and 83–12, and using the

grid job bases as a framework, the court should have remanded for a determination of whether the remaining job base was significantly closer to one or the other job bases, thus dictating a result.

16 *Swenson*, 876 F.2d at 688 (citing 20 C.F.R. pt. 404, subpt. P, app. 2, § 200.00(e)(2)).

17 *Id.* A year earlier, the court remanded a grid exception case where the agency had denied a claimant based on direct application of the grid without procuring VE testimony to ascertain the erosive effects of nonexertional limitations. *See* Desrosiers v. Sec'y of HHS, 846 F.2d 573 (9th Cir. 1988). In a concurring opinion, Judge Pregerson observed:

> When the Secretary is required to call a vocational expert, the [grid] Guidelines "provide an overall structure" and a "frame of reference" within which the vocational expert must evaluate and the ALJ must decide individual cases. 20 C.F.R. pt. 404, subpt. P, app. 2, § 200.00(d) (1987). If either a vocational expert's testimony or an ALJ's decision appears to be inconsistent with the overall structure provided by the Guidelines, a claimant may challenge the testimony or the decision on that basis.

Id. at 578–79 (Pregerson, J., concurring).

18 *Swenson*, 876 F.2d at 688 (emphases added). By suggesting that the VE's testimony was "inconsistent" by both identifying thousands of performable jobs while simultaneously finding that the job incidence totals were below those in the applicable grid rule's job base, the court reflected some confusion about the full nature of the grid's adjudicative premises. The court's reasoning fails to acknowledge that a claimant can be deemed unable to make a work adjustment to a sufficient number of jobs in the grid, even when the number of jobs such a claimant can perform may number into the millions. In other words, performability alone is not the endpoint of the grid rules; adaptability based on age and the combination of other adverse vocational factors are also noticed in the grid's work adjustment presumptions. In addition, the court's last sentence erroneously suggests that the agency could conceivably accept VE testimony that was "significantly inconsistent" with the grid's overall framework if proper reasons were supplied. Under the grid framework erosion approach, the agency may not accept a VE's adaptability and work adjustment findings that are contrary to those derived from the grid. The grid's assumptions are the product of binding administrative notice embodied in legislative rules and made expressly applicable to grid exception cases through binding SSRs. *Swenson*'s more basic holding has been followed. *See* Distasio v. Shalala, 47 F.3d 348, 349–50 (9th Cir. 1995) (ruling that where the VE only identified sedentary jobs in a grid exception case, and the claimant would be found unable to make work adjustment under the sedentary grid rule, *Swenson* mandates an award of benefits).

19 880 F.2d 1152 (9th Cir. 1989).

20 *See id.* at 1154.

21 *Id.* at 1158.

22 *Id.* at 1154–55.

23 *See id.* at 1155.
24 *See Cooper*, 880 F.2d at 1157–58.
25 *Id.* at 1158.
26 *See id.* (suggesting that an individual "closely approaching advanced age" who possesses the same physical limitations as the claimant would receive "slightly different" treatment under the job adaptability regulations).
27 *Id.*
28 *Id.* at 1157–58 (second emphasis added) (quoting 20 C.F.R. pt. 404, subpt. P, app. 2, § 202.00(c) (1988)).
29 216 F.3d 864 (9th Cir. 2000).
30 *Id.* at 870–71 ("Moore argues . . . that the upper category, 'light' work, was so reduced that it was essentially equivalent to the lower category, 'sedentary' work, which would have meant he was classified as 'disabled.'").
31 *Id.* at 870.
32 *Id.*
33 *Id.* at 869–70. *Moore* has been followed. *See* Thomas v. Barnhart, 278 F.3d 947, 960 (9th Cir. 2002) (applying *Moore* without citing *Swenson*).
34 468 F.3d 1111 (9th Cir. 2006).
35 *Id.* at 1116–17 (quoting 20 C.F.R. pt. 404, subpt. P, app. 2, § 200.00(c) (referencing n.2 to Rule 202.07)).
36 *Id.* at 1113.
37 *Id.* at 1113 n.1.
38 20 C.F.R. § 404.1566(b) (2021) (emphasis added).
39 Lounsburry v. Barnhart, 468 F.3d at 1117 (quoting Social Security Ruling 83-10). Section 404.1566(b) could also be reconciled with the occupational base range directives of SSR 83-10 and the applicable grid transferable skills explanatory sections by interpreting the general clause referencing "at least one occupation" as an acknowledgment of the possibility that a single occupation or two might represent the bulk of a range of work such as the sedentary range. It is conceivable that a common occupation or occupations like sedentary clerk or receptionist could eventually represent a substantial majority of the actual jobs in the fragile and diminishing unskilled sedentary work occupational base. So, for example, in a case involving a younger individual and a determination under SSR 96-9p of sedentary job base erosion that is below the full range, it is conceivable that eventually one or more occupations might include enough of the occupational base range to establish a significant majority of the total unskilled sedentary job base and justify a work adjustment finding).
40 533 F.3d 1035 (9th Cir. 2008).
41 *Id.* at 1043.
42 *See id.* (relying on Rule 201.07, which states that claimants of advanced age who can perform sedentary skilled or semiskilled work and possess a high-school degree are not disabled).
43 *Id.*

44 *See id.* at 1044 (stating that a contrary conclusion would lead to confusion and inconsistency in applying grid rules).
45 *See* 20 C.F.R. pt. 404, subpt. P, app. 2, § 201.00(e) (2021).
46 533 F.3d at 1044 n.5.
47 *Id.*
48 *Id.* at 1044.
49 *Id.*
50 971 F.3d 1128 (9th Cir. 2020).
51 *Id.* at 1131–32.
52 *Id.*
53 *Id.*
54 *Id.*
55 867 F.2d 1040, 1045 (7th Cir. 1989).
56 *See id.*
57 397 F.3d 468, 469 (7th Cir. 2005).
58 *Id.* at 471
59 *Id*
60 *Id.*
61 988 F.2d 789 (7th Cir. 1993).
62 *Fast*, 397 F.3d at 472.
63 *Id.*
64 *Id.* at (emphasis in original).
65 Social Security Ruling 85-15, at *1 (emphasis added).
66 *Id.* at *3 (emphasis added).
67 Social Security Ruling 85-15 also provides some examples of using its terms for entirely nonexertional mental impairment profiles. Some of the examples expressly include references to grid rules to provide reasoning regarding the occupational base available to claimants in the listed examples. *Id.* at *5 (Example 3 referencing grid Rule 203.10; Example 4 referencing grid Rules 201.07, 202.07, 203.07; Example 5 referencing grid rules 203.11–203.17).
68 *See* Lee v. Sullivan, 988 F.2d 789, 794 (7th Cir. 1993) (citing cases finding a significant number of jobs based on VE testimony ranging from only 174 jobs to 1,266 jobs).
69 *See* Boone v. Barnhart, 353 F.3d 203, 204–210 (3d Cir. 2004).
70 *See* Wright v. Massanari, 321 F.3d 611, 615–16 (6th Cir. 2003); *see also* Wilson v. Comm'r of Soc. Sec., 378 F.3d 541, 549–50 (6th Cir. 2004).
71 *See, e.g.*, Trimiar v. Sullivan, 966 F.2d 1326, 1330–32 (10th Cir. 1992) (850–1,000 jobs is a significant number); Jenkins v. Bowen, 861 F.2d 1083, 1087 (8th Cir. 1988) (500 jobs is a significant number); Allen v. Bowen, 816 F.2d 600, 602 (11th Cir. 1987) (174 jobs is a significant number). Underscoring the ad hoc, standardless nature of this work adjustment approach, a supervisory staff attorney at the SSA's hearings and appeals unit published an article in the agency's office of hearings and appeals reporter, provided to hearing and appeals adjudicators across the

country, offering his "impression that some courts will accept a clearly credible expert's testimony that jobs exist in significant numbers *without even discussing any actual numbers*." Palestini, at 24 (emphasis added).

72 The Court has not ruled on the proper approach for evaluating the relevant Social Security Rulings' legal significance. However, Social Security Rulings are a superior form of nonpromulgated interpretive agency authority over the agency's internal rules for the lower levels of agency adjudication known as the Program Operations Manual System (POMS), or the "claims manual." The agency has not bound its adjudicators by regulation to the claims manual, and the Court has held that it lacks the force of law. *See* Schweiker v. Hansen, 450 U.S. 785, 789 (1981). Nevertheless, the Court has also held that a court evaluating SSA interpretive guidance, even in a POMS, should at least accord the POMS "respect" based on Skidmore v. Swift & Co., 323 U.S. 134, 139–40 (1944), and sometimes deference pursuant to Auer v. Robbins, 519 U.S. 452, 461 (1997). *See* Wash. State Dep't of Health & Soc. Servs. v. Guardianship Estate of Keffeler, 537 U.S. 371, 385–87 (2003). The Court has explained the "respect" required by *Skidmore* as a function of "the thoroughness evident in [the agency guidance's] consideration, the validity of its reasoning, its consistency with earlier and later pronouncements, and all those factors which give it power to persuade, if lacking power to control." *Skidmore*, 323 U.S. at 140.

Auer mandates deference to agency rules as reflected in the Court's decision in Chevron U.S.A., Inc. v. Natural Resources Defense Council, Inc., 467 U.S. 837 (1984). Under *Chevron*, an agency rule that interprets a statute, and does not conflict with it, should be followed by the courts if the rule reflects a reasonable interpretation of the statute. *See* 467 U.S. at 842–43. *Auer* mandates *Chevron* deference to certain sufficiently authoritative forms of nonpromulgated agency interpretive guidance that interprets ambiguous agency regulations. *See also* Kisor v. Wilkie, 139 S. Ct. 2400 (2019) (explaining the scope of the *Auer* doctrine). Thus, at a minimum, SSRs must be accorded *Skidmore* respect and sometimes usually more decisive *Auer/Chevron* deference. *See, e.g.*, Bray v. Comm'r of SSA, 554 F.3d 1219, 1225 (9th Cir. 2009) (applying *Auer* deference to SSR 82-41). However, the Court has also clarified that agency counsel's mere litigation positions on how an act, regulation, or ruling should be interpreted are entitled to no special consideration. *See* Bowen v. Georgetown Univ. Hosp., 488 U.S. 204, 212–13 (1988).

73 Social Security Rulings "are binding on all components of the [SSA]." 20 C.F.R. § 402.35(b)(1), (2) (2021); Heckler v. Edwards, 465 U.S. 870, 873 n.3 (1984).

74 The Sixth Circuit has stated:

> It is an elemental principle of administrative law that agencies are bound to follow their own regulations. . . . The Supreme Court has long recognized that a federal agency is obliged to abide by the regulations it promulgates. *See* Vitarelli v. Seaton, 359 U.S. 535, 545 (1959); Service v. Dulles, 354 U.S. 363, 372 (1957); Accardi v. Shaughnessy, 347 U.S. 260, 267 (1954). An agency's failure

> to follow its own regulations "tends to cause unjust discrimination and deny adequate notice" and consequently may result in a violation of an individual's constitutional right to due process. Where a prescribed procedure is intended to protect the interests of a party before the agency, "even though generous beyond the requirements that bind such agency, that procedure must be scrupulously observed." *Vitarelli*, 359 U.S. at 547 (Frankfurter, J., concurring).

Wilson v. Comm'r of Soc. Sec., 378 F.3d 541, 545 (6th Cir. 2004) (quotation and select citations omitted).

75 Santise v. Schweiker, 676 F.2d 925, 930 (3d Cir. 1982) (quoting MASHAW, HEARINGS, at 19); *see also* TRAVER, at § 1708 ("Strange as it may seem, in an Agency that is interested in consistency in adjudication, the simple fact of how many jobs equals a 'significant number' at a specific age, education, and work experience . . . is a factual issue to be decided on a case by case basis by adjudicators.").

76 The Fifth Amendment incorporates equal protection concepts to the federal government through its Due Process Clause. *See* Bolling v. Sharpe, 347 U.S. 497, 498–99 (1954).

77 *See* Social Security Ruling 83-10.

78 *See, e.g*, Cleburne v. Cleburne Living Ctr., 473 U.S. 432, 439–47 (1982) (holding that the selective special use permit requirement for mentally disabled group homes lacked a rational relationship to a legitimate government purpose); U.S. Dep't of Agric. v. Moreno, 413 U.S. 528, 534 (1973) (holding that a federal amendment removing food stamps from households containing a person unrelated to other household members lacked a rational relationship to a legitimate government interest); *see also* U.S. v. Vaello-Madero, 956 F.3d 12 (1st Cir. 2020), cert. granted, 141 S. Ct. 1462 (2021) (statutory exclusion of residents of Puerto Rico from the SSI program lacks a rational basis in violation of Fifth Amendment equal protection principles); Stieberger v. Sullivan, 738 F. Supp. 716, 730, 757–60 (S.D.N.Y. 1990) (SSA's de facto or "informal non-acquiescence" practice, resulting when the agency declines to issue an acquiescence ruling (AR) on a circuit precedent since agency adjudicators are forbidden from applying circuit precedents that are not embodied in ARs, creates a dual system of law for those who do not appeal agency decisions and are thereby denied equal benefit of circuit precedent for which there is no rational basis, in violation of equal protection principles).

8. THE ADJUDICATIVE USE OF THE OFFICIAL NOTICE/ ADMINISTRATIVE NOTICE DOCTRINE IN GRID EXCEPTION CASES

1 By "off the grid," I mean where a grid rule is not directly dispositive and vocational expert testimony may be needed. As explained in chapter 7 above, the grid should always be applicable as a framework in such situations as mandated in the processes set out in the SSA's applicable social security rulings and regulations.

2 While this section's focus is on the de facto or announced use of the official notice doctrine to determine that nonexertional limitations do not remove a claimant

from direct application of an unfavorable exertional grid rule, the analysis would apply equally to other, less common grid exceptions. This would include use of official notice to determine that: (1) Exertional limitations that place a claimant between two exertional ranges with differing work adjustment conclusions do not remove a claimant from direct application of the unfavorable higher range grid rule (*see* Social Security Ruling 83-12); or (2) exertional limitations that prevent performance of a full range of sedentary work do not preclude direct unfavorable application of a sedentary grid rule (*see* Social Security Ruling 96-9p); or (3) transferable skills that expand the grid's unskilled job base permit denial based on the grid rules that reference the potentially expanded job bases (*see* Social Security Ruling 82-41).

3 Agency regulations and rulings mandate that claimants with both exertional and nonexertional limitations must be accorded the "lock-in" favorable evaluation to assess whether they meet the grid's per se rules for demonstrating inability to make a work adjustment on exertional grounds alone.

4 The step 2 severity standard and severity regulations are discussed in chapter 6.

5 *See* Hoopai v. Astrue, 499 F.3d 1071, 1075–76 (9th Cir. 2007). *Hoopai* is one of the clearest cases sanctioning de facto unannounced non-rebuttable administrative notice that severe nonexertional limitations do not significantly erode the grid's occupational or job bases. However, it is predicated on a few faulty assumptions. First, the Ninth Circuit conflated a step 2 severity finding with a step 4 finding of inability to perform past relevant work that satisfies the claimant's prima facie case. *See id.* at 1076. Then, the court determined that if a finding of a step 2 severe nonexertional impairment would require use of a VE at step 5, the two steps would collapse and a vocational expert would be required in every case in which a step 2 determination of severity is made. This would defeat the purpose of the grids because a claimant could not reach the step 5 determination without making out a prima facie case of a severe disability at step 2. *Id.*

This reasoning fails to recognize that claimants with only severe exertional impairments or limitations at step 2 would still proceed to a step 5 determination based solely on the grid and without a VE. In the situation where a claimant has nonexertional limitations, the grid by its express terms does not provide a direct rule of decision because the grid was not based on administrative notice of the effects of such limitations. Thus, direct application of the grid to claimants with severe limitations separate and apart from those upon which the grid was based cannot be properly deemed "the purpose of the grids."

6 *See, e.g.*, Ortiz v. Sec'y of HHS, 890 F. 2d 520, 524 (1st Cir. 1989) (even "significant non-strength" limitations do not preclude exclusive reliance on the grid unless they are found to preclude a wide range of the grid's job bases).

7 In this context, as the First Circuit has recognized that, "[d]espite what may be suggested by the use of the word 'framework,' whenever an ALJ fails to take vocational testimony, he must be deemed '[i]n reality' to have 'relied exclusively

on the grid to show the existence of jobs claimant could perform.'" *Id.* at 524 n.4 (quotation omitted).

8 Brock v. Astrue, 674 F.3d 1062, 1065 (8th Cir. 2012); King v. Astrue, 564 F.3d 978, 979 (8th Cir. 2009).

9 *See* Loza v. Apfel, 219 F.3d 378, 398–99 (5th Cir. 2000).

10 *See, e.g.*, Phillips v. Barnhart, 357 F.3d 1232, 1242 (11th Cir. 2004) ("Exclusive reliance on the grids is not appropriate *either* when [the] claimant is unable to perform a full range of work at a given level *or* when a claimant has non-exertional impairments that significantly limit basic work skills.") (quoting Francis v. Heckler, 749 F.2d 1562, 1566 (11th Cir.1985)).

11 *See, e.g.*, Villano v. Astrue, 556 F.3d 558, 564 (7th Cir. 2009) ("When a claimant has nonexertional limitations that *might* significantly reduce the range of work she can perform, the ALJ may not rely on the Grid to find a claimant not disabled but must instead consult a VE to determine whether the claimant can perform a significant number of jobs.") (emphasis added) (citations omitted).

12 *See, e.g.*, Smalls v. Shalala, 966 F.2d 413, 417 (D.C. Cir. 1993) ("If a claimant suffers from non-exertional limitations that *could* limit the claimant's ability to perform jobs of which she would be otherwise capable, mechanical application of the grids is inappropriate.") (emphasis added).

13 *See, e.g.*, Bapp v. Bowen, 802 F.2d 601, 605–06 (2d Cir. 1986).

14 *See, e.g.*, Walker v. Bowen, 889 F.2d 47, 49 (4th Cir. 1989).

15 *See, e.g.*, Abbot v. Sullivan, 905 F.2d 918, 926–27 (6th Cir. 1990).

16 *See, e.g.*, Channel v. Heckler, 747 F.2d 577, 579–81 (10th Cir. 1984).

17 *See, e.g.*, Jordan v. Comm'r of Soc. Sec., 548 F.3d 417, 424 (6th Cir. 2008); Rosa v. Callaghan, 168 F.3d 72, 82 (2d Cir. 1999); *Channel*, 747 F.2d at 580–81.

18 *See, e.g.*, Sykes v. Apfel, 228 F.3d 259, 271–72 (3d Cir. 2000); *see also* Poulos v. Comm'r of Soc. Sec., 474 F.3d 88, 95 (3d Cir. 2007) ("This lack of supporting evidence highlights why we require an ALJ either to take vocational evidence or to follow the proper steps to take official notice, providing the claimant with an opportunity to see the evidence on which the ALJ relies and with an opportunity to challenge the ALJ's conclusion."); Allen v. Barnhart, 417 F.3d 396, 401–08 (3d Cir. 2005). Several other courts have identified, on occasion, that this issue implicates official notice principles. *See, e.g.*, Warmouth v. Bowen, 798 F.2d 1109, 1110–13 (7th Cir. 1986) ("[W]e only require that there be reliable evidence of some kind that would persuade a reasonable person that the limitations in question do not significantly diminish the employment opportunities otherwise available. . . . We therefore conclude that the Secretary erred *when he in effect summarily took administrative notice* that there is a significant number of unskilled, sedentary jobs in the national economy that Warmoth can perform.") (emphasis added and citations omitted); Delgado v. Barnhart, 305 F. Supp. 2d 704, 710 (S.D. Tex. 2004) ("In instances in which the Guidelines merely serve as a decisional framework (*e.g.*, when significant nonexertional limitations are involved), the ALJ *may not simply take administrative notice of jobs existing in the economy* and must, therefore,

satisfy his burden of proof in some other fashion, most typically via the testimony of a vocational expert.") (emphasis added); *cf.* Wilson v. Califano, 617 F.2d 1050, 1053 (4th Cir. 1980) ("In *Taylor v. Weinberger*, [512 F.2d 664 (4th Cir. 1975),] *we expressly rejected the contention* that the *Secretary may establish specific vocational ability solely through medical evidence or by 'administrative notice.'* Implicit in *Taylor* is the recognition that the ALJ is not qualified to provide affirmative vocational evidence.") (emphasis added); Kuwahara v. Bowen, 677 F. Supp. 553, 562 (N.D. Ill. 1988) ("Appellate courts properly frown on efforts to take judicial notice of the availability of jobs with specific vocational requirements. This Court has no desire to play armchair vocational expert.") (citations omitted).

19 The ALJ found, and the commissioner did not contest, that the claimant's nonexertional visual impairment reflected a "severe" impairment under the agency's step 2 nonseverity regulations. *See Sykes*, 228 F.3d at 261. In the 1980s, the agency implemented, but then withdrew, a Social Security Ruling that had established that monocular vision and nineteen other impairments or conditions should never be deemed severe impairments and were thus per se nonsevere under the agency's regulations. *See* Social Security Ruling 82-55 (rescinded and replaced by SSR 85-28, which deleted the twenty per se nonsevere conditions). *See generally* Dixon v. Shalala, 54 F.3d 1019, 1023–33 (2d Cir. 1995) (describing SSR 82-55's rescission and legal problems with its application). A determination that a nonexertional limitation or impairment is severe at step 2 has vocational implications; it means that the claimant has a limitation that has more than a slight or trivial impact on ability to perform at least one of the several "basic work activities" in the agency's regulations.

20 *Sykes*, 228 F.3d at 270.

21 *Id.* The court relied on a similar case in the Eleventh Circuit involving application of the grid to a claimant with monocular vision to underscore the absence of an evidentiary basis for the non-erosion finding. *See id.* (citing Francis v. Heckler, 749 F.2d 1562, 1567 (11th Cir.1985)). Several other courts have found that neither ALJ intuition nor medical evidence can supply an appropriate evidentiary basis for the labor market facts of job base erosion or job incidence. *See, e.g.*, Foreman v. Callahan, 122 F.3d 24, 26 (8th Cir. 1997) ("[T]he ALJ's unsupported assertion that Foreman's mental impairment would not limit his ability to perform the full range of jobs contemplated in the grids 'invaded the province of the vocational expert.'"); DeFrancesco v. Bowen, 867 F.2d 1040, 1045 (7th Cir. 1989) (finding that the ALJ failed to procure a VE "either because of his belief—untenable given the record—that DeFrancesco's medical condition impaired his ability to perform light work but slightly, or because the [ALJ] confused a medical advisor with a vocational specialist"); *cf. Wilson*, 617 F.2d at 1053 (reiterating that the agency may not "establish specific vocational ability solely through medical evidence" and the "ALJ is not qualified to provide affirmative vocational evidence").

22 *Sykes*, 228 F.3d at 272 (citing Union Elec. Co. v. FERC, 890 F.2d 1193, 1202 (D.C. Cir. 1989) (quoting Oh. Bell Tel. v. Pub. Util. Comm'n, 301 U.S. 292, 301–302)).

23 *Id.*
24 *See id.* at 273.
25 *Id.*
26 *Id.* at 273. Because the court left open the question of the substantive propriety of the administrative notice doctrine's application in this context, presumably that issue could still be challenged on remand and on future appeals.
27 *See id.* at 268–69 n.12 (citing cases in the First, Second, Fifth, Seventh, and Tenth Circuits and explaining the rejection of their holdings—that ALJs may determine that nonexertional limitations do not significantly erode the grid's occupational bases without taking vocational evidence or proper official notice—due to inconsistency with *Campbell*).
28 *See Poulos*, 474 F.3d at 94 n.4.
29 *See* Social Security Acquiescence Ruling 01-1(3).
30 20 C.F.R. § 404.985(b) (2021).
31 *See* SSAR 01–1(3), at 517–18.
32 *See id.* at 517 ("The court stated that it was not deciding the issue of 'whether Social Security Rulings can serve the same function as the rulemaking upheld in Campbell.' The court further stated that it need not resolve the issue of whether 'the Commissioner can properly refer to a ruling for guidance as to when nonexertional limitations may significantly compromise the range of work that an individual can perform.'"); *Sykes*, 228 F.3d at 271 & n.15. In *Sykes*, the agency argued on appeal that SSR 85-15 supported the non-erosion conclusion. *Id.* This ruling is written in a flexible, nonconclusive fashion, providing generally that visual impairments that only prevent performance of jobs requiring good vision do not preclude a substantial number of jobs at all exertional levels. At the same time, the ruling provides that some persons with adverse vocational characteristics who have worked in jobs requiring good vision will be so precluded. *See* Social Security Ruling 85-15. The court found that this ruling did not purport to supply a definitive or conclusive decisional rule applicable to Sykes's situation but merely a "factor for consideration." *Sykes*, 228 F.2d at 271. Moreover, since the ALJ had not applied this ruling in the decision, its use for the first time on appeal violated the settled administrative law principle precluding post hoc justifications for agency decisions. *Id.* (citing SEC v. Chenery, 318 U.S. 80 (1943)).
33 *See* POMS DI 52735.000, https://secure.ssa.gov/apps10/poms.NSF/lnx/0452735000 (referencing SSAR 01-1(3)).
34 *See* SSAR 01–1(3).
35 417 F.3d 396 (3d Cir. 2005).
36 *Id.* at 397.
37 The ALJ's only apparent reference to Social Security Ruling 85-15 to support his non-erosion conclusion was a citation in his penultimate finding that

> given the claimant's age, level of education, work skills and residual functional capacity for a full range of work at all exertional levels. 20 C.F.R. § 404.1569 and Medical–Vocational Rule 204.00, Appendix 2, Subpart P,

Regulations No. 4, used as a framework for decisionmaking, warrants a conclusion of not disabled. The claimant's mental limitations do not significantly erode the base of unskilled jobs available (SSR 85-15).

Brief of Appellee, Allen v. Barnhart, No. 04–2163, 2004 WL 4990654, at *6 (Aug. 23, 2004). On appeal, the agency expanded the ALJ's reasoning to suggest that language paraphrased from example four in Social Security Ruling 85-15 "provides substantial evidence to determine the impact of Allen's nonexertional limitations." *Id.* at *17. Example four of Social Security Ruing 85-15 provides the following:

Example 4: Someone who is of advanced age, has a high school education, and did skilled work as manager of a housing project can no longer, because of a severe mental impairment, develop and implement plans and procedures, prepare budget requests, schedule repairs or otherwise deal with complexities of this level and nature. Assuming that, in this case, all types of related skilled jobs are precluded but the individual can do work which is not detailed and does not require lengthy planning, the remaining related semiskilled jobs to which skills can be transferred and varied unskilled jobs, at all levels of exertion, constitute a significant vocational opportunity. A conclusion of "not disabled" would be appropriate. (Compare rules 201.07, 202.07, and 203.13 of Appendix 2.).

Social Security Ruling 85-15. Apart from *Allen*, the agency apparently takes the nationwide position that its SSRs' non-erosion examples are "evidence" as opposed to simply legal interpretive rules. *See, e.g.*, Jordan v. Comm'r of Soc. Sec., 548 F.3d 417, 424 (6th Cir. 2008) ("SSA argues on appeal that SSR 85-15 constituted the necessary 'reliable evidence' that Jordan's nonexertional limitations did not significantly limit her ability to perform light work."). Indeed, in *Sykes*, the Third Circuit noted that the *Skidmore* "respect" doctrine might not be "entirely apposite" with reference to the non-erosion examples in SSR 85-15 because "we deal here with a prior agency determination of fact" as opposed to an interpretation of law. 228 F.3d at 271 n.14.

38 *Allen*, 417 F.3d at 407.

39 *Id.* at 407–08.

40 *Id.*

41 *Id.*

42 *Compare* Martinez v. Comm'r of Soc. Sec., 2014 WL 7896423, *9–10 (D.N.J. 2014) (advance notice and right to rebut SSRs required under *Allen*) *with* Rzonca v. Colvin, 2015 WL 71154, at *7 (D.N.J. 2015) ("while the ALJ should provide notice of intention to rely upon an SSR as evidence of an undiminished occupational base, failure to do so [only] means the court should apply close scrutiny to the ALJ's reliance on an SSR.").

43 *See* Heckler v. Campbell, 461 U.S. 458, 469 (1983) (citing APA, 5 U.S.C. § 556(e)); Goldberg v. Kelly, 397 U.S. 254, 271 (1970); *see also* 42 U.S.C. § 405(b)(1) (commissioner "shall" base SSA decision after hearing on "evidence adduced at the hearing").

44 *Campbell*, 461 U.S. at 470.

45 *See* Office of Chief Admin. Law Judge, CJB-09–03, Prohibition on the Use of "Generic" Vocational Expert Interrogatories by Administrative Notice (2009) (citing *Campbell*, 461 U.S. at 467, 470), https://secure.ssa.gov/apps10/public/reference.nsf/links/05262009025802PM.

46 *See, e.g.*, Minard Run Oil Co. v. U.S. Forest Service, 670 F.3d 236, 254–55 (3d Cir. 2011) ("Legislative rules are subject to the notice and comment requirements of the APA because they work substantive changes in prior regulations, or create new law, rights, or duties. . . . [T]he District Court properly found that appellees were likely to succeed on the merits of their claim that the Settlement Agreement and the Marten Statement . . . must be promulgated pursuant to the notice and comment procedures of the APA."); *see generally* American Mining Congress v. Mine Safety & Health Admin., 995 F.2d 1106. 1108–13 (D.C. Cir. 1993) (describing many of the circumstances distinguishing substantive legislative rules from mere interpretive rules including amendments of substantive rules); U.S. v. Fla. E. Coast Ry. Co., 410 U.S. 224 (1973) (describing the differences between formal "on the record" rulemaking under 5 U.S.C. §§ 556, 557 and informal "notice and comment" legislative rulemaking under 5 U.S.C. § 553); *cf.* Christensen v. Harris County, 529 U.S. 576, 588 (2000) (an agency may not attempt "under the guise of interpreting a regulation, to create a new de facto regulation").

47 Some Social Security Rulings contain examples of various nonexertional limitations that "generally" or "usually" substantially limit or do not substantially restrict various occupational bases. *See generally* TRAVER, at ch. 12 (describing these examples). The Social Security Rulings thus include both "lock-in" and "lock-out" examples or general guidance on grid occupational base erosion or non-erosion from certain nonexertional limitations. The examples do not appear to reflect definitive erosion/non-erosion conclusions. *Compare* TRAVER, at § 1200.1 (suggesting that use of the modifiers "generally" or "usually" coupled with the agency's burden of proof on this issue should require a persuasive demonstration by the agency that a disability finding is not mandated for a claimant with an SSR profile where substantial erosion "usually" or "generally" occurs), *with* Lauer v. Apfel, 169 F.3d 489, 493 (7th Cir. 1999) (suggesting that a "lock-in" job base erosion example in SSR 96-9p based on presumed job base erosion from inability to stoop is only advisory and does not mandate a favorable decision by agency adjudicators). The agency may choose to bind itself to the SSRs' "lock-in" examples of presumed job base erosion as a matter of administrative convenience as it has done with the medical listings at step 3 of the sequential evaluation process. This would presumably serve adjudicative efficiency interests and generally reduce agency time and resources from a more prolonged individualized assessment. As with the listings, the Social Security Rulings' application might be overinclusive and benefit some people who might arguably have been rejected thereunder if given a more individualized medical-vocational labor market work adjustment assessment. That possibility would be part of the agency's cost-benefit calculation.

However, use of the "lock-out" examples to deny claims based on presumed non-erosion of the job bases implicates issues of substantive and procedural fairness to claimants under due process and APA principles.

48 *See* Stieberger v. Sullivan, 738 F. Supp. 716, 757–60 (S.D.N.Y. 1990) (noting that the agency's current announced policy of acquiescence in circuit court precedent still results in de facto or informal nonacquiescence when the agency declines to issue an acquiescence ruling on a circuit precedent since agency adjudicators are forbidden from applying circuit precedents that are not embodied in ARs).

49 In *Sykes v. Apfel*, the Third Circuit suggested in a footnote that even nonsevere, nonexertional limitations might still have a significant impact on the grid's occupational bases, and it did not exempt cases involving such nonsevere restrictions from its holding's requirement of either producing vocational evidence or taking proper official notice. 228 F.3d 259, 268 n.12 (3d Cir. 2000). However, the agency's acquiescence ruling appeared to limit *Sykes*'s application to its narrow factual context—a case where a nonexertional limitation was deemed "severe" or nontrivial at step 2. *See* Social Security Acquiescence Ruling 01-1(3) ("In view of the ALJ's finding that the claimant had a severe nonexertional impairment, the court stated that we cannot establish the existence of other jobs in the national economy that Sykes can perform by relying on the grids alone, even if [we use] the grids only as a framework instead of to direct a finding of no disability.").

50 See Bowen v. Yuckert, 482 U.S. 137 (1987) (rejecting facial challenge to the SSA's nonseverity regulations and sustaining the agency's authority to establish a de minimis, slightness medical severity threshold at step 2).

51 The step 2 severity standard and the notion that the effects of multiple nonsevere impairments can be cumulatively severe are discussed in chapter 6.

52 *See* Bowen v. City of N.Y., 476 U.S. 467, 475 (1986) ("[T]he court stated that evidence of the 'fixed clandestine policy against those with mental illness' was overwhelming."), *aff'g sub nom.* City of New York v. Heckler, 742 F.2d 729 (2d Cir. 1984), *aff'g* City of New York v. Heckler, 578 F. Supp. 1109 (E.D.N.Y. 1984); *see also* Mental Health Ass'n of Minn. v. Schweiker, 554 F. Supp. 157 (D. Minn. 1982), *aff'd*, 720 F.2d 965 (8th Cir. 1983) (finding a Department of Health and Social Services policy, which presumed that persons whose mental impairment did not meet or equal listings of impairment could do unskilled work, to be a violation of the Social Security Act and "arbitrary, capricious, irrational, and an abuse of discretion").

9. THE DICTIONARY OF OCCUPATIONAL TITLES IN WORK ADJUSTMENT ASSESSMENTS

1 A review of the occupations in the 1991 DOT (the fourth edition) reveals, however, that many of the occupational descriptions and requirements in that edition have not been reevaluated and updated since the 1970s when viewing the designation of "DLU" (date of last update) in the occupational title. For example, in the (frequently sought-out) unskilled, sedentary work category, the job of "assembler/

final assembler" (affixing pads and temple pieces to optical frames by hand with screwdrivers) or "addresser" (addressing envelopes, cards, and packages by hand or typewriter) have each not been updated since 1977. *See* DOT REVISED 4TH ED., DOT ## 713.687–018, 209.587–010.

2 *See* 42 Fed. Reg. 55,349, 55,351–54, 55,360–61 (Nov. 28, 1978). The agency administratively noticed other publications to support its conclusions in the grid, such as Census Reports and County Business Patterns published by the Bureau of the Census, as well as the Occupational Outlook Handbook published by the Bureau of Labor Statistics. *Id.* at 55,351. However, the only comprehensive occupational classification system noticed was the DOT, and thus the agency and all commentators properly recognized the DOT as the agency's primary source for the grid's occupation-based rules.

3 *Id.* at 55,360–61.

4 *Id.*

5 The grid regulation's assumption of 200 (as opposed to 137) sedentary occupations was called into question even before the grid became effective in 1979. The grid regulations have always acknowledged that "sedentary work represents a significantly restricted range of work." 20 C.F.R. pt. 404, app. 2, § 201.00(b) (2020); *cf.* TRAVER, § 1200.3.5 ("The occupational base for unskilled sedentary work is likely non-existent and certainly fragile."). The DOT still includes questionable sedentary occupations such as "dowel inspector" (DOT # 669.687–014) and "vamp strap ironer" (DOT #788.687–158) in its occupations list. *See* DOT REVISED 4TH ED.

6 *See* 20 C.F.R. pt. 404, subpt. P, app. 2 (2021).

7 DOT REVISED 4TH ED., at v.

8 *Id.*

9 *Id.*

10 Social Security Ruling 96-9p, 1996 WL 374185, at n.5 (July 2, 1996); *see also* 57 Fed. Reg. 43,005 (Sept. 17, 1992) ("The range of work (of which the medical-vocational rules take administrative notice) continues to represent more occupations than would be required to represent significant numbers. . . . [W]e have received no significant data or other evidence to indicate that . . . the unskilled occupational base . . . has changed substantially."); 53 Fed. Reg. 51,097 (Dec. 20, 1988) (same).

11 *See* Sherwin v. Sec'y of Health & Human Servs., 685 F.2d 1, 6–7 (1st Cir. 1982).

12 *Id.*

13 *See* English v. Shalala, 10 F.3d 1080, 1084–85 & n.3 (4th Cir. 1993); Townley v. Heckler, 748 F.2d 109, 113–14 (2d Cir. 1984).

14 *Townley*, 748 F.2d at 113–14; *English*, 10 F.3d at 1084–85 (quoting *Townley*, 748 F.2d at 113–14).

15 *See* NAT'L RESEARCH COUNCIL, WORK, JOBS AND OCCUPATIONS: A CRITICAL REVIEW OF THE DICTIONARY OF OCCUPATIONAL TITLES (1980) [hereinafter CRITICAL REVIEW]. One popular social security disability treatise also questions the SSA's reliance on the 1965 DOT, which the agency used to support the grid's 1978 rule promulgation without ever having deter-

mined that the DOT and related data and assumptions were accurate. DAVID F. TRAVER, SOCIAL SECURITY DISABILITY ADVOCATE'S HANDBOOK § 1403, 1403.1.3 (2009) (*citing* CRITICAL REVIEW). The treatise's author, David Traver, is both a former vocational evaluator and a disability lawyer. The treatise is a practice manual focusing on the evaluation and litigation of vocational issues in disability benefits cases. It includes a scathing critique of the DOT. *See id.* §1403.1 ("The Social Security Administration figures the DOT and its related data are 'better than nothing.' But 'better than nothing' is not a reliable basis to award or deny life-sustaining benefits to the disabled and disadvantaged."); *see id.* (noting the SSA's continuing reliance on the DOT and related data that derives from a time "when the Beatles ruled the AM pop charts, and Elvis was still the king"). Traver also provides detailed analysis of methodological deficiencies in the secondary documentary sources, other than the DOT, relied upon to supply empirical support for the grid. *Id.* at ch.15; *see* 20 C.F.R., Pt. 404, app.2, § 200.00(b) (2021) (listing documentary sources of which the agency took administrative notice to support labor market work adjustment rules in the grid).

16 *See* CRITICAL REVIEW, at 145–47, 191–94.

17 *Id.* at 195.

18 Julie L. Bose, Thomas A. Grzesik, Glen O. Geist & David R. Bryant, *Misuse of Occupational Information in Social Security Disability Cases*, 30 REHAB. COUNSELING BULL. 83 (1986).

19 *Id.* at 88–89. A "self-contained," unskilled, sedentary job is one in which there are no tasks involved in the job that involve either exertional requirements more strenuous than sedentary or the use of any skills. *See id.* at 89.

20 *Id.* at 90–91.

21 *Id.* at 89.

22 *Id.* at 91–92.

23 MICHAEL J. HANDEL, METHODOLOGICAL ISSUES RELATED TO THE OCCUPATIONAL REQUIREMENTS SURVEY 10 (February 26, 2015) [hereinafter HANDEL, OCCUPATIONAL REQUIREMENTS SURVEY].

24 *Id.*

25 *See* Angela M. Heitzman et al., *A Call to Update the DOT: Findings of the IARP Occupational Database Committee*, 17 REHAB. PROF. 63, 64 (2009) [hereinafter Heitzman et al., *A Call to Update the DOT*] (explaining that the DOL convened the Advisory Panel for the Dictionary of Occupational Titles (APDOT), which recommended in 1993 that the DOT be replaced).

26 *Id.* at 77; *see also id.* at 71 ("The Structure of the DOT doesn't work well with career planning."); *see generally* U.S. DEP'T OF LABOR, ADVISORY PANEL FOR THE DICTIONARY OF OCCUPATIONAL TITLES (APDOT) A NEW DOT: A DATABASE OF OCCUPATIONAL TITLES FOR THE TWENTY-FIRST CENTURY (1993) [hereinafter A NEW DOT] (APDOT's recommendations).

27 *Id.* at 71. Instead of the nine levels of specific vocational preparation utilized in the DOT, which focus on the time required to learn and perform job tasks, the

O*NET has five job "zones," which "are more abstract and include: little or no preparation needed; some preparation needed; medium needed; considerable preparation needed; and extensive preparation needed." *Id.* at 72.

28 *Id.* at 72.

29 *See* COMM. ON NAT'L STATISTICS, NAT'L RESEARCH COUNCIL (NRC), A DATABASE FOR A CHANGING ECONOMY: REVIEW OF THE OCCUPATIONAL INFORMATION NETWORK (O*NET) 164–65 (NANCY T. TIPPINS & MARGARET L. HILTON, EDS. 2010) [hereinafter CHANGING ECONOMY], www.nap.edu (describing the O*NET's use of the concept of static strength as opposed to RFC); Heitzman et al., *A Call to Update the DOT*, at 72 (noting that in "O*NET the occupational unit may include jobs that are sedentary all the way up to heavy in the same grouping").

30 Heitzman et al., *A Call to Update the DOT*, at 72.

31 *Id.*

32 The methodological problems generated from efforts to fit the DOT's approximately 13,000 occupational titles into only approximately 800 occupational groupings in the present-day DOL occupational classification system are discussed in chapter 5.

33 An assistant commissioner from the DOL's Bureau of Labor Statistics confirmed in 2007 that the BLS regards the DOT as "obsolete since much of the information contained in the most recent version is based on research conducted at least two decades ago." Letter from Dixie Somers, Assistant Commissioner, U.S. Department of Labor, Office of Occupational Statistics, to David Lowery (Nov. 26, 2007) (on file with author). Indeed, since it has been thirty years since the last DOT revision (1991), the SSA's regulations on past relevant work suggest that the information supplied has become outdated for SSA's purposes too. *See* 20 C.F.R. §§ 404.1565(a), 416.965(a) (2021) (jobs performed more than fifteen years from the onset of disability are no longer "relevant" because "[a] gradual change occurs in most jobs so that after 15 years it is no longer realistic to expect that skills and abilities acquired in a job done then continue to apply"); *see* Cunningham v. Astrue, 360 Fed. Appx. 606, 614–16 (6th Cir. 2010) ("[C]ommon sense dictates that when such [DOT] descriptions appear obsolete, a more recent source of information should be consulted. . . . [W]e conclude that the VE's dependence on the DOT listings alone does not warrant a presumption of reliability.").

34 *See* Jeffrey A. Truthan & Sylvia E. Karman, *Transferable Skills Analysis and Vocational Information During a Time of Transition*, 6 J. FORENSIC VOCATIONAL ANALYSIS 17, 20 (2003) (noting that, until a new occupational information instrument is developed, "the DOT cannot be retired or written off for rehabilitation, forensic, and disability adjudication [purposes]"); *see also* U.S. GEN. ACCOUNTING OFFICE (GAO), SSA & VA DISABILITY PROGRAMS: RE-EXAMINATION OF DISABILITY CRITERIA NEEDED TO HELP ENSURE PROGRAM INTEGRITY 14 (Aug. 2002) [hereinafter RE-EXAMINATION NEEDED], www.gao.gov/ ("The agencies have discussed ways that O*NET might

be modified or supplemental information collected [sic] to meet SSA's needs, but no definitive solution has been identified. SSA officials have indicated that an entirely new occupational database could be needed to meet SSA's needs, but such an effort could take many years to develop, validate, and implement."); DISABILITY RESEARCH INST., SOCIAL SECURITY JOB DEMANDS PROJECT METHODOLOGY TO IDENTIFY AND VALIDATE CRITICAL JOB FACTORS 5, 11 (Nov. 2002), www.paq.com (explaining that DOL's abandonment of the DOT and use of the O*NET creates a "dilemma for the SSA[;] O*NET does not adequately describe job demands to meet SSA's current program requirements").

10. PROGRESS TOWARD A NEW OCCUPATIONAL TAXONOMY FOR WORK ADJUSTMENT ASSESSMENTS

1 Heitzman et al., *A Call to Update the DOT*, at 63.

2 *Id.*

3 CHANGING ECONOMY, at 162.

4 *See id.* at 103.

5 *Id.* The NRC observed a marked decline in "communication and collaboration between DOL and SSA regarding a common occupational database." *Id.*

6 *Id.* at 163.

7 *See* id. at 159–70. After an inexplicably unsuccessful attempt to collaborate with the DOL on a mutually workable occupational taxonomy earlier in the decade, the SSA went off on its own in 2009 and assembled an advisory committee to explore the creation of an independent additional occupational taxonomy to support the SSA's own disability adjudicative needs. *See* Meeting Notice, 74 Fed. Reg. 3666-03 (Jan. 21, 2009) (announcing SSA's convening of the first meeting of the Occupational Information Development Advisory Panel that will "advise the Agency on creating an occupational information system tailored specifically for SSA's disability programs and adjudicative needs [and will provide] . . . recommendations . . . in the following areas: medical and vocational analysis of disability claims; occupational analysis, including definitions, ratings and capture of physical and mental/cognitive demands of work and other occupational information critical to SSA disability programs; data collection; use of occupational information in SSA's disability programs; and any other area(s) that would enable SSA to develop an occupational information system suited to its disability programs and improve the medical-vocational adjudication policies and processes").

8 *See* CHANGING ECONOMY, at 161, 163.

9 *See id.* at 168. There may have been political obstacles to agency collaboration on a project, which could significantly alter the nature and scope of millions of disability determinations in an enormous social welfare program. There are less inherent structural mechanisms in government for facilitating better collaboration between the SSA—which is an independent agency—and executive departments. Indeed, in 1994, when Congress removed the SSA from the executive cabinet as a component of the Department of Health and Human Services and

established it as an independent agency with only a single commissioner who could be removed only for cause, President Bill Clinton questioned the Act's constitutionality and its consistency with the Article II executive power. *See* The American Presidency Project, William J. Clinton: Remarks on Signing the Social Security Independence and Program Improvements Act of 1994 (Aug. 15, 1994), www.presidency.ucsb.edu. In President Clinton's view, the new scheme created a structure with the potential for unusually minimal and limited presidential involvement and direction in the policy and operation of one of the largest agencies in the federal government. In 2020, the Supreme Court held in a case challenging the Consumer Financial Protection Bureau's (CFPB) enforcement authority that the CFPB's "leadership by a single individual, removable only for [cause,] violates separation of powers." Seila Law LLC v. Consumer Financial Protection Bureau, 140 S. Ct. 2183, 2197 (2020). In so doing, the majority expressly cited President Clinton's 1994 signing statement but also distinguished the SSA from independent regulatory agencies like the CFPB as "lacking enforcement authority to bring actions against persons and limited only to adjudicating claims for social security benefits." *Id.* at 2202. The partial dissent derisively challenged the suggestion of lesser executive functioning and policy implications from the SSA, vis-à-vis the CFPB, stating: "Consider: would a President lose more votes from a nonfunctioning SSA or CFPB?" *Id.* at 2241 (Kagan, J., joined by Ginsburg, Breyer, and Sotomayor, JJ., concurring in the judgment with respect to severability and dissenting in part). After *Seila Law*, the SSA's current single-commissioner structure is likely unconstitutional. Seven members of the Court concluded in *Seila Law*, however, that the CFPB's for-cause removal provision could be severed from the rest of the statute and thus did not require invalidation of the agency itself; *id.* at 2209–11 (Roberts, C.J. joined by Alito and Kavanaugh, JJ, plurality opinion on severability); *id.* at 2245 (concurring opinion on the judgment with respect to severability and partial dissent). Presumably, SSA's for-cause removal provision would be severed as well, and the agency otherwise salvaged, if the Court were to find SSA to possess the same constitutional defect as the CFPB. and Congress will likely need to pursue other options reflected as permissible under the majority's reasoning to create a new structure for the SSA. *See id.* at 2199–00. This could entail returning to one of its historical structures as either an independent bipartisan board or as part of an executive cabinet level department such as HHS (as it was prior to 1994). It could also be elevated to its own executive department.

10 Changing Economy, at 161.

11 *Id.* at 168. For discussion of potential methodological concerns with O*NET, *compare* Robert J. Harvey, *The O*NET: Do Too-Abstract Titles + Unverifiable Holistic Ratings + Questionable Raters + Low Agreement + Inadequate Sampling + Aggregation Bias =(a) Validity, (b) Reliability, (c) Utility, or (d) None of the Above?* (2009), http://harvey.psyc.vt.edu, *with* Suzanne Tsacoumis, *Responses to Harvey's Criticisms of HumRRO's Analysis of the O*NET Analysts' Ratings* (2009), www7.nationalacademies.org.

12 Occupational Information System Project, www.ssa.gov.
13 *Id.*
14 *See* www.bls.gov.
15 *See* www.ssa.gov.
16 *See* www.bls.gov.
17 *See* www.bls.gov; https://www.bls.gov/ors/home.htm.
18 Handel, Occupational Requirements Survey, at 1.
19 *Id.* at 75–78.
20 *Id.* at 1.
21 *Id.* at 89
22 *See id.* at 1.
23 *See Chavez*, 895 F.3d at 965 (citing Soc. Sec. Admin., Occupational Information System Project, www.ssa.gov.
24 *Id.*
25 *See* www.ssa.gov.
26 *Id.*
27 *Id.*
28 80 Fed. Reg. 55050, 55051 (September 14, 2015).
29 The 2020 regulatory and SSR changes deleting inability to communicate in English and contracting the illiteracy category's scope in the grid are discussed in chapter 6.
30 Deputy Commissioner Warshawsky was also the former assistant secretary for economic policy in the George W. Bush administration. *See* www.ssa.gov.
31 *See* https://fee.org.
32 Mark J. Warshawsky and Ross A. Marchand, *Modernizing the SSDI Eligibility Criteria: A Reform Proposal That Eliminates the Outdated Medical–Vocational Grid* 34–35 (April 2015), www.mercatus.org [hereinafter Warshawsky and Marchand, *Modernizing the SSDI Eligibility Criteria*].
33 *Id.*
34 On the day of President Biden's 2021 inauguration, Andrew Saul, the commissioner of Social Security appointed by President Trump, issued a memorandum to SSA senior staff announcing Deputy Commissioner Warshawsky's departure effective immediately and his replacement with Kilolo Kijakazi from the Urban Institute and formerly from the Center on Budget and Policy Priorities. *See* Memorandum from SSA Commissioner Andrew Saul to Senior Staff, dated January 20, 2021 (on file with the author). Presumably, the nonpublic (albeit leaked to reporters) late 2020 proposed regulations to modify the SSA's grid and reduce reliance on vocational factors, stemming in part from the Warshawsky and Marchand paper and reported as moving forward after the presidential election and in the Trump administration's lame duck period, are now, at least, suspended. *See* David A. Weaver, *Social Security Administration Is Preparing to Bar 500,000 Americans from Getting Benefits*, The Hill (Dec. 7, 2020), thehill.com (speculating, based on an earlier leaked proposal, that the proposed SSA regulations sent

to the Office of Management and Budget during the first weekend in December 2020 would likely utilize "the buzzword 'modernization'" and "suggest that the 'modern' economy provides many jobs that even a displaced and disabled older worker can do").

Commissioner Saul's status is also uncertain. Saul is a businessman, former garment firm executive, Republican fundraiser, and former college classmate of President Trump with no previous experience in the Social Security Administration before being appointed in 2019. *See* Roger Sollenberger, *Social Security Commissioner Invested in Company That Makes COVID Test Touted by Trump*, SALON (June 25, 2020), www.salon.com. He was a board member of the Manhattan Institute—a right-wing think tank that advocated reductions in social security coverage. *See id.* Although Saul has four years remaining on his six-year appointment and is dischargeable only for cause in that period, at the time of this writing, the Biden administration has placed him on a list of "temporary government leaders" and referenced Saul with an "acting" title. *See* Lisa Rein and Anne Gearan, *Biden Is Firing Some Top Trump Holdovers but in Some Cases, His Hands May Be Tied*, WASHINGTON POST (Jan. 24, 2021), www.washingtonpost.com; *see also* Joe Davidson, *Some Groups Want Biden to Fire Trump's Social Security Commissioner. It's Not That Easy to Do*, WASHINGTON POST (Dec. 18, 2020), www.washingtonpost.com (describing opposition to Saul, obstacles to his removal, and fears of continuation of some Trump administration agency policies if he remains); *see also* Michael Hiltzik, *Biden Needs to Clean House at the Social Security Administration, and Fast*, LOS ANGELES TIMES (Jan. 29, 2021) (delineating reasons Biden should seek Saul's resignation or dismissal).

The Supreme Court's 2020 decision in *Seila Law* (described above in chapter 10, note 9), holding that an independent agency headed by single leader removable only for cause violates separation of powers principles in certain circumstances and requiring severance of the for-cause removal restrictions) may supply leverage for a change in SSA leadership if sought by President Biden. However, even prior to Trump's election, Saul's appointment as commissioner, or Warshawsky's tenure as deputy commissioner, the SSA announced in 2015 that it was considering altering reliance on vocational factors in labor market work adjustment assessments through an advance notice of proposed rulemaking on these factors. (The 2015 ANPRM is discussed above in chapter 10 and note 28). Accordingly, it would be premature to assume that these issues have been fully abandoned in the SSA's pending policy agenda, even after a change in much of SSA's top leadership from the Trump administration.

35 Professor Gellhorn's analysis is discussed in chapter 4.

11. INTRODUCTION TO THE DEBATE OVER ALTERNATIVES TO THE CURRENT DISABILITY STANDARD AND PROGRAM

1 The concept of the "social obligation of work" is discussed in note 14 in the Introduction.

2 *See* Capowski, *Categorical Decision-making*, at 374–75; Liebman, *The Definition of Disability*, at 852–53; *see also* Jerry Mashaw, *The Supreme Court's Due Process Calculus for Administrative Adjudication in* Mathews v. Eldridge: *Three Factors in Search of a Value*, 44 U. CHI. L. REV. 28, 45 (1976) ("SSA disability adjudications should perhaps be viewed as really concerned with difficult value judgments—individualized exemptions from the moral, social and economic constraints of the work ethic, determined by a complex of medical, vocational and environmental factors as they impinge on particular individuals."). Thus, the notion that a person might be quite disabled, but still capable of doing some things for which others will pay, is not inconsistent with the Act's conception or recognition of a normative justification for an exemption from the social obligation of work. *See* Liebman, *The Definition of Disability*, at 852 ("[V]irtually every disabled person can do something for which another person will pay. He is 'totally' disabled because the market value of his labor, given such alternatives as machines and healthy persons, is so low."); Diller, *Dissonant Disability Policies*, at 1009 (disability benefit recipients "may be capable of working if they exceed social expectations"); BERKOWITZ, DISABLED POLICY, at 100 (noting that, while a person who suffered "loss of his arms and legs, his eye and his hearing,[] might have his trunk conveyed to a busy street corner and make a little money by selling such small objects as post cards, candy or cigars," Congress would not require as much under the SSA's disability standard); Smith v. Califano, 637 F.2d 968, 971 (3d Cir. 1981) ("[S]tatutory disability does not mean that a claimant must be a quadriplegic or an amputee. Similarly, shopping for the necessities of life is not a negation of disability and even two sporadic occurrences such as hunting might indicate merely that the claimant was partially functional on two days. Disability does not mean that a claimant must vegetate in a dark room excluded from all forms of human and social activity."); Butler v. Flemming, 288 F.2d 591, 594 (5th Cir. 1961) ("I do not interpret the Act to apply only to the totally helpless and bedridden nor to those at death's door.").

3 Boatner v. Berryhill, No. 3:16-CV-243-CWR-RHW, 2018 WL 2191804, *2 (S.D. Miss., May 11, 2018); *cf.* Devah Pager, Bruce Western & David Pedulla, *Employment Discrimination and the Changing Landscape of Low-Wage Labor Markets*, 1 U. CHI. LEGAL F. 317, 343 (2009) [hereinafter cited as Pager, Western & Pedulla, *Employment Discrimination*] (concluding that "discrimination remains a significant barrier to employment facing minority low-wage workers").

4 John M. Meisburg, Jr., *Ten Ways to Improve the Social Security Disability Law and Save Billions of Dollars*, 47 FED. LAWYER 38, 40 (2000) [hereinafter Meisburg, *Ten Ways*]; *cf.* Robert E. Rains, *Debating Disability Design: A Response*, 47 FED. LAWYER 39, 43–45 (2000) (challenging ALJ Meisburg's assumptions and noting that Meisburg supplies no data, study, or suggestion that the work adjustment and job incidence presumptions based on the mix of vocational factors in the sedentary grid rules are too generous).

5 *See* SUBCOMM. ON SOC. SEC. OF HOUSE COMM. ON WAYS & MEANS, 97TH CONG., 1ST SESS., REAGAN ADMINISTRATION DISABILITY PROPOSALS 3–13 (Comm. Print 1981); *see* Capowski, *Categorical Decision-making*, at 373–74 and n.195 (describing the proposal). For another reasonably contemporary call to consider reviving this proposal, see David H. Autor & Mark G. Duggan, *The Growth in the Social Security Disability Rolls: A Fiscal Crisis Unfolding*, 20 J. ECON. PERSP. 71, 92–93 (2006) [hereinafter Autor & Duggan, *Growth in Social Security*].

6 Report of the 1971 Advisory Council on Social Security, H.R. DOC. NO. 92–80, at 29–30 (Apr. 5, 1971); Reports of the Quadrennial Advisory Council on Social Security, H.R. DOC. NO. 94–75, at 38–40 (Mar. 10, 1975).

12. AMENDMENTS TO SIMPLIFY WORK ADJUSTMENT ASSESSMENTS BY RESTRICTING ELIGIBILITY

1 *See* STAFF OF THE HOUSE SUBCOMM. ON ADMIN. OF THE SOC. SEC. LAWS, 86TH CONG., DISABILITY INSURANCE FACT BOOK 23 (1959) ("The law does not authorize the use of a rating schedule or the adoption of an 'average man' concept of total disability. The question in every case is whether the individual in spite of his impairment has sufficient capacity to function so that considering his age, education and experience, he is able to engage in any substantial gainful activity.") (quoting DEP'T OF HEALTH, EDUC. & WELFARE, DISABILITY AND SOCIAL SECURITY (1958)); *see also* MASHAW, BUREAUCRATIC JUSTICE, at 75 (explaining inapplicability of "average person" concept to SSA disability program).

2 *See* NAS, PAIN AND DISABILITY, at 11 ("Pain is inherently subjective; there are no thoroughly reliable ways to measure it; and the correlation between the severity of pain and the level of dysfunction is imperfect."). The courts have recognized that at a certain, albeit difficult to quantify, point it is reasonable for society to excuse workers from enduring further pain, suffering, or substantial discomfort in the job market. In a series of early cases shortly after the Act's passage, courts rejected Judge Learned Hand's "now famous aphorism" in a case under the War Risk Insurance Act that "[a] man may have to endure discomfort or pain and not be totally disabled; much of the best work of life goes on under such disabilities.'" Page v. Celebrezze, 311 F.2d 757, 762 (5th Cir. 1963) (quoting Theberge v. United States, 87 F.2d 697, 698 (2d Cir. 1937)). In *Page*, the Fifth Circuit observed that the notion that pain must be endured—that pain, no matter how severe or overpowering, is not disabling unless it will "substantially aggravate" a condition—is "contrary to the standard announced in" cases from this and other circuits since "the purpose of much social security legislation" including this Act "is to ameliorate some of these rigors that life imposes." *Id.*; *see generally* Jon C. Dubin, *Poverty, Pain and Precedent: The Fifth Circuit's Social Security Jurisprudence*, 25 ST. MARY'S L.J. 81, 112–16 (1993) (analyzing judicial and regulatory history and treatment of pain in SSA disability programs).

3 Warshawsky & Marchand, *Modernizing the SSDI Eligibility Criteria*, at 33.
4 Capowski, *Categorical Decision-making*, at 374.
5 *See id.* at 374 n.201.
6 *See* Peter V. Lee, Sheri Porath & Joan E. Schaffner, *Engendering Social Security Determinations: The Path of A Woman Claimant*, 68 TUL. L. REV. 1477, 1521 (1994) ("Poor claimants, as well as increasingly many working-class claimants, are not likely to have the financial resources to establish an ongoing relationship with a physician of the type envisioned by the SSA regulations. Often they can only afford to go to a public clinic where physicians are not likely to have the same detailed knowledge of the patient's condition that would be expected of a private doctor. The clinic physician who sees a claimant once may not, for example, be able to describe adequately how a particular medical ailment uniquely affects the claimant's ability to function. Doctors who are unfamiliar with a patient's medical history may be less likely to perform diagnostic tests, which can be important to the claimant seeking to build a record of objective medical evidence of her impairment. Additionally, when there is no long-term relationship between a claimant and a physician, the testimony or reports of the physician can be more easily discredited by decisionmakers in the disability determination process." (citations omitted)).
7 *See* U.S. GEN. ACCOUNTING OFFICE, SOCIAL SECURITY: RACIAL DIFFERENCE IN DISABILITY DECISIONS WARRANTS FURTHER INVESTIGATION 5 (1992), http://archive.gao.gov ("GAO recommends that the [SSA] Commissioner . . . investigate the reasons for the racial difference in allowance rates . . . and that the Commissioner act to correct and prevent any unwarranted disparities."); *see also* U.S. GEN. ACCOUNTING OFFICE, SSA DISABILITY DECISION MAKING: ADDITIONAL MEASURES WOULD ENHANCE AGENCY'S ABILITY TO DETERMINE WHETHER RACIAL BIAS EXISTS (2002), www.gao.gov (finding that "[t]he steps SSA has taken over the last decade have not appreciably improved the agency's understanding of whether . . . racial bias exists in its disability decision-making process"); *see also* Community Legal Services of Philadelphia, *Racial Disparities in Access to Supplemental Security Income Benefits for Children* (Dec. 2020), clsphila.org (describing racial disparities in SSI disability for children due to factors including substantive revision and significant and unjustified increase in the stringency of sickle cell anemia step 3 listing requirements and other step 3 listed conditions disproportionately afflicting African American children; underdiagnosis of children of color leading to less medical proof of disability, and overcriminalization of children of color resulting in forms of custody rendering children of color ineligible for SSI); Elaine Golin, Note, *Solving the Problem of Gender and Racial Bias in Administrative Adjudication*, 95 COLUM L. REV. 1532 (1995); For discussion of gender disparities, see Lee et al., at 1524 (concluding that the disability process "is based on male research models and . . . does not account for differences that may exist between men and women, leaving medical advisors with inadequate

information about women's health issues"); THE EFFECTS OF GENDER IN THE FEDERAL COURTS: FINAL REPORT OF THE NINTH CIRCUIT GENDER BIAS TASK FORCE (July 1993), *reprinted in* 67 S. CAL. L. REV. 857, 869–70 (1994) ("[T]he Advisory Committee concluded that many of the 'facially neutral' aspects of the SSA determinations may have gendered impacts—given current social expectations and roles of women and men, and moreover, that not all women are treated equally; race, class, and ethnicity may further disable women claimants.").

8 *See generally*, D. STANLEY EITZEN, MAXINE BACA ZINN & KELLY EITZEN SMITH, SOCIAL PROBLEMS 184–219 (11th ed. 2008) (describing disproportionate representation of racial minorities and women living in poverty, without access to adequate health care, and with less adequate educational opportunities); *see also* Capowski, *Categorical Decision-making*, at 374 n.201 (describing anticipated harm to African Americans from Reagan's proposal).

9 Warshawsky & Marchand, *Modernizing the SSDI Eligibility Criteria*, at 36–37.

10 *See* www.bls.gov.

11 *See, e.g.*, WILLIAM C. WOOD, LITERACY AND THE ENTRY LEVEL WORKFORCE: THE ROLE OF LITERACY AND POLICY IN LABOR MARKET SUCCESS (JUNE 2010); NATIONAL CENTER FOR EDUCATION STATISTICS, LITERACY IN EVERYDAY LIFE: RESULTS FROM THE 2003 NATIONAL ASSESSMENT OF ADULT LITERACY 46 (2007) ("At least 50 percent of adults with Below Basic literacy, on each of the three scales, were not in the labor force."); NATIONAL CENTER FOR EDUCATION STATISTICS, ADULT LITERACY IN AMERICA: A FIRST LOOK AT RESULTS FROM THE NATIONAL ADULT LITERACY SURVEY 68 (1993) ("individuals who performed in the lower levels of literacy proficiency were more likely than their more proficient counterparts to be unemployed or out of the labor force. They also tended to earn lower wages and work fewer weeks per year, and were more likely to be in craft, service, laborer, or assembler occupations than respondents who demonstrated higher levels of literacy performance.").

12 *See* https://beta.bls.gov.

13 *Id.*

14 The elimination of the category of ability to communicate in English from the grid and the need for English-language communication skills in certain unskilled occupations frequently identified by vocational experts in work adjustment assessments are discussed in chapter 6.

15 83 Fed. Reg. 51114, 51195 (October 10, 2018).

16 83 Fed. Reg. 51114, 51195 (October 10, 2018).

17 Most work adjustment adjudication focuses on claimants without transferable skills who have mostly performed unskilled past work, and the disability inquiry focuses on adjustment to unskilled "other work" in the economy. Agency regulations clarify that "[a] person does not gain work skills by doing unskilled jobs." 20 C.F.R. § 404.1568(a) (2021).

18 The Warshawsky/Marchand proposal provides no reasoning, independent of discussion of the education category, for the elimination of past-work experience as a factor in work adjustment assessments. SSA's current policy rests on the common sense assumptions that claimants with acquired skills from work can adjust to a wider array of other work when those skills are transferable. *See* chapter 6 and discussion of the relevance of transferable skills. It also acknowledges that those who have been unable to work or with only temporally remote work history are going to have a more difficult adjustment to performance of consistent competitive work than those have been in the work force more regularly or recently. *See id.*

19 Warshawsky & Marchand, *Modernizing the SSDI Eligibility Criteria*, at 33–34.

20 *Id.* at 35.

21 Paul N. Van De Water, Center on Budget and Policy Priorities, *The Realities of Work for Individual with Disabilities: Impact of Age, Education, and Work Experience* 6 (November 20, 2015), www.ssa.gov [hereinafter Van De Water, *The Realities of Work*] (quoting Hilary Waldron, *Trends in Mortality Differentials and Life Expectancy for Male Social Security-Covered Workers, by Average Relative Earnings*, Social Security Administration, ORES Working Paper No. 108, October 2007, www.ssa.gov); *see also* NATIONAL ACADEMY OF SCIENCE, THE GROWING GAP IN LIFE EXPECTANCY BY INCOME: IMPLICATIONS FOR FEDERAL PROGRAMS AND POLICY RESPONSES 2 (NATIONAL ACADEMY OF SCIENCES, 2015), www.nap.edu ("better-educated, higher-income people live longer, on average than less educated lower income people. In recent decades, however, the *gap* in life expectancy between higher-income individuals and those lower on the socioeconomic distribution has been expanding."); National Academy of Science, *The Role of Inequality, in* EXPLAINING DIVERGENT LEVELS OF LONGEVITY IN HIGH-INCOME COUNTRIES Ch. 9 (NATIONAL ACADEMY OF SCIENCES, 2011) www.nap.edu.

22 Van de Water, *The Realities of Work*, at 6.

23 *See* 20 C.F.R., Pt. 416, subpart K (income limits); Subpart L (resource limits) (2021).

24 Chart Book: Social Security Disability Insurance, Center on Budget and Policy Priorities (September 6, 2019), www.cbpp.org (approximately 50 percent of disability beneficiaries would be below the poverty line without SSDI and 20 percent remain at incomes below the poverty line even after receipt of SSDI benefits).

25 *See id.*; *see also* Erica Steinmetz, U.S. Census Bureau, Current Population Reports Americans with Disabilities: 2002 7–10 (May 2006) (finding a higher uninsured rate, lower high-school completion rate, and higher poverty rate among those with severe disabilities compared to those without disabilities).

26 The relevance of age in work adjustment assessments is discussed in chapters 4, 5, and 6.

27 Rachel O. Coats, Andrew D. Wilson, Winona Snapp-Childs, Aaron J. Fath & Geoffrey P. Bingham, *The 50s Cliff: The Perceptuo-Motor Learning Rate Across the Lifespan* (January 16, 2014), https://doi.org.

28 *Id.*
29 Miki Malul, *Older Workers' Employment in Dynamic Technology Changes*, 38 J. OF SOCIO-ECON. 809, 809 (2009)
30 Jacob J. Sosnoff & Karl M. Newell, *Age-Related Loss of Adaptability to Fast Time Scales in Motor Variability*, 63B J. OF GERONTOLOGY 344, 344 (2008).
31 Neil Charness & Sara J. Czaja, AARP Public Policy Institute, *Older Worker Training: What We Don't Know* 16 (October 2006), assets.aarp.org.
32 Jody Schimmel Hyde, April Yanguan Wu, & Lakhpreet Gill, *The Benefit Receipt Patterns and Labor Market Experiences of Older Workers Who Were Denied Social Security Disability Insurance Benefits on the Basis of Work Capacity*, 80 SOC. SEC. BULL. 25, 40–41 (2020).
33 The proposed and withdrawn regulation to restrict eligibility by increasing the age requirements in the grid is discussed in chapter 6, note 43.

13. THE TWENTY-FIRST CENTURY LABOR MARKET FOR LOW-SKILL WORK

1 Warshawsky & Marchand, *Modernizing the SSDI Eligibility Criteria*, at 33.
2 *Id.* at 35.
3 RE-EXAMINATION NEEDED, at 13; *see also* VIRGINIA RENO, NATIONAL ACADEMY OF SOCIAL INSURANCE, SOCIAL SECURITY AS PART OF AN INTEGRATED NATIONAL DISABILITY POLICY: IS THE SOCIAL SECURITY DEFINITION OUT OF SYNC? 15 (Apr. 14, 2004) [hereinafter RENO, OUT OF SYNC?], www.ssab.gov (noting that the current labor market is harder on persons with mental limitations because it requires that employees be "highly flexible"—one employee may be expected to perform and shift between the varied activities previously performed by two or three workers—and perform with an enhanced emphasis on speed and productivity).
4 David H. Autor and David Dorn, *The Growth of Low-Skilled Service Jobs and the Polarization of the U.S. Labor Market*, 103 AMER. ECON. REV. 1553, 1555 (2013).
5 *Id.*
6 *Id.*
7 *Id.*
8 *Id.* at 1588.
9 *Id.* at 1559.
10 *Id.*; *see also id.* at 1590.
11 *Id.* at 1559 n.9.
12 *See* 20 C.F.R. pt. 404, subpt. P, app. 2, §§ 201.00–203.00 (2021).
13 *See* https://beta.bls.gov.
14 *Id.*
15 *See generally* KUBITSCHEK & DUBIN, chs. 5, 3 (collecting cases on vocational expert assessments in cases involving mental impairments).
16 The case law is legion with examples of VE work adjustment assessments for claimants limited to "simple, routine, repetitive tasks" (SRRT). *See id.* As a mat-

ter of practice, the agency takes the position that all claimants whose mental impairments produce moderate restrictions on concentration persistence and pace (CPP) can adjust to work involving SSRT. *See generally id.* This is so even though there are no meaningful regulatory definitions for the terms "simple" or "moderate." The circuits are divided on this presumptive agency appellate position that a moderate limitation in CPP—a work production output- and performance speed-based limitation—is always accounted for through a VE's skill level restriction to SRRT jobs. *Compare* O'Connor-Spinner v. Astrue, 627 F.3d 614, 620–21 (7th Cir. 2010) ("The ability to stick with a given task over a sustained period is not the same as the ability to learn how to do tasks of a given complexity" [and] "the ALJ should refer expressly to limitations on concentration, persistence and pace in the hypothetical in order to focus the VE's attention on these limitations and assure reviewing courts that the VE's testimony constitutes substantial evidence of the jobs a claimant can do."); Mascio v. Colvin, 780 F.3d 632, 638 (4th Cir. 2015) (same); and Ramirez v. Barnhart, 372 F.3d 546, 553 (3d Cir. 2004) (same) *with* Stubbs-Danielson v. Astrue, 539 F.3d 1169, 1173–74 (9th Cir. 2008) (ALJ's hypothetical to VE including ability to perform "simple, routine, repetitive tasks" adequately captured claimant's limitations in pace-of-work performance from mental impairment). The agency's announced policy is more nuanced and acknowledges that "the skill level of a position is not necessarily related to the difficulty an individual will have in meeting the demands of the job." *See* SSR 85-15. It posits the example of a busboy who might be able to perform simple table-clearing tasks, but mental restrictions on pace may preclude performance without significant mistakes or at a competitive level, no matter how "simple" those tasks may seem. *See id.* Current low-skill labor market trends should moot this circuit-splitting debate, because the unskilled SRRT job market is rapidly becoming extinct due to automation.

17 *See* https://beta.bls.gov.

18 OECD SKILLS OUTLOOK 2013 FIRST RESULTS FROM THE SURVEY OF ADULT SKILLS 46 (2013), www.oecd.org.

19 *Id.* at 55.

20 THE WORLD BANK, THE WORLD DEVELOPMENT REPORT 2019: THE CHANGING NATURE OF WORK vii (2019); *see also* Daron Acemoglu and Pascual Restrepo, *Robots and Jobs: Evidence from the Labor Market* 36 (March 2017), www.nber.org ("Because there are relatively few robots in the US economy, the number of jobs lost due to robots has been limited so far (ranging between 360,000 and 670,000 jobs . . .)[;] [h]owever, if the spread of robots proceeds as expected by experts [] over the next two decades the future aggregate implications of the spread of robots could be much more sizable.").

21 Pager, Western & Pedulla, *Employment Discrimination*, at 333.

22 *See id.* at 343.

23 For a personal case study of the difficulty adjusting to work in the twenty-first century's low-skill labor market, even for a white worker without any medical im-

pairments or vocational impediments, and with an advanced education (graduate degree), no dependents or child care responsibilities, and an otherwise extraordinarily successful work history, *see* BARBARA EHRENREICH, NICKEL AND DIMED: ON (NOT) GETTING BY IN AMERICA (2001).

14. THE DISABILITY REFORM DEBATE

1 FRANK S. BLOCH AND JON C. DUBIN, SOCIAL SECURITY LAW, POLICY AND PRACTICE, CASES AND MATERIALS 67 (2016) ("[T]he Social Security Trust Funds are not trust funds in the usual sense where money is contributed to—and remains in—a fund to be used for specified limited purposes; instead the money in the Funds is in constant circulation with older money being spent regularly and new money coming in to (more or less) replace the money that went out. In effect, the Funds are a cash-flow management tool.").

2 *See id.*; *see generally* THE BOARD OF TRUSTEES, FEDERAL OLD-AGE AND SURVIVORS INSURANCE AND FEDERAL DISABILITY INSURANCE TRUST FUNDS, THE 2015 ANNUAL REPORT OF THE BOARD OF TRUSTEES OF THE FEDERAL OLD-AGE AND SURVIVORS INSURANCE AND FEDERAL DISABILITY INSURANCE TRUST FUNDS, H.R. DOC. NO. 114–51 (2015).

3 *See* Kathy Ruffing & Paul N. Van De Water, Center on Budget and Policy Priorities, *Congress Needs to Boost Disability Insurance Share of Payroll Tax by 2016* (July 31, 2014), www.cbpp.org (describing (a) Congress's eleven reallocations between the OASI and SSDI trust funds in both directions—six from OASI to SSDI, five from SSDI to OASI—in actions in the years 1968, 1970, 1978, 1979, 1980, 1982, 1983, 1984, 1994, 1997, and 2000; and (b) a projection in 1994 of the need to rebalance from OASI to SSDI in 2016 due to demographic trends); *see also* THE WHITE HOUSE, : A LIFELINE FOR MILLIONS OF AMERICAN WORKERS AND THEIR FAMILIES 10–11 (2015) [hereinafter THE WHITE HOUSE, SOCIAL SECURITY DISABILITY INSURANCE], www.whitehouse.gov (explaining the reasons behind the long-anticipated and actual increase in SSDI benefit outlays as attributable largely to aging of the baby boom generation into disability-prone years; substantial growth in the percentage of women in covered employment from 1970 to 2013; and increases in the retirement age; and noting that fraud is "extremely rare" and not identified as a factor).

4 Kathy Ruffing, *The Disability Insurance Non-crisis*, Center on Budget and Policy Priorities (Feb. 10, 2015), www.cbpp.org.

5 *See* H.R. RES. 5, 114th Cong. § 3(q) (2015).

6 National Academy of Social Insurance, *Social Security Finances: Findings of the 2015 Trustees Report*, 45 SOCIAL SECURITY BRIEF 1, 6–7 (July 2015) [hereinafter NASI, *Social Security Finances*].

7 *See* Social Security Benefit Protection and Opportunity Enhancement Act of 2015, Pub. L. No. 114–74, Title VIII, Sec. 801, et seq., www.congress.gov; *see also* Bipartisan Budget Act of 2015, Pub. L. 114-74, § 833, 129 Stat. 584, 613–14 (2015), www.ssa.gov/legislation/legis_bulletin_110315.html.

8 *See* The Board of Trustees, Federal Old-Age and Survivors Insurance and Federal Disability Insurance Trust Funds, The 2016 Annual Report of the Board of Trustees of the Federal Old-Age and Survivors Insurance and Federal Disability Insurance Trust Funds, H.R. Doc. No. 14-145 3–4 (2016).

9 *See* The Board of Trustees, Federal Old-Age and Survivors Insurance and Federal Disability Insurance Trust Funds, The 2020 Annual Report of the Board of Trustees of the Federal Old-Age and Survivors Insurance and Federal Disability Insurance Trust Funds (2020), www.ssa.gov (2020) [hereinafter cited as 2020 Trustees Report].

10 *Id.* The report indicates that its projections do not take account of the impacts and potential downward adjustments in trust fund revenues due to the COVID-19 pandemic. *Id.* at 1. The OASI trust fund is projected to be able to cover 100 percent of benefits through 2034. *Id.* at 5. As the Democratic presidential candidate, Joe Biden proposed lifting the social security (FICA) 2020 payroll tax cap on income over $137,700 ($142,800 in 2021) and taxing income over $400,000 to raise approximately $1 trillion to shore up the OASI trust fund after 2034. *See Understanding Joe Biden's 2020 Tax Plan*, Committee For a Responsible Federal Budget, www.crfb.org (July 30, 2020). For discussion of measures to bolster the OASI trust fund after 2035, see Kathleen Romig, Center on Budget and Policy Priorities, *What the 2020 Trustees' Report Shows About Social Security* (May 13, 2020), www.cbpp.org; *see generally*, Kathryn J. Moore, *The Future of Social Security: Principles to Guide Reform*, 41 J. Marshall L. Rev. 1061 (2008).

11 2020 Trustees Report, at 32.

12 An Open Letter from Former Commissioners of the Social Security Administration (April 4, 2013), www.c-c-d.org [hereinafter cited as SSA Commissioners' Open Letter]; former SSA commissioner Michael Astrue, who served in appointed positions in the Reagan, George H. W. Bush and George W. Bush administrations, the latter as SSA chief for a full six-year term, explained his view that the disability criteria "is a *very* tough standard; and you can argue about whether it should be the standard or not but I am stuck with it." *"Failing the Disabled," Investigation: Disability Benefits System Harbors Culture of Denying Help to Even the Most Unfit to Work*, CBS News (Jan. 15, 2008), www.cbsnews.com (emphasis in original verbal statement).

13 SSA Commissioners' Open Letter.

14 *See* Mark C. Weber, *Disability and the Law of Welfare: A Post Integrationist Examination*, 2000 U. Ill. L. Rev. 889, 896 nn.45–46 [hereinafter Weber, *Disability and the Law of Welfare*] (citing studies showing that one-eighth of claimants who obtained disability insurance in a twelve-month period died within two years and that "[t]he proportion of individuals dying within the first six months on [the program] is fourteen times that of persons in their first six months on the Social Security old-age insurance program").

15 *See* Diller, *Dissonant Disability Policies*, at 1071 n.310 (citation omitted).

16 *Id.* at 1071 n.311 (citation omitted).

17 *See* Autor & Duggan, *Growth in Social Security*, at 92–93.

18 Warshawsky & Marchand, *Modernizing the SSDI Eligibility Criteria*, at 38.

19 Jerry L. Mashaw, 20 J. HEALTH POL'Y & L. 225, 226 (1995) (reviewing EDWARD H. YELIN, DISABILITY AND THE DISPLACED WORKER (1993)); *see also* RENO, OUT OF SYNC?, at 7 (recognizing that, while "any wage-replacement system can be characterized as a disincentive to work to some degree . . . [disability] benefits are not a strong deterrent to work . . . [because] benefits and replacement rates are relatively modest," anecdotal evidence shows people turn to disability benefits "only as a last resort," and "empirical studies show people often remain on jobs after the onset of disability and many change jobs or continue looking for work before applying for benefits"); Weber, *Disability and the Law of Welfare*, at 911 ("[T]he prospect of benefits is not enough of an incentive to induce individuals to become disabled to obtain benefits."); *see generally id.* at 930 (noting that SSI benefits pay only approximately 70 percent of the federal poverty level). Indeed, 2020 benefits level were approximately $1,200 per month for DI ($1,258) and $800 per month for SSI ($783) as the maximum benefit for a single individual. *See* www.ssa.gov (2020 DIB average amount); www.ssa.gov (2020 SSI maximum). Therefore, the average DI recipient garnered only 50 percent, or one-half, of the $600 per week deemed essential in the Spring 2020 Cares Act for *extra* extended unemployment benefits due to the COVID-19 pandemic, and an SSI recipient at the federal maximum received only 33 percent, or one-third. *See* Chad Stone, Center on Budget and Policy Priorities, *Cares Act Measures Strengthening Unemployment Insurance Should Continue While Need Remains* (June 9, 2020), www.cbpp.org.

20 SSA Commissioners' Open Letter.

21 In the wake of the major welfare reform legislation, the Personal Responsibility and Work Opportunity Reconciliation Act of 1996, which "ended welfare as we know it," extreme poverty has steadily climbed. H. Luke Shaefer & Kathryn Edin, Nat'l Poverty Center, *Extreme Poverty in the U.S., 1996 to 2011* 2 (2012), www.npc.umich.edu (reporting the number of households in extreme poverty has increased from 636,000 in 1996 to about 1.46 million in 2011). When included as income, SNAP (food stamps) reduces extreme poverty; however, since much of its success relies on relaxed eligibility requirements by the states, stricter standards could prove damaging. *Id.* at 1–2; Jasmine Aguilera, *How Trump's New Food Stamp Rule Could Impact Nearly 700,000 Vulnerable Americans*, TIME (Dec. 9, 2019), https://time.com (finding that Trump administration rules where states can no longer temporarily waive the restrictions unless for high (10 percent) unemployment rates and requiring twenty hours of work per week could harm 700,000 citizens). The United States has also continued to struggle with homelessness and hunger. "Between 1999 and 2002, the number of households that experienced food insecurity increased from 10.5 million to 12.1 million." Shawn Fremstad, Center

on Budget and Policy Priorities, *Recent Welfare Reform Research Findings* (Jan. 31, 2004), www.cbpp.org. Food insecurity rose to 14.3 million U.S. households in 2018. U.S. DEP'T OF AGR., ECONOMIC RESEARCH SERVICE: FOOD SECURITY STATUS OF U.S. HOUSEHOLDS IN 2018, www.ers.usda.gov. In 2019, the Department of Housing and Urban Development estimated a 3 percent increase in homelessness since 2018. Despite the number of people in shelters falling by .05 percent between 2018 and 2019, the number of unsheltered homeless people rose by 9 percent. *See* https://nlihc.org. Public housing programs have fallen short in their ability to address the growing need for affordable housing. JOINT CENTER FOR HOUSING STUDIES OF HARVARD U., THE STATE OF THE NATION'S HOUSING 35 (2017), www.jchs.harvard.edu ("According to HUD's 2015 Worst Case Housing Needs report, the number of very low-income renters increased from 18.5 million to 2013 to 19.2 million in 2015, but the share of assistance declined from 25.7 percent to 24.9 percent."). While TANF aimed to "end welfare as we know it," states' latitude in determining eligibility requirements and benefit levels have reduced program assistance: "In 1996, 68 families received TANF for every 100 families in poverty; in 2018, only 22 families received TANF for every 100 families in poverty." Center on Budget and Policy Priorities, *Policy Basics: Temporary Assistance for Needy Families*, (Feb. 6, 2020), www.cbpp.org. In addition, imposing strict work requirements creates a weaker cash safety net, resulting in "half to two-thirds of families [having] their cash assistance grants reduced or eliminated due to a work-orientated sanction." Landonna Pavetti, Center on Budget and Policy Priorities, *TANF Studies Show Work Requirements Proposals for Other Programs Would Harm Millions, Do Little to Increase Work* (Nov. 13, 2018), www.cbpp.org. Similar work requirements on adult Medicaid enrollees have proven to have a severely disproportionate impact on people with disabilities when enforced. Center on Budget and Policy Priorities, *Taking Away Medicaid for Not Meeting Work Requirements Harms People with Disabilities*, (Mar. 10, 2020), www.cbpp.org (finding that in Arkansas, the first state to implement such requirements, more than 18,000 Medicaid beneficiaries lost coverage in 2018 under the state's policy, compelling a federal court to intervene).

22 *See* Jon C. Dubin and Robert E. Rains, *Scapegoating Social Security Claimants (and the Judges Who Evaluate Them)*, 6 ADVANCE: J. AM. CONST. SOC. ISSUE GROUPS 109, 111–12 (2012), www.acslaw.org [hereinafter cited as Dubin & Rains, *Scapegoating Social Security Claimants*]; *Work or Die*, N.Y. TIMES, May 23, 1983, www.nytimes.com; *see generally* Schweiker v. Chilicky, 487 U.S. 412, 416–17 (1988) (describing "the terrible effects on individual lives" from wrongful disability benefits denial decisions).

23 Dubin & Rains, *Scapegoating Social Security Claimants*, at 112.

24 *See* Warshawsky & Marchand, *Modernizing the SSDI Eligibility Criteria*, at 9; Autor & Duggan, *Growth in Social Security*, at 71; *see also* Richard J. Pierce, Jr., *What Should We Do About Social Security Disability Appeals?*, REGULATION (Fall 2011), at 34 [hereinafter cited as Pierce, *What Should We Do?*].

25 The most significant amendments to the SSA's disability benefits programs' substantive standard and eligibility since 1967 were the Social Security Disability Benefits Reform Act of 1984, Pub. L. No. 98–460, 98 Stat. 1794 (codified at various subsections of 42 U.S.C. §§ 423, 1382 (2006)) (establishing a substantive medical improvement standard for evaluating whether to terminate benefits; requiring that the combined or cumulative effects of a claimant's impairments and limitations be considered throughout the disability evaluation process, including in the determination of threshold medical severity; providing an interim standard for evaluation of pain and subjective symptomology; directing the SSA to rewrite its mental impairment criteria; and extending an administratively imposed moratorium on mental disability benefit terminations until the new criteria were in place); the Contract with America Advancement Act of 1996, Pub. L. No. 104–121, § 105, 110 Stat. 847 (codified at 42 U.S.C. §§ 423(d)(2)(C), 1382c(a)(3)(J) (2006)) (precluding persons from receiving benefits "if alcoholism or drug addiction would . . . be a contributing factor material to the [SSA commissioner's] determination that the individual is disabled"); and the Personal Responsibility and Work Opportunity and Reconciliation Act of 1996, Pub. L. No. 104–193, § 402, 110 Stat. 2105 (1996) (codified at various subsections of 42 U.S.C. §§ 423(a)(1)(C), (d)(2)(A), 1382(e)(B), 1382(e)(4)(A) (2006)) (imposing sweeping restrictions on noncitizen eligibility; narrowing eligibility for children's SSI disability; and removing from SSI eligibility persons fleeing prosecution, custody, or confinement for a felony); *see also* Social Security Protection Act of 2004, Pub. L. No. 108–203, §203, 118 Stat. 493 (2004) (extending fleeing felon prohibitions to the disability insurance program); *see generally* BLOCH, BLOCH ON SOCIAL SECURITY, at §§ 1.8, 1.9 (describing statutory amendments affecting the disability programs from 1984 to present); L. Scott Muller, Brett O'Hara & John R. Kearney, *Trends in the Social Security and Supplemental Security Income Disability Programs*, SOC. SEC. ADMIN. 79–80 (Aug. 2006), www.ssa.gov (describing all amendments to the Act from 1970 to 2003).

26 *See, e.g.*, 81 Fed. Reg. 66138–01 (January 17, 2017) (repealing mental/cognitive listing 12.05(C) for borderline cognitive IQ (60–70) plus an additional impairment causing significant work related limitations); 64 Fed. Reg. 46,122 (Aug. 24, 1999) (repealing the obesity listing (former listing 9.09)); 65 Fed. Reg. 42772, 42774, 42780 (July 11, 2000) (codified at 20 C.F.R. §§ 404.1520(b), 404.1592(d)(2)(ii)–(iii) (2003)) (precluding eligibility for disability insurance claimants with disabling impairments who commence substantial gainful activity within twelve months of disability onset and preventing commencement of a trial work period within that first twelve-month period); 65 Fed. Reg. 17,994, 17,995 (Apr. 6, 2000) (deleting reference to a "highly marketable skills" requirement for finding transferable skills for older workers, thereby rendering eligibility for older workers more stringent).

27 The former president of the National Organization of Social Security Claimants' Representatives has explained a perceived movement toward greater disability

program eligibility restrictions and disability standard stringency from the perspectives of longtime attorneys representing claimants:

> [G]etting disability approval is harder than ever. Undocumented pain, alcoholism and drug abuse have been disqualified. Mental retardation and HIV standards are tougher. Diabetes and obesity are no longer distinct disabilities. Illegal immigrants are now disqualified. Applicants must now present objective medical evidence of disability. This is no rubber-stamp process.

Charles Martin, *Opposing View: Disability Benefits Remains a Vital Lifeline*, USA TODAY, Feb. 3, 2012, www.usatoday.com.

28 *See* 68 Fed. Reg. 51,153, 51,159 (Aug. 26, 2003) (codified at 20 C.F.R. §§ 404.1560(b)(3), 416.960(b)(3) (2003)); Barnhart v. Thomas, 540 U.S. 20 (2003) (sustaining agency denial based on ability to perform previous job as elevator operator, even though the job no longer exists in significant numbers in the American economy and the claimant was found unable to adjust to alternative work).

29 The SSA's deletion of the "inability to communicate in English" category from the grid in 2020 is discussed in chapter 6.

30 *See* Warshawsky & Marchand, *Modernizing the SSDI Eligibility Criteria*, at 9; Autor & Duggan, *Growth in Social Security*, at 71–72; see Pierce, *What Should We Do?*, at 34; Richard V. Burkhauser, American Enterprise Institute for Public Policy Research, *SSDI Program Growth Will Continue Unless Fundamental Reforms are Implemented*, statement before the United States Committee on Finance Hearing titled "Social Security: A Fresh Look at Worker's Disability Insurance SSDI Program Growth Will Continue Unless Fundamental Reforms Are Implemented" (July 24, 2014), at 5 [hereinafter cited as Burkhauser, *SSDI Program Growth*].

31 SSA Commissioners' Open Letter, at 1.

32 *See* Warshawsky & Marchand, *Modernizing the SSDI Eligibility Criteria*, at 9; Pierce, *What Should We Do?*, at 34; Autor & Duggan, *Growth in Social Security*, at 71. Autor & Duggan also attribute some disability program growth in the 2000s to the demographic factors of greater women's labor force participation and baby boomers aging into more disability likely age categories, but they only view women's participation as a significant factor in the increases. *See also* Burkhauser, *SSDI Program Growth*, at 7 (suggesting growth due to baby boomer aging was only a minor factor in overall program growth at the time).

33 Warshawsky & Marchand, *Modernizing the SSDI Eligibility Criteria*, at 27.

34 Pierce, *What Should We Do?*, at 3–4.

35 Burkhauser, *SSDI Program Growth*, at 5.

36 *Id.*

37 Most prominent among the unique political circumstances that motivated the 1984 Disability Benefits Reform Act's passage by a unanimous vote in each house was the huge public outcry against the perceived excesses of the Reagan administration's program to massively reduce the disability roles by terminating the benefits of proven disability program beneficiaries. *See* Schweiker v. Chilicky, 487 U.S. 412, 414–19 (1988); SUSAN G. MEZEY, NO LONGER DISABLED: THE

FEDERAL COURTS AND THE POLITICS OF SOCIAL SECURITY (1988). Accordingly, the principal new claimant-protective provision from the 1984 Reform Act was the enactment of a medical improvement standard to be used before benefits could be terminated. *See* Pub. L. No. 98–460, § 2(a), 98 Stat. 1794 (1984) (codified at 42 U.S.C.§ 423(f)). That act also enacted a requirement, long recognized by the courts, that the combined, synergistically limiting effects of a claimant's multiple impairments be considered in the disability assessment. *See* Pub. L. No. 98–460 § 4(a)(1), 98 Stat.1794 (1984) (codified at 42 U.S.C. § 423(d)(2)(B)). The combined-effects requirement is based on the common-sense rejection of isolated and separate consideration of impairments, which could result in the implied conclusion that "in much the same way a mathematician might prove that because two does not equal four, two plus two never equals four." Dixon v. Heckler, 589 F.2d 1494, 1508 (S.D.N.Y. 1984).

38 Social Security Act Amendments of 1967, Pub. L. No. 90–248, 81 Stat. 821, § 158(b) (codified at 42 U.S.C. § 423(d)(4)–(5) (2006)) (emphasis added).

39 *See* Dubin, *Poverty, Pain and Precedent*, at 114–15 & nn.160, 164 (collecting cases).

40 BLOCH, BLOCH ON SOCIAL SECURITY, at § 1.8 (citation omitted).

41 Bloch, *Medical Proof*, at 206 n.105 (citations omitted); *see* Statement of Mariana La Conforma, Acting Deputy Commissioner, Office of Retirement and Disability Policy, Social Security Administration, in Hearing Before the Committee on Finance of the United States Senate, 113th Cong., titled "Social Security: A Fresh Look at Worker's Disability Insurance" (July 24, 2014), at 105, www.finance.senate.gov. She stated:

> We respectfully disagree with the [CBO's] characterization of the effects of the Social Security Disability Benefits Reform Act of 1984 (1984 Amendments). Prior to the enactment of those amendments, we had already had a policy for evaluating pain and other symptoms; the 1984 Amendments codified that existing policy on a temporary basis. Moreover, Section 223(d)(5) of the Social Security Act (Act) prohibits us from approving a disability claim unless there is objective medical establishing the existence of the disability, such as medical signs and findings established by medically acceptable clinical or laboratory techniques. If we review a disability claim and the evidence does not establish a medically determinable impairment, the statute requires us to deny the claim.

Id.

42 New York-Presbyterian Hospital, Department of Neurology and Neurosurgery, *Spine Disorders: Symptoms and Diagnosis*, www.nyp.org.

43 COMMISSION ON THE EVALUATION OF PAIN, U.S. DEP'T OF HEALTH AND HUMAN SERVS., REPORT 12 (1986); *see id.* at 71–72 (elaborating on commission's conclusion that malingering is not a significant problem in the disability evaluation process); *see also* NAS, PAIN AND DISABILITY 152 (Marian Osterweis et al. eds., 1987) (finding that "there is no evidence that malingering is common in the SSA disability context"); STONE, THE DISABLED STATE, at

135 ("The clinical literature frequently discusses the problem of distinguishing genuine from faked pain . . . [and] [t]here is fairly wide agreement that clinicians can recognize patient deception.").

44 Dubin & Rains, *Scapegoating Social Security Claimants*, at 116.

45 *See* SUBCOMMITTEE ON THE ADMINISTRATION OF SOCIAL SECURITY LAWS FOR THE USE OF THE COMMITTEE ON WAYS AND MEANS, DISABILITY INSURANCE FACT BOOK 31–32 (1959).

46 Bowen v. City of New York, 476 U.S. 467, 474–75 (1986).

47 Pub. L. No. 98–460, § 5(a), 98 Stat. 1805 (1984).

48 *Id.*

49 *See generally* Max Selver, Note, *Disability Benefits and Addiction: Resolving an Uncertain Burden*, 91 N.Y.U. L. REV. 954 (2016) (discussing proof burdens in disability benefit cases involving decoupling substance abuse disorders from other potentially disabling impairments in comorbidity cases under the 1996 act's amendments and regulations).

50 *See* 81 Fed. Reg. 66138–01 (January 17, 2017) (repealing mental/cognitive listing 12.05(C) for borderline cognitive IQ (60–70) plus an additional impairment causing significant work related limitations).

51 *See* DIAGNOSTIC AND STATISTICAL MANUAL OF MENTAL DISORDERS (5TH ED. 2013); 20 C.F.R. pt. 404, subpt. P., app. 1 (Listings 12.02–08) (2021).

52 *See* Rebecca Vallas, Center for American Progress, *Social Security Disability Insurance: A Bedrock of Security for American Workers*, Statement Before the U.S. Congress Joint Economic Committee at Hearing titled "Ensuring Success for the Social Security Disability Insurance Program and Its Beneficiaries" 5 (November 15, 2015), www.jec.senate.gov [hereinafter Vallas, *Social Security Disability Insurance*] (noting 30.5 percent of DI beneficiaries have a primary diagnosis of musculoskeletal or connective tissue disorder and 31.5 percent have a primary diagnosis of a mental disorder); see also *Social Security Advisory Board, Disability Chartbook* ch. 6, Chart 2 (Jan. 24, 2017), www.ssab.gov (31 percent of DI beneficiaries have mental impairments (4.1 percent cognitive mental impairments; 26.9 percent psychiatric and other mental impairments) and 57.4 percent of adult SSI beneficiaries had mental impairments (18.8 percent cognitive mental impairments; 38.6 percent psychiatric and other mental impairments)).

53 *See* ORGANIZATION FOR ECONOMIC COOPERATION AND DEVELOPMENT, SICKNESS, DISABILITY AND WORK: BREAKING THE BARRIERS (A SYNTHESIS OF FINDINGS ACROSS OECD COUNTRIES) (Nov. 24, 2010), www.oecd.org, at 62–83 [hereinafter OECD, SICKNESS, DISABILITY AND WORK].

54 Vallas, *Social Security Disability Insurance.*

55 *See* Michael Diehl, Comment, *Screening Out Worthy Social Security Claimants and Its Effect on Homelessness*, 45 U. MIAMI L. REV. 617, 639–40 (1990–91) (discussing deinstitutionalization of the mentally ill and impact on homelessness and potential eligibility for disability benefits).

56 *See* Vallas, *Social Security Disability Insurance.*

57 Mark C. Weber, *Disability Rights, Disability Discrimination and Social Insurance*, 25 GA. ST. U. L. REV. 575, 601(2009); *see* ERKULWATER, DISABILITY RIGHTS, at 236–38; *see generally* RENO, OUT OF SYNC?, at 9–10 (noting the significantly greater expenditures of gross national product on disability benefit programs in European countries notwithstanding the presence of a much wider variety of expensive European safety-net alternatives such as general assistance welfare benefits, more expansive unemployment benefits, and universal health care—all of which lessen the need for disability benefits).

58 OECD, SICKNESS, DISABILITY AND WORK, at 89; Vallas, *Social Security Disability Insurance*, at 7.

59 *See* OECD, SICKNESS, DISABILITY AND WORK, at 85.

60 Mark J. Warshawsky and Ross A. Marchand, *Disability Claim Denied? Find the Right Judge*, WALL ST. J., March 8, 2015, www.wsj.com [hereinafter cited as Warshawsky and Marchand, *Find the Right Judge*].

61 Pierce, *What Should We Do?*.

62 Warshawsky & Marchand, *Find the Right Judge.*

63 *Id.* at 3–4.

64 *Id.* at 2–3.

65 *See id.*

66 *See id.*

67 OFFICE OF THE INSPECTOR GENERAL, AUDIT REPORT: ADMIN. LAW JUDGE ALLOWANCE RATES, QUALITY, AND LENGTH OF SERVICE [1] (2017), https://oig.ssa.gov (finding the percentage of favorable ALJ decisions has diminished since reporting a high of 75.2 percent in FY 1994 to 53.5 percent in FY 2015): "The 53.3-percent decisional average allowance rate in FY 2015 was the lowest rate in 23 years."

68 *See* SOC. SEC. ADMIN., FY Fiscal Year 2021 Congressional Justification (2020), 156, www.ssa.gov.

69 *See* Dubin & Rains, *Scapegoating Social Security Claimants*, at 111.

70 SOC. SEC. ADMIN., ALJ DISPOSITION DATA, FY 2020 (For Reporting Purposes: 9/28/2011 through 6/26/2020), www.ssa.gov.

71 *See, e.g.*, U.S. GENERAL ACCOUNTING OFFICE, DEATH PENALTY SENTENCING, RESEARCH INDICATES PATTERN OF RACIAL DISPARITIES (Feb. 1990), www.gao.gov.

72 *See, e.g.*, Jaya Ramji-Nogales, Andrew I. Schoeholtz & Philip G. Schrag, *Refugee Roulette: Disparities in Asylum Adjudication*, 60 STAN. L. REV. 295 (2007).

73 *See, e.g.*, Damian Paletta, *Disability-Claim Judge Has Trouble Saying 'No,'* WALL ST. J., May 19, 2011, http://online.wsj.com; Damian Paletta, *Social Security Judge Retires Amid Probe*, WALL ST. J., July 18, 2011, http://online.wsj.com; Damian Paletta, *Ex-Judge's Disability Rulings Probed*, WALL ST. J., Nov. 25, 2011, http://online.wsj.com.

74 Pierce, *What Should We Do?*, at 8.

75 United State Department of Justice Press Release, *Former Social Security Administrative Law Judge Sentenced to Four Years in Prison For Role in $550 Million Fraud Scheme* (Aug. 25, 2017), www.justice.gov.
76 *Id.*
77 111 F.Supp. 2d 556 (M.D. Pa. 2000).
78 *Id.* at 559.
79 *Id.*
80 *Id.* at 559–60
81 *Id.* at 570.
82 917 F.Supp. 103 (D.P.R. 1996).
83 *Id.* at 110–11 and n.4.
84 U.S. Gen. Accounting Office, Social Security: Racial Difference in Disability Decisions Warrants Further Investigation 5 (1992), http://archive.gao.gov.
85 *Id.*
86 U.S. Gen. Accounting Office, SSA Disability Decision Making: Additional Measures Would Enhance Agency's Ability to Determine Whether Racial Bias Exists (2002), www.gao.gov.
87 Meisburg, *Ten Ways*, at 40. He stated: "The Grid Rules should also be made advisory and not mandatory—which would give more flexibility and quasi-judicial discretion to the ALJs to determine if disability is really warranted in a particular case." *Id.*
88 *See* 42 U.S.C. §§ 405(b); 423(g).
89 397 U.S. 254 (1970). Moreover, it is highly unlikely that the agency and Congress would fail to extend comparable hearing rights to DI claimants that would be extended to SSID claimants. When the Court distinguished *Goldberg* on the procedural due process necessity of a pretermination hearing for benefit recipients of the non–welfare based DI program in Matthews v. Eldridge, 424 U.S. 319 (1976), Congress stepped in to provide pretermination hearing rights by statute to DI recipients. *See* 42 U.S.C. §423(g).
90 *See* Stieberger v. Heckler, 615 F.Supp. 1315, 1393–98 (S.D.N.Y. 1985).
91 *See* Nash v. Bowen, 869 F.2d 675, 681 (2d Cir. 1989).
92 *See* Dubin & Rains, *Scapegoating Social Security Claimants*, at 110.
93 *See, e.g.*, Soc. Sec, Admin. Office of Hearing and Appeals v. Anyel, 58 M.S.P.R. 261 (1993) (finding that ALJ's decisional independence did not extend to systematic disregard of binding law and governing procedure and that a high rate of adjudicatory error can establish good cause for removal and recommending suspension or greater sanction).
94 Aman v. Cort Furniture Rental Corp., 84 F.3d 1074, 1081–82 (3d Cir. 1996).
95 Jerry Kang, Rachel Godsil, Devon Carbado, et al., *Implicit Bias in the Courtroom*, 59 U.C.L.A. L. Rev. 1124, 1126 (2012) [hereinafter Kang et al., *Implicit Bias*].
96 *See* Pager, Western & Pedulla, *Employment Discrimination*, at 329–31.

97 *Id.* at 331–43.

98 For a menu of practical and concrete steps and corrective actions for ameliorating implicit bias in judicial decision-making, see Kang et al., *Implicit Bias*, at 1172–86.

99 Warshawsky & Marchand, *Modernizing the SSDI Eligibility Criteria*, at 27.

100 SOCIAL SECURITY ADMINISTRATION, OFFICE OF THE INSPECTOR GENERAL, THE SOCIAL SECURITY ADMINISTRATION'S ABILITY TO DETECT AND PREVENT FRAUD (SEPTEMBER 2014), https://oig.ssa.gov.

101 *See id.*; *see, e.g.*, Stephen R. Brown "*Former NY Cop Pleads Guilty to Disability Scam While Working at Strip Club*," N.Y. DAILY NEWS, April 19, 2019. www.nydailynews.com; U.S. Department of Justice Press Release, *Former NYPD Police Officer Pleads Guilty to Fraudulently Obtaining Disability Benefits and Tax Evasion* (April 19, 2019), www.justice.gov; U.S. Department of Justice Press Release, *Second Former NYPD Officer Sentenced to Federal Prison for Federal Disability Fraud and Tax Evasion* (Aug. 9, 2019), www.justice.gov.

102 *See id.*

103 *See* SSA Commissioners' Open Letter, and accompanying text; THE WHITE HOUSE, SOCIAL SECURITY DISABILITY INSURANCE, at 11 ("[F]raud is extremely rare in SSDI.").

104 NASI, *Social Security Finances*, 7.

105 *See, e.g.*, UNDER SECRETARY OF DEFENSE FOR ACQUISITION, TECHNOLOGY AND LOGISTICS, REPORT TO CONGRESS ON CONTRACTING FRAUD (OCTOBER 2011), https://fas.org (finding that fifty-four Department of Defense (DOD) contractors were charged with criminal fraud between 2001 to 2011 with over $254 million lost, and over 300 DOD contractors entered into settlements or had civil judgments entered against them in those ten years with obligations after judgment of approximately $400 billion).

106 Kathy Ruffing, Center on Budget and Policy Priorities, *Disability Insurance Has Many Safeguards Against Fraud and Abuse*, www.cbpp.org.

15. AMENDMENTS TO SIMPLIFY WORK ADJUSTMENT ASSESSMENTS BY EXPANDING ELIGIBILITY

1 *See* H.R. 805, 89th Cong. (1st Sess. 1965); *accord* H.R. 911, 89th Cong.(1st Sess. 1965); *see generally Burden of Proof*, at 1473 n.46 (describing these bills); *see also* H.R. 18008, 89th Cong. (2d Sess. 1966) (providing eligibility for claimants at least age 55 whose impairments prevent performance of substantial gainful activity "requiring skills or abilities comparable to those of any gainful activity in which [they have] previously engaged with some regularity and over a substantial period of time"); *Three Current Problems*, at 180–81 n.103 (describing H.R. 18008 and its failure to secure passage because it was "introduced too late in the session to get adequate consideration").

2 *Id.*

3 *See* NAS, PAIN AND DISABILITY, at 33 (comparing cultural conceptions of disability based on social status and prestige-focused occupational standards in Ger-

many and the Netherlands with "[t]he very stringent [SSA disability] definition [that] expresses the dominant American ethos of the primacy of work"); STONE, THE DISABLED STATE, at 61–68 (describing class- and status-based cultural assumptions in Germany's occupational disability standard). The greater use of occupational disability standards or other, more lenient criteria likely accounts for the diminished use of vocational factors in several other countries. According to a survey of the use of vocational factors in the disability programs of eleven countries (United States, Canada, Australia, United Kingdom, Ireland, Denmark, Finland, Netherlands, Norway, Sweden, and Switzerland), only work experience was a vocational factor used by all, and few used either age or education in the assessment. *See* David Rajnes and Tony Nataro, *Vocational Factors in Disability Claim Assessment: A Comparative Survey of 11 Countries*, 79 SOCIAL SECURITY BULL. 1, 44 (2019). However, of the eleven countries surveyed, the study found only Canada and Ireland "used a similarly restrictive definition of disability." *Id.* at 25.

4 Chapter 6 describes step 4 of the sequential evaluation process and points out that claimants will be deemed capable of performing past relevant work at step 4 if they can perform their prior work as it is generically performed in the economy, even though they are incapable of performing the specific tasks of their former jobs. Thus, in the SSA disability program's step 4 assessment, a department store clerk who is fired because of a hip impairment, which precludes performance of the required task of climbing a ladder to post a window display, might be denied benefits. Such a claimant could still be deemed capable of performing past relevant department store sales clerk work as that work is "generically" performed in the economy. By contrast, an airline pilot with an inner-ear impairment that precludes flying would be deemed incapable of performing such specialized, highly skilled past relevant work and could be excused from the further obligation to work under an occupational disability standard.

5 *See generally* 20 C.F.R.§ 416.920(g)(1)(2021).

6 *See generally* 20 C.F.R. § 416.987 (2021) (describing the process for the mandatory reevaluation under adult criteria of persons receiving SSI benefits as children upon turning eighteen).

7 Liebman, *The Definition of Disability*, at 854–55.

8 *Id.* at 855.

9 *Id.*

10 Weber, *Disability and the Law of Welfare*, at 943–51.

11 *See id.* at 950–55; *see generally* Moore v. Ganim, 660 A.2d 742, 755 n.39 (Conn. 1995) (noting that only twenty-three states still had general assistance residual welfare programs and many of those remaining programs had been significantly limited by the mid-1990s).

12 Diller, *Dissonant Disability Policies*, at 1075–80.

13 *See id.*; *see generally* BRIAN STEENSLAND, THE FAILED WELFARE REVOLUTION: AMERICA'S STRUGGLES OVER GUARANTEED INCOME POLICY

(2007) (describing the guaranteed income proposals from the late 1960s to the early 1970s and reasons for their legislative defeat).

14 Diller reached a similar conclusion about the unlikely political success of his own proposal over two decades ago. *See* Diller, *Dissonant Disability Policies*, at 1080 n.349. For discussion of universal basic income (UBI) and its increased popularity during the coronavirus pandemic, *see* Joseph Zeballos-Rois, *Spain Is Moving to Establish Permanent Basic Income in the Wake of the Coronavirus Pandemic*, Business Insider (April 6, 2020), www.businessinsider.com; Sarah Holder, *Stockton Extends Its Universal Basic Income Pilot*, Bloomberg CityLab, (June 2, 2020), www.bloomberg.com ("A pioneering universal basic income pilot in the low-income California city was scheduled to expire soon. But the coronavirus crisis made the case to extend it."); *but cf.* Robert Greenstein, Center on Budget and Policy Priorities, *Universal Basic Income May Sound Attractive But If It Occurred, Would Likelier Increase Poverty Than Reduce It*, June 13, 2019, www.cbpp.org (suggesting UBI would be prohibitively expensive and likely coupled with elimination or reduction in the safety net for low-income persons, which would likely push more people into poverty and more extreme poverty).

15 *See, e.g.*, Bill Clinton, *How We Ended Welfare, Together*, N.Y. Times, Aug. 22, 2006, at A23; Ron Haskins, *Welfare Reform, Success or Failure? It Worked*, Brookings Institution (Mar. 15, 2006), www.aphsa.org. Among other provisions, PRWORA ended the Aid to Families with Dependent Children (AFDC) entitlement program and replaced it with the Temporary Assistance to Needy Families program. TANF includes mandatory work requirements, a five-year lifetime time limit on benefits, and time frames and incentives for states to have claimants engaged in work activities, among other new restrictions. *See generally* Weaver, Ending Welfare (describing PRWORA's provisions).

16 Jeneen Interlandi, *Employer-Based Health Care, Meet Massive Unemployment: The Coronavirus Pandemic Is Exposing a Central Flaw in America's Health Care System*, N.Y. Times, June 29, 2020, www.nytimes.com ("The nation spends an average of $3.5 trillion per year on health care—more than Japan, Germany, France, China, the United Kingdom, Italy, Canada, Brazil, Spain and Australia combined—and still loses more people to preventable and treatable medical conditions than any of those countries do."); Jeffrey Martin, *87 Percent of Democrats Support "Medicare for All" Though Joe Biden Doesn't*, Newsweek, August 4, 2020, www.newsweek.com ("In total, Medicare for All was supported by 67 percent of registered voters and opposed by 33 percent."); Alison P. Galvania et al., *The Imperative for Universal Health Care to Curtail the COVID-19 Outbreak in the USA*, Eclinical Medicine, May 17, 2020, www.thelancet.com (pointing out deficiencies of the current employer-provided health insurance system and large and growing number of uninsured and arguing "that universal health care would alleviate the cost barriers that are impeding control of this pandemic").

16. PROPOSALS TO IMPOSE A "WELFARE REFORM" MANDATORY WORK INCENTIVES MODEL

1 *See, e.g.*, Paul Armstrong, *Toward a Unified and Reciprocal Disability System*, 25 J. NAT'L ADMIN. L. JUDGES 157, 171 (2005) ("[C]hanging attitudes about the possible productivity of disabled individuals, induced in part by the rhetoric of the ADA supporters and their repeated use of successfully productive examples of disabled individuals, together with the experience of declining caseloads of former AFDC recipients under the mandatory work requirements of TANF, may lead to public support for mandatory vocational evaluations and work referrals for disability applicants and recipients."); *Social Security Disability: Management Action and Program Redesign Needed to Address Long-Standing Problems, Testimony Before the Subcomm. on Social Security of the House Ways and Means Comm.*, 104th Cong. (1995) (statement of Jane L. Ross, Director of Income Security Issues for the Health, Education, and Human Services Division), www.gao.gov ("Time limits are intended to set the expectation that disability benefits are to be considered temporary. This expectation is intended to encourage beneficiaries to take some responsibility, such as obtaining treatment and pursuing rehabilitation, to overcome their disabling conditions and return to productive employment.").

2 TANF's "success" is dependent on a frame of reference. If success is measured by reductions from the AFDC/TANF welfare roles, or some increased, largely temporary, involvement in the workforce in unstable low-wage jobs by single mothers in less than all four quarters of a year, or the vindication of a newer emerging social consensus on the unworthiness of impoverished single mothers with children for relief from work obligations, then TANF has been quite successful. By contrast, if success is measured by long-term, significant reduction in poverty and extreme poverty and improvement in the quality of former recipient families' lives, a declaration of success is at best premature and at worst patently inaccurate. *See* SHARON PARROT & ARLOC SHERMAN, CENTER ON BUDGET AND POLICY PRIORITIES, TANF AT 10: PROGRAM RESULTS ARE MORE MIXED THAN OFTEN UNDERSTOOD (Aug. 17, 2006), www.cbpp.org. While TANF initially increased work activity by former AFDC single mothers, the 2000 economic slowdown again diminished work participation. *Id.* at 1. Further, there is a greatly increased number and percentage of persons lacking either welfare or work, as well as persons, especially children, living in extreme poverty (defined as living below one-half of the poverty line). *Id.* at 1. The percentage of families eligible for cash assistance who are receiving benefits has also diminished from 80 percent in the early 1990s to only 48 percent in 2002. *Id.* at 2; *see also* Peter B. Edelman, *Changing the Subject from Welfare to Poverty to a Living Income*, 4 N.W. J.L. & SOC. POL'Y 14, 18–23 (2009) (citing similar studies making similar findings and concluding that "TANF remains a deeply flawed program"); *see* Liz Schott, *Summary of Final TANF Rules: Some Improvements Around the Margins*

(Feb. 20, 2008), www.cbpp.org. *See generally* Joel Berg, *Welfare Reform: The Promise Unfulfilled*, 11 J. Gender Race & Just. 47, 47–48 (2007) [hereinafter Schott, *Summary of Final TANF Rules*] ("[J]udging the success of welfare reform solely by how many people leave welfare is a bit like judging the success of a hospital by how many people leave it, without differentiating between how many people leave it cured, ill or dead . . . [T]his issue has become the social policy equivalent of Bush's 'mission accomplished.'"). Rules implementing state work participation rates and time limits under TANF also provide incentives to states to terminate assistance to disabled TANF applicants who have not yet been found eligible for disability benefits and are not in work activities, including those applicants in the SSA's labyrinthine disability benefits application process. *See* Schott, *Summary of Final TANF Rules*. Data examining the life circumstances of TANF participants twenty years after TANF's enactment reveal similar findings and show that TANF has failed to help most unemployed parents to obtain and maintain work and that proposals for adding work requirements to other benefit programs would harm millions and do little to increase work. *See* Ladonna Pavetti, Center on Budget and Policy Priorities, *TANF at 20, Part 2: Failing to Help Most Unemployed Parents Find and Maintain Work* (Aug. 16, 2016), www.cbpp.org; Ladonna Pavetti, Center on Budget and Policy Priorities, *TANF Studies Show Work Requirement Proposals for Other Programs Would Harm Millions, Do Little to Increase Work* (Nov.13, 2018), www.cbpp.org.

3 Americans with Disabilities Act, Pub. L. No. 101–336, 104 Stat. 327 (codified at 42 U.S.C. §§ 12,101–12,213 (2006)).

4 *See, e.g.*, Social Security Advisory Board, A Disability System for the 21st Century 6 (Sept. 2006), www.ssab.gov ("[W]e have heard widespread agreement that the current overall approach to disability is harmful to people with disabilities, is contrary to basic societal values, and in particular, contradicts the policies and values of the *Americans with Disabilities Act*.") (emphasis in original); Edward Berkowitz, *Implications for Income Maintenance Policy*, *in* Implementing the Americans with Disabilities Act 193, 195 (Jane West ed. 1996) [hereinafter Berkowitz, *Implications*] ("If we are to allow the ADA to set the tone for our disability policy . . . [w]e must create a climate in which people with disabilities expect to work and employers expect to hire them. The only way to do that is to change the rules for awarding SSI and SSDI benefits."). Diller argues that the implicit or explicit assumption that the ADA disability discrimination protections in the workplace are necessarily inconsistent with the SSA's provision of disability benefits to persons not working is misguided. *See* Diller, *Dissonant Disability Policies*, at 1059–75. Because the disability standard more properly reflects an exemption from the social obligation to work as opposed to an objectively verifiable determination of complete inability to perform any work, there are circumstances in which a claimant can justifiably claim entitlement to benefits while still retaining belief in his or her ability to engage in some work activity. *Id.*; *see also* Cleveland v. Policy Systems Management

Corp., 526 U.S. 795, 803–07 (1999) (rejecting assertion of necessary inconsistency between ADA and disability benefits programs as would justify presumed judicial estoppel from one program to the other and citing examples that reflect lack of conflict). There are at least five explicit situations where a claimant could both claim an entitlement to benefits and but still assert a belief in the ability to perform some work activity: (1) claimant is working (i.e., part-time or sheltered work) but is not performing and cannot perform at step 1 substantial gainful activity levels; (2) claimant's condition meets or equals a listing and the inability to engage in SGA is merely presumed; (3) claimant fulfills the "worn-out manual laborer" profile and the non-adaptability to lighter work is merely presumed; (4) claimant can adjust to some relatively small number of other jobs but cannot adjust to "work which exists in significant numbers" in the economy based on the grid or individualized vocational testimony or evidence; or (5) claimant is working at SGA levels but is participating in a trial work period or related eligibility preserving voluntary work incentive.

5 *See* Berkowitz, *Implications,* at 193–226.

6 The disability programs currently contain a variety of voluntary work incentives such as a nine-month trial work period for disability insurance beneficiaries; a ticket to work program providing a voucher for professional rehabilitation and employment services and extended Medicare or Medicaid benefits while working; an expedited reentitlement period; and an extended period of eligibility, among other incentives. *See* Barbara Samuels, SOCIAL SECURITY DISABILITY CLAIMS: PRACTICE & PROCEDURE Ch. 29 (2020) (describing these work incentive programs for SSA disability benefit program recipients); *see generally* Diller, *Dissonant Disability Policies,* at 1067–68 (discussing proposal to strengthen voluntary work incentives "to promote the goals of the ADA without compromising the income support of the disability benefit programs").

7 *See* RENO, OUT OF SYNC?, at 7 (recognizing that, while "any wage-replacement system can be characterized as a disincentive to work to some degree . . . [disability] benefits are not a strong deterrent to work . . . [because] benefits and replacement rates are relatively modest," anecdotal evidence shows people turn to disability benefits "only as a last resort," and "empirical studies show people often remain on jobs after the onset of disability and many change jobs or continue looking for work before applying for benefits"); Weber, *Disability and the Law of Welfare,* at 911 ("[T]he prospect of benefits is not enough of an incentive to induce individuals to become disabled to obtain benefits."); *see generally id.* at 930 (noting that SSI benefits pay only approximately 70 percent of the federal poverty level).

8 *See* Samuel R. Bagenstos, *The Americans with Disabilities Act as Welfare Reform,* 44 WM. & MARY L. REV. 921, 1017–19 (2003) [hereinafter Bagenstos, *ADA as Welfare Reform*] (citing studies showing a small decline in employment participation by disabled persons since the ADA's passage).

9 *See* Weber, *Disability and the Law of Welfare,* at 910 (noting that only the most medically and vocationally limited claimants are eligible for benefits and are thus

less likely to be persons qualified for jobs for which reasonable accommodation may be required under the ADA since "qualification" requires ability to perform the jobs' essential functions).

10 Schweiker v. Chilicky, 487 U.S. 412, 417 (1988); Diller, *Dissonant Disability Policies*, at 1073.

11 *See* Mashaw, Bureaucratic Justice, at 26–29, 38 (describing a professional treatment model option for SSA disability program administration and concluding that "[o]utside some matrix of bureaucratic standards, routines, and structures, the vocational professionals' decisional behavior might be both unpredictable and inconsistent. Simple delegation to professionals did not seem a responsible strategy").

12 Bagenstos, *ADA as Welfare Reform*, at 1025.

13 Samuel R. Bagenstos, The Future of Disability Law, 114 Yale L.J. 1, 23 (2004); *see also id.* ("Antidiscrimination laws like the ADA are a singularly ineffective means of eliminating such structural barriers.").

14 The process of distinguishing between disability beneficiaries who are realistic candidates for rehabilitation and those who are not would also create significant decisional or adjudicative complexity and expense. It would also create "perverse" incentives for recipients to be found incapable of rehabilitation to avoid a classification that would result in time-limited, significantly delayed, or otherwise restricted benefits, thereby likely inhibiting voluntary rehabilitation or labor market reentry efforts. Diller, *Dissonant Disability Policies*, at 1073.

15 Richard V. Burkhauser & Mary C. Daly, The Declining Work and Welfare of People with Disabilities, What Went Wrong and a Strategy for Change 109–13 (2011) [hereinafter cited as Burkhauser & Daly, Declining Work]; Burkhauser, *SSDI Program Growth*, at 8–11.

16 Burkhauser, *SSDI Program Growth*, at 10.

17 *Id.*

18 *Id.*

19 Burkhauser & Daly, Declining Work, 33. It is unclear what types of "discouraged entry" measures adopted in TANF programs after welfare reform would be encompassed within this observation. In the nation's largest TANF program—New York City while under Mayor Rudolph Giuliani—the experience with "discouraged entry" or deterrence and diversion from entry into the TANF, SNAP (food stamps), and Medicaid programs after welfare reform's adoption and as implemented systematically, was successfully challenged as disentitling otherwise eligible claimants and producing unjustified and excessive delays in benefit receipt, in violation of federal law and constitutional due process principles. *See* Reynolds v. Giuliani, 35 F. Supp. 2d 331 (S.D.N.Y. 1999); *see generally* Vicki Lens, *Bureaucratic Disentitlement After Welfare Reform: Are Fair Hearings the Cure?*, 12 Geo. J. on Poverty. L.& Pol'y 13 (2005) (describing the practice of "bureaucratic disentitlement" by benefactory and social welfare agencies and identifying how the 1996 welfare reform legislation incentivized the practice and produced

additional mechanisms to facilitate it). The imposition of excessive delays in entry to and at various stages in the SSDI and SSI process can also produce substantial, unnecessary human suffering and has legal consequences. *See, e.g.*, Heckler v. Day, 467 U.S. 107, 111 (1983) (SSA concedes before the U.S. Supreme Court that a ninety-day or greater period between reconsideration request and reconsideration decision violates the Social Security Act's requirement in 42 U.S.C. § 405(b) that SSA agency action not be unreasonably delayed); White v. Mathews, 434 F. Supp. 1252, 1259–61 (D. Conn. 1976) (excessive delays in SSA hearing decision times violate both the Fifth Amendment's Due Process Clause and 42 U.S.C. § 405(b)), *aff'd on other grounds*, 559 F.2d 852 (2d Cir. 1977), *cert. denied sub nom.*, Califano v. White, 435 U.S. 908 (1978). Court decisions finding SSA delays in individual cases to be unlawful are abundant. *See., e.g.*, Davenport v. Bowen, 709 F.Supp. 634 (E.D. Pa. 1989); Mason-Page v Bowen, 655 F. Supp. 255 (D.N.J. 1987) Mills v. Heckler, 595 F. Supp. 952 (S.D.N.Y. 1984); Cohen v. Heckler, 599 F.Supp. 837 (S.D.N.Y. 1984); Gomaz v. Heckler, 591 F.Supp. 1122 (E.D. Wis. 1984); Labonne v. Heckler, 574 F.Supp. 1016 (D. Minn. 1983).

20 *Id.*

21 *See, e.g.*, Elaine Fultz, Center on Budget and Policy Priorities, *Disability Insurance in the Netherlands: A Blueprint for U.S. Reform,* (Sept. 16, 2015) [hereinafter Fultz, *Disability Insurance in the Netherlands*]; Kathy Ruffing, Center on Budget and Policy Priorities, *Netherlands Not a Model for U.S. Disability Reforms* (Feb. 18, 2015) [hereinafter Ruffing, *Netherlands Not a Model*], www.cbpp.org; Paul N. Van De Water, *4 Reasons Why Netherlands Isn't a Model for Disability Insurance*, Center for Budget and Policy Priorities (Sept. 17, 2015) [hereinafter Van De Water, *4 Reasons*], www.cbpp.org.

22 Van De Water, *4 Reasons.*

23 Ruffing, *Netherlands Not a Model.*

24 Van De Water, *4 Reasons.*

25 Ruffing, *Netherlands Not a Model.*

26 Fultz, *Disability Insurance in the Netherlands.*

27 Burkhasuer & Daly, DECLINING WORK, at 111.

28 *Id.* at 112.

29 *Id.* at 110–11.

30 David H. Autor & Mark Duggan, *Supporting Work: A Proposal for Modernizing The U.S. Disability System* 5–7 (December 2010), www.brookings.edu; *see also* Peter Orszag, *Making Disability Work*, N.Y. TIMES, Dec. 9, 2010 (describing this program).

31 *Id.* For discussion of the Compassionate Allowance Program, *see* POMS DI 11005.604 Processing Compassionate Allowances (CAL) in the Field Office (FO) (Oct. 20, 2020) ("The CAL initiative is designed to quickly identify diseases and other medical conditions that invariably qualify under the Listing of Impairments based on minimal, but sufficient, objective medical information. If the condition does not meet these strict criteria, it is not designated as a CAL case.").

32 *Id.*
33 *Id.* at 18–24.
34 *Id.* at 26–27.
35 *See* Burkhauser, *SSDI Program Growth*, at 10–11 (comparing the Burkhauser & Daly proposal to the Autor & Duggan PDI proposal and observing that both "are in the spirit of Dutch reforms" and that the messages of each program are the same).
36 Jagadeesh Gokhale, *Disability Insurance Must Be Restructured to Protect Vulnerable, Incentivize the Fit*, INVESTOR'S BUS. DAILY, Dec. 17, 2010, www.investors.com (suggesting the Autor & Duggan PDI proposal would involve larger up-front costs, much longer delays and unnecessary impediments in qualifying for social security disability insurance benefits, and some hidden costs); see also Burkhauser, *SSDI Program Growth*, at 10 (suggesting that the Autor & Duggan PDI proposal "could result in substantial added costs to the system").
37 *See* Gay Gellhorn, *Disability and Welfare Reform: Keep The Supplemental Security Income Program But Reengineer The Disability Determination Process*, 22 FORDHAM URB. L.J. 961, 992–95 (1995) (discussing disability advocates' frustration with the agency for disclaiming an intent to alter the substantive disability standard but then filtering substantive proposals through an ostensibly process-based project).
38 *See* 59 Fed. Reg. 47887 (Sept. 19, 1994).
39 *Id.* at 47911.
40 *Id.* at 47912
41 *Id.* at 47912.
42 *Id.*
43 *Id.*
44 *Id.* at 47913.
45 *Id.*
46 *Id.*
47 *See* Daniel F. Solomon, *Vocational Testimony in Social Security Hearings*, 18 J. NAT'L ASS'N. ADMIN. L. JUDGES 197, 253 (1998) [hereinafter Solomon, *Vocational Testimony*].
48 Diller, *Dissonant Disability Policies*, at 1049–50 n.211.
49 *Id.*
50 *Id.* at 1050.
51 *See id.*; *see also Cleveland*, 526 U.S. at 803 ("[T]he matter of 'reasonable accommodation' may turn on highly disputed workplace-specific matters; and an SSA misjudgment about that detailed, and often fact-specific matter would deprive a seriously disabled person of the critical financial support the statute seeks to provide."). The SSA has embraced *Cleveland* and reaffirmed that potential "reasonable" employer accommodations under the ADA play no role in step 5 labor market work adjustment assessments. *See, e.g.*, Social Security Ruling 00-1c (adopting Cleveland); Social Security Ruling 11-2p, § D.1.e ("When we determine

whether a person can do other work that exists in significant numbers in the national economy, we do not consider whether he or she could do so with accommodations, even if an employer would be required to provide reasonable accommodations under the Americans with Disabilities Act of 1990.").

52 *Solomon, Vocational Testimony, at 253.*

53 *Id.* at n.88.

54 *See* U.S. General Accounting Office, SSA Disability Redesign: Focus Needed On Initiative Most Crucial To Reducing Costs And Time (Dec. 20, 1996), www.gao.gov.

55 This conclusion is based on conversations with agency personnel "to the best of their knowledge."

CONCLUSION

1 *See* 42 U.S.C. § 406(e).

2 *Campbell*, 461 U.S. at 467 (citing "42 U.S.C. § 423(d)(2)(A) (specifying consideration of each individual's condition).").

INDEX

Page numbers in *italics* indicate Tables.

ADA. *See* Americans with Disabilities Act
adaptability assumptions, 78
adaption by necessity principle, 192n10
ad hoc approach: for claimants, 74–75, 80–81; for courts, 79, 84–85; in gridding, 208n7; for Social Security Act, 82; for workplace adjustments, 212n71
adjudicative facts, 32–33
administrative law judges (ALJs), 2; authority of, 90–91; case-by-case basis for, 214n75; claimants for, 197n64, 201n9, 210n17, 215n7, 217n19; in *Cooper v. Sullivan*, 77–78; for courts, 34–35, 184n25, 217n21; decisional independence of, 245n93; discretion for, 245n87; DOT for, 35, 40; evidence for, 163, 216n18; facts for, 32; for GAO, 161; gridding for, 89–90, 216n11; light work for, 187n47; methodology for, 198n69; nonexertional limitations for, 218n26; obligations of, 192n4; official notice for, 93; policy for, 234n16; reform for, 61; skills for, 79–80; for SSA, 185n35, 193n24; SSRs for, 79, 95–96, 98, 218n37, 219n42; statistics on, 244n67; testimony for, 45; VE for, 20–21, 49–58, 72, 192n6, 197nn62–63; for Warshawsky/Marchand proposal, 143–49, *144*; workplace adjustments for, 19–20
administrative notice. *See* official notice
Administrative Procedure Act (APA), 19; in courts, 96, 220n46; evidence in, 38; facts related to, 32–33; gridding in, 97, 164; history of, 182n5; for SSA, 184n25, 187n47; in SSRs, 85–86; violations of, 98
advance notice of proposed rule making (ANPRM), 110–11
AFDC. *See* Aid to the Families with Dependent Children
age: blindness related to, 178n4; burden of proof related to, 190n61; for claimants, 211n26, 211n42; disability related to, 132–33, *133*; employment related to, 193n24; in gridding, 123, 205n43; for impairment, 178n2; in sedentary work, 37, 116; skills related to, 218n37; for SSA, 129–30; SSDI and, 156–57; transferable skills related to, 240n26; in U.S., 241n32; in Warshawsky/Marchand proposal, 121–23, *123*; work experience related to, 188n56
Aid to the Families with Dependent Children (AFDC), 248n15, 249nn1–2
Aid to the Permanently and Totally Disabled (APTD), 9–10
ALJs. *See* administrative law judges
Allen v. Barnhart, 94, 96–97
Altmeyer, Arthur, 10–11, 15, 171n20
Americans with Disabilities Act (ADA), 249n1; for claimants, 251n9; against discrimination, 252n13; history of, 154–55, 159; policy for, 250n4; in SSRs, 254n51
ANPRM. *See* advance notice of proposed rule making

APA. *See* Administrative Procedure Act
Apfel, Kenneth S., 184n25
applications, 31, 131, *132*, 172n29, 214n2
APTD. *See* Aid to the Permanently and Totally Disabled
Astrue, Michael, 237n12
authority: of ALJs, 90–91; for OASDI, 169n3; of SSA, 195n30, 227n34, 231n6, 252n11; for SSI program, 169n4
automation, 126–28, 234n16, 235n20
Autor, David, 125–26, 157

Bapp v. Bowen, 93
benefits decisions, 48–49
Bernoski, Ronald G., 184n25
Biden, Joe, 227n34, 237n10
Biestek, Michael, 1
Biestek v. Berryhill, 1, 51–56, 163
blindness, 178n4
BLS. *See* Bureau of Labor Statistics
Brace v. Saul, 57, 163
burden of proof, 176n10; age related to, 190n61; for claimants, 26–27, 177n19, 181n1; evidence for, 97; fairness applied to, 33; Federal Rules of Evidence and, 199n103; official notice and, 39, 185n29; for SSA, 1, 20, 42; in workplace adjustments, 37–38, 62, 91
Bureaucratic Justice (Mashaw), 62
bureaucratic rationality, 201n11
Bureau of Labor Statistics (BLS), 46, 108–11, 162, 224n33
Burkhauser, Richard, 137, 155–57

Capowski, John, 188n57
Chavez v. Berryhill, 46–48, 54–57, 163
Chefs de Froids standard, 47
children, 170n15
claimants: ADA for, 251n9; ad hoc approach for, 74–75, 80–81; age for, 211n26, 211n42; for ALJs, 197n64, 201n9, 210n17, 215n7, 217n19; applications for, 214n2; burden of proof for, 26–27, 177n19, 181n1; commutes for, 179n5; for courts, 202n13; DI for, 240n26; DOT for, 50; due process for, 147; eligibility for, 178n2, 240n27; employment for, 25; evaluations of, 18–19; evidence for, 26–27, 34, 176n14, 190n61; exertional requirements for, 91; false positives for, 204n28; gridding for, 74–76, 80–81, 128, 206n52, 221n49; hearing rights for, 245n89; impairment for, 247n4; job incidence for, 41; light work for, 186n40; medical challenges for, 66; mental limitations for, 86–87, 90; methodology for, 78–79; nonexertional limitations for, 65, 126–27, 216n10, 216n12; occupational definitions for, 25–26; occupations of, 197n53; official notice for, 72–73, 186n41, 187n47, 202n14; pain for, 192n10; personal experience of, 43–44; PRW for, 65; psychology of, 238n19, 250n4, 251n7; regulation for, 97–98, 191n3; restrictions for, 37–38; RFC for, *68–69*, 68–71, 81; SGA for, 63–64; skills for, 74–75, 187n49, 233n18; SOC for, 56–57; Social Security Act for, 115–17, 136; SSA for, 198n68; SSI program for, 151; SSRs for, 95; strictness for, 13; transferable skills for, 67–68, 72, 79, 84, 208n10; for VE, 215n5; vocational challenges for, 10–11; vocational profiles for, 71; work experience for, 40, 70–71, 241n28; workplace adjustments for, 36–37, 80–81, 176n15, 177n18
Clinton, Bill, 225n9
collaboration, 225n9
common sense, 41–42, 79, 208n6
communication, 232n14, 241n29
commutes, 179n5
Compassion Allowance Program, 253n31
Congress: DI for, 175n62; disability freeze program by, 12, 172n31; Disability Reform Act for, 242n41; eligibility for, 9–10, 140; hearing rights for, 245n89; history of, 173n45; House Ways and

Means Committee for, 24, 62, 200n5; impairment for, 16–17; medical expertise for, 14–15, 174n49; Obama with, 130–31; politics of, 172n36, 173n46; requirements for, 173n43; Social Security Act for, 184n25; SSA for, 22–27, 118–19, 225n9, 229n2; SSB for, 171n20; SSDI for, 10–11; work experience for, 13
Contract with American Advancement Act, 240n25
Cooper v. Sullivan, 77–78
courts: adaption by necessity principle for, 192n10; ad hoc approach for, 79, 84–85; ALJs for, 34–35, 184n25, 217n21; APA in, 96, 220n46; Chefs de Froids standard in, 47; claimants for, 202n13; data in, 45, 104–5; DOT in, 38, 195n29; due process in, 202n15; evaluations for, 213n72; evidence in, 52–53, 137–38, 195n33; fairness in, 33; Federal Rules of Evidence for, 182n13, 183n22; gridding in, 72–74, 76–79, 81–85, 164–65, 201n9, 202n14, 210n17, 215n7; impairment in, 230n1; job availability for, 41–42; job incidence for, 43–44, 57–58; medical expertise in, 177n25, 197n64; mental limitations in, 98–99; nonexertional limitations in, 90–92; official notice for, 182n3, 185n35, 216n18, 218n26; pain in, 230n2; policy in, 115–17; precedent from, 177n1; reform in, 225n9; regulation for, 213n74; revisions for, 187n49; sedentary work in, 18; Social Security Act for, 26–27, 63; SSA in, 18–21, 31–32, 61–62, 89, 145–48, 212n71; SSRs in, 218n32; statistics for, 193n11, 193n14; substantial evidence test for, 55–56, 199n103; TANF in, 252n19; testimony in, 195n34; VE in, 42–43, 181n1, 196n42, 198n69, 208n15; Vocational Expert Handbook in, 53–54; work experience for, 194n27, 215n5; workplace adjustments in, 24–25, 232n17. *See also specific cases*
COVID-19 pandemic, 135, 153, 237n10, 238n19, 248n14
cross-examination, 197n58

Daly, Mary, 155–57
data: collection of, 46; in courts, 45, 104–5; on DI, 170n18; for DOL, 103–4; employment, 39; from GAO, 146, 148–49; for gridding, 203n19; on low-skill work, 162; methodology for, 207n58; OES, 46; ORS, 120, 127; on racism, 231n7; for SSA, 188n57; in SSRs, 222n10; for testimony, 195n33; for VE, 51–52
Daubert v. Merrell Dow Pharmaceuticals, Inc, 45, 51
Davis, Kenneth Culp, 32–33, 183n17, 183n22, 190n61
day care, 170n15
decisional independence, 245n93
DeFrancesco v. Bowen, 82–83
Department of Health and Social Services, 221n52
Department of Homeland Security (DHS), 120–21
Department of Labor (DOL), 27; data for, 103–4; DOT for, 186n44, 196n38; OIS for, 162–63; O*NET for, 105–7; reasonable dispute for, 183n16; SSA for, 224n34, 225n7; studies, 186n41
DHS. *See* Department of Homeland Security
DI. *See* Disability Insurance
Dictionary of Occupational Titles (DOT): for ALJs, 35, 40; for BLS, 224n33; for claimants, 50; in courts, 38, 195n29; for DOL, 186n44, 196n38; employment for, 46; exertional requirements in, 64–65; gridding in, 222n2; history of, 103–4, 221n1; job descriptions in, 48; job incidence in, 37–38; job performability in, 36; O*NET compared to, 223n27; SOC in, 46; for SSA, 43–44, 48–49, 222n15; for VE, 27, 44–45,

Dictionary of Occupational Titles (*cont.*) 189n60, 192n5, 196n38; in workplace adjustments, 103–6
Diller, Matthew, 152–53, 158–59, 188nn56–57, 248n14
disability freeze program, 12, 172n31
Disability Insurance (DI): applications, 131, *132*, 172n29; for claimants, 240n26; for Congress, 175n62; COVID-19 pandemic for, 135, 238n19; data on, 170n18; GDP for, 141, *142*; impairment for, 122–23, *123*; OASI compared to, 2, 129–31; reform of, 131–32, *132–33*; SSI with, 170n16; statistics on, 243n52; in U.S., 143, *143*
Disability Reform Act, 136–40, 241n37, 242n41
discrimination, 229n3, 252n13
Dixon, Robert, 22, 37
documentary basis, 35
DOL. *See* Department of Labor
Donahue v. Barnhart, 44–45
Dorn, David, 125–26
DOT. *See* Dictionary of Occupational Titles
due process: in applications, 31; for claimants, 147; in courts, 202n15; facts related to, 183n22; official notice as, 94, 98, 184n25; rebuttal rights, 33, 186n41; in Social Security Act, 229n2; in U.S., 63, 96
Duggan, Mark, 157
Dutch model, 156–57

education, 119–20, 233n21
Eisenhower, Dwight, 172n36, 174n49
eligibility: for claimants, 178n2, 240n27; for Congress, 9–10, 140; criteria, 180n23; definitions, 23–24; for Medicare, 23; mental limitations for, 172n31; moral judgment of, 188n57; for permanent disability, 173n45; politics of, 25–26; for public assistance, 171n4; reform of, 157–59; in Social Security Act, 22–23; for workplace adjustments, 118–23, *123*, 151–53, 161
employment: age related to, 193n24; availability, 35; for claimants, 25; data, 39; discrimination in, 229n3; for DOT, 46; employer practices, 25, 155–56, 177n17; exertional requirements in, 64–65; illiteracy for, 66–67; with medical challenges, 1–5; with mental limitations, 234n3; OES, 46; politics of, 170n15; scarcity of, 193n12; for SSA, 188n56, 254n51; for unskilled workers, 37, 69–70; in U.S., 13–15, 156–57; with vocational challenges, 1–5, 26; for women, 241n32
England, 9
Entitlement (Diller), 188n57
erosion approach, 69–71, 72–76, 80–82, 179n5, 208n11
evaluations: of claimants, 18–19; for courts, 213n72; nonexertional limitations in, 83–84; sequential evaluation process, 63–66; of skills, 70–71; for SSA, 172n35, 247n4; SSRs for, 73–74; for VE, 200n5
evidence: for ALJs, 163, 216n18; in APA, 38; for burden of proof, 97; for claimants, 26–27, 34, 176n14, 190n61; in courts, 52–53, 137–38, 195n33; facts and, 185n28; Federal Rules of Evidence, 33, 44, 182n13, 183n22, 195n35, 199n103; for official notice, 31–32; policy for, 190n67; preponderance of the, 55; Rule 201 for, 33; for SSA, 39, 191n1; for SSRs, 97; substantial evidence test, 55–56, 58, 199n103, 254n37; testimony as, 49–51, 53–54, 181n1; work experience in, 176n16
exertional requirements, 64–65, 91

facts, 182n14; APA related to, 32–33; due process related to, 183n22; evidence

and, 185n28; in *Heckler v. Campbell*, 62–63; legislative, 32–33, 183n22, 202n15; in methodology, 195n34
fairness, 33, 39
fake pain, 242n43
false positives, 204n28
Fast v. Barnhart, 82–83
Federal Insurance Contribution Act (FICA), 2
Federal Rules of Evidence: burden of proof and, 199n103; for courts, 182n13, 183n22; Rule 201 for, 33; for SSA, 195n35; for testimony, 44
FICA. *See* Federal Insurance Contribution Act
fraud, 145, 149–50, 246n105
Friendly, Henry, 18–21
Fultz, Elaine, 156

GAO. *See* General Accounting Office
GDP. *See* gross domestic product
Gellhorn, Ernest, 33, 39, 112, 185n28, 254n37
General Accounting Office (GAO), 124–25, 146, 148–49, 159, 161
George, Walter, 13–14, 173n43
Germany, 178n3, 246n3
Ginsburg, Ruth Bader, 55–56
Giuliani, Rudolph, 252n19
globalization, 127–28, 178n3, 244n57, 246n3, 248n16
Goldberg v. Kelly, 147
Goode v. Commissioner of Social Security, 56, 163
Gorsuch, Neil, 55–56
Goss, Stephen C., 130, 136
Grant v. Commissioner, Social Sec. Admin, 145–46, 148
Great Depression, 11
greater-than-slightness threshold, 203n23
gridding, 201n8; ad hoc approach in, 208n7; age in, 123, 205n43; for ALJs, 89–90, 216n11; in APA, 97, 164; for claimants, 74–76, 80–81, 128, 206n52, 221n49; in courts, 72–74, 76–79, 81–85, 164–65, 201n9, 202n14, 210n17, 215n7; data for, 203n19; in DOT, 222n2; erosion approach for, 210n18; flexibility in, 245n87; history of, 188n54; policy for, 111–12, 119–20, 147–48, 202n15; regulation of, 98–99, 146–47, 190n61; sedentary work in, 79, 81, 208n10, 208n15, 222n5, 229n4; skills in, 79–80; for SSA, 85–88, 103, 201n9, 220n47; SSRs on, 211n39; testimony in, 214n1; transferable skills in, 81, 206n52, 211n39, 214n2; for workplace adjustments, 61–71, *68–69*, 87–88
gross domestic product (GDP), 141, *142*, 156

Handel, Michael, 109
health care, 248n16
hearing rights, 245n89
Heckler v. Campbell, 35, 62–63, 96–97
Henkel, Paul, 23
history: of ADA, 154–55, 159; of APA, 182n5; of Congress, 173n45; of Disability Reform Act, 136–40, 241n37; of DOT, 103–4, 221n1; of gridding, 188n54; of nonmedical vocational challenges, 115–16; of occupational base erosion approach, 69–71; of official notice, 31–39, 181n1, 185n27; of PRWORA, 180n23; of regulation, 175n63, 180n22; of Social Security Act, 9–17, 22–23, 171n20, 176n10, 181n31, 204n28, 242n41; of Social Security Council, 174n56; of SSA, 224n33, 240n25; of SSRs, 208n11; of U.S., 172n36; of VE, 191n1; of Warshawsky/Marchand proposal, 111–12; of workplace adjustments, 4–5
homelessness, 238n21, 243n55
House Ways and Means Committee, 24, 62, 200n5

illiteracy, 66–67, 119–20
impairment: age for, 178n2; for claimants, 247n4; in Compassion Allowance Program, 253n31; for Congress, 16–17; in courts, 230n1; for DI, 122–23, *123*; in Disability Reform Act, 241n37; levels of, 64; mental, 180n23; physical, 177n17; severe, 204n24; skills compared to, 178n4, 186n40, 246n1; for VE, 177n18
income: education and, 233n21; in politics, 237n10; proposals, 247n13; taxes, 171n4; universal basic, 248n14; work experience and, 121–22
industry, 176n16, 177n18, 234n16
Inter-Organizational Task Force (IOTF), 107

Jaffe, Louis L., 185n28
job adaptability, 36–38, 188n57, 190n61
job availability, 41–42
job incidence, 36; for claimants, 41; for courts, 43–44, 57–58; in DOT, 37–38; for SSRs, 69–70; testimony, 45–46, 51–52, 54–55
job performability, 36
job polarization, 125
Johnson, Lyndon, 172n36
junk science, 199n100

Kerner v. Flemming, 18–22, 24–26, 177n19
Kijakazi, Kilolo, 227n34
Klein, Ezra, 170n15
Kumho Tire Co. v. Carmichael, 51

Lee v. Sullivan, 83
Leftwich v. Gardner, 23–24
legislative facts, 32–33, 183n22, 202n15
Liebman, Lance, 152
light work, 186n40, 187n47
litigation facts, 32
Losing Ground (Murray), 135
Lounsburry v. Barnhart, 79–82
Lowry, David B., 196n38
low-skill work, 124–28, 154–55, 162, 235n23

mandatory work incentives model, 154–60
manual tasks, 125–26
Marchand, Ross, 26, 111–12, 116, 118. *See also* Warshawsky/Marchand proposal
Mashaw, Jerry, 20, 35, 61–62, 134–35, 192n6, 201n11
mass justice challenges, 2–3
Mathews v. Eldridge, 21
Maxwell v. Saul, 82
Meaney, George, 23
Medicaid, 251n6, 252n19
medical challenges: for claimants, 66; employment with, 1–5; for House Ways and Means Committee, 24; RFC related to, 64–65; for SSA, 62; symptomatology as, 14–15
medical expertise, 12; for Congress, 14–15, 174n49; in courts, 177n25, 197n64; official notice related to, 185n34; subjectivity of, 14; testimony of, 20–21; for VE, 194n16, 217n21
Medicare, 23, 251n6
mental impairment, 180n23, 214n78
mental limitations: for claimants, 86–87, 90; in courts, 98–99; in Disability Reform Act, 136–37; for eligibility, 172n31; employment with, 234n3; homelessness related to, 243n55; for SSA, 138–40; statistics on, 170n18; in U.S., 140–41
Metcalf, Lee, 23–24
methodology: for ALJs, 198n69; for claimants, 78–79; for data, 207n58; deficiencies in, 189n60; facts in, 195n34; of RFC, 66–71, *68–69*; in SSRs, 84; for VE, 199n100
Mitt Romney Flashback (Klein), 170n15
moral judgment, 188n57
Murray, Charles, 135

National Academy of Social Insurance, 130
National Center on Administrative Justice, 20, 35, 61
National Research Council (NRC), 104–5, 107–8
Netherlands, 156–57, 178n3, 246n3
Nixon, Richard, 172n36
nonacquiescence, 177n1, 221n48
nonexertional limitations: for ALJs, 218n26; for claimants, 65, 126–27, 216n10, 216n12; in courts, 90–92; in evaluations, 83–84; official notice for, 214n2; for SSA, 89–90; SSRs on, 94, 212n67, 217n19, 220n47; VE related to, 75–76; in workplace adjustments, 86–87
nonlisted conditions, 118
nonlitigation facts, 32
nonmedical vocational challenges, 15–17, 115–16
NRC. *See* National Research Council

OASDI. *See* Old Age, Survivors, and Disability Insurance
OASI. *See* Old Age and Survivors Insurance
Obama, Barack, 130–31
occupational base erosion approach, 69–71, 72–76, 80–82, 179n5, 208n11
occupational definitions, 22, 25–26
Occupational Employment Statistics (OES), 46
Occupational Information Network (O*NET), 105–8, 223n27, 224n29
Occupational Information System (OIS) project, 108–11, 162–63
Occupational Requirements Survey (ORS), 108–11, 120, 127, 162
OECD. *See* Organization for Economic Cooperation and Development
OES. *See* Occupational Employment Statistics
Office of Disability Policy, 112
Office of the Inspector General (OIG), 149–50
official notice: for ALJs, 93; burden of proof and, 39, 185n29; for claimants, 72–73, 186n41, 187n47, 202n14; for courts, 182n3, 185n35, 216n18, 218n26; as due process, 94, 98, 184n25; history of, 31–39, 181n1, 185n27; medical expertise related to, 185n34; for nonexertional limitations, 214n2; in *Ohio Bell Telephone Co. v. Public Utilities Commission of Ohio*, 92–93; reasonable dispute with, 183n16; for SSA, 33–34, 189n60
Ohio Bell Telephone Co. v. Public Utilities Commission of Ohio, 31–35, 38, 92–93, 182n12
OIG. *See* Office of the Inspector General
OIS project. *See* Occupational Information System project
Old Age, Survivors, and Disability Insurance (OASDI), 1–5, 129–30, 169n3
Old Age and Survivors Insurance (OASI), 2, 129–31, 236n3, 237n10
O*NET. *See* Occupational Information Network
Operation Common Sense, 203n20
Organization for Economic Cooperation and Development (OECD), 127, 140–41, *141–43*, 143
ORS. *See* Occupational Requirements Survey

pain, 192n10, 230n2, 242n43
Pain Commission report, 138–39
past relevant work (PRW), 3, 27, 65
PDI. *See* private disability insurance
Pennsylvania, 145–46
permanent disability, 173n45
personal experience, 43–44
Personal Responsibility and Work Opportunity Reconciliation Act (PRWORA), 153–56, 171n6, 180n23, 238n21, 240n25

Pestrana v. Chater, 146, 148
physical impairment, 177n17
Pierce, Richard, 136–37, 144, 147
policy: for ADA, 250n4; for ALJs, 234n16; in courts, 115–17; for Department of Health and Social Services, 221n52; for evidence, 190n67; in Germany, 246n3; globalization of, 127–28; for gridding, 111–12, 119–20, 147–48, 202n15; nonacquiescence as, 177n1, 221n48; Office of Disability Policy, 112; for OIS project, 108–11; for poverty, 248n14; reengineering of, 157–59; from Social Security Act, 93–94; SSA, 5, 134, 206n45; unemployment, 152–53; in Warshawsky/Marchand proposal, 233n18; for workplace adjustments, 9–17
politics: of collaboration, 225n9; of Congress, 172n36, 173n46; of eligibility, 25–26; of employment, 170n15; income in, 237n10; of reform, 174n56, 175n62; of SSDI, 130–31, 149–50; in U.S., 115–17, 151–53, 165; for Warshawsky/Marchand proposal, 133–34, 227n34; of workplace adjustments, 4, 23–24. *See also* Congress
POMS. *See* Program Operations Manual System
Poor Laws, of England, 9
Posner, Richard, 3, 45, 72
poverty: policy for, 248n14; PRWORA, 238n21; SSA for, 169n2; for SSDI, 121–22, 233n24; SSI related to, 238n19; statistics on, 233n25; in U.S., 232n8
preponderance of the evidence, 55
Presidential Administration Bill, 23
private disability insurance (PDI), 157, 254n36
procedural steps, for VE, 34–35
Program Operations Manual System (POMS), 213n72
PRW. *See* past relevant work
PRWORA. *See* Personal Responsibility and Work Opportunity Reconciliation Act
psychology, 238n19, 250n4, 251n7, 252n14
public assistance, 171n4

racism, 146–49, 231n7
range of work, 80
Reagan, Ronald, 25–26
reasonable dispute, 183n16
recessions, 172n29
reengineering, of policy, 157–59
reform: for ALJs, 61; analysis of, 249n2; in courts, 225n9; of DI, 131–32, *132–33*; Disability Reform Act, 136–40; of eligibility, 157–59; for fraud, 149–50; of OASI, 129–31; for OECD, 140–41, *141–43*, 143; politics of, 174n56, 175n62; with PRWORA, 171n6; of RFC, 158; for SSA, 137–40, 143–49, *144*, 161–65, 180n23; Warshawsky/Marchand proposal for, 133–37; welfare, 154–60
regulation: ambiguity in, 213n72; for claimants, 97–98, 191n3; for courts, 213n74; of gridding, 98–99, 146–47, 190n61; history of, 175n63, 180n22; for SSA, 76–77, 175n62, 200n5, 215n3; in U.S., 182n5; for Warshawsky/Marchand proposal, 143– 148
rehabilitation, 11, 252n14
residual functional capacity (RFC): assessment, 204n30; for claimants, *68–69*, 68–71, 81; medical challenges related to, 64–65; methodology of, 66–71, *68–69*; PRW related to, 27; reform of, 158; sedentary work related to, 72, 76, 205n43; SSRs for, 66–67; workplace adjustments and, 75
restrictions, for claimants, 37–38
retirees, 10
revisions, 187n49
RFC. *See* residual functional capacity
Romney, Ann, 170n15

Romney, Mitt, 170n15
Rowland, Landon H., 176n10
Ruffing, Kathy, 156
Rule 201, Federal Rules of Evidence, 33

Samuels, Barbara, 43–44
Saul, Andrew, 227n34
scarcity, of employment, 193n12
sedentary work: age in, 37, 116; in courts, 18; in gridding, 79, 81, 208n10, 208n15, 222n5, 229n4; O*NET and, 224n29; RFC related to, 72, 76, 205n43; skills for, 51, 186n40, 211n42, 223n19; standing time in, 126, 205n31
sequential evaluation process, 63–66
service economy, 5, 124–25
severe impairment, 204n24
SGA. *See* substantial gainful activity
Sims v. Apfel, 50–51
skills: acquisition of, 232n17; age related to, 218n37; for ALJs, 79–80; for claimants, 74–75, 187n49, 233n18; communication, 232n14; evaluations of, 70–71; in gridding, 79–80; impairment compared to, 178n4, 186n40, 246n1; low-skill work, 124–28, 154–55, 162, 235n23; for sedentary work, 51, 186n40, 211n42, 223n19; for SSA, 66–67; SSRs on, 214n2; statistics related to, 121–23, *123*; unskilled workers, 37, 69–70, 105, 206n52; for VE, 206n52; workplace adjustments related to, 67–68. *See also* transferable skills
Slichter, Sumner, 15
slightness standard, 64
SOC. *See* Standard Occupational Classification
social security. *See specific topics*
Social Security Act: ad hoc approach for, 82; blindness in, 178n4; for claimants, 115–17, 136; common sense in, 208n6; for Congress, 184n25; for courts, 26–27, 63; due process in, 229n2; eligibility in, 22–23; history of, 9–17, 22–23, 171n20, 176n10, 181n31, 204n28, 242n41; OASIDI in, 129–30; policy from, 93–94; PRW in, 3; slightness standard in, 64; workplace adjustments in, 25
Social Security Administration (SSA): administrative hearings for, 173n46, 201n11; age for, 129–30; ALJs for, 185n35, 193n24; APA for, 184n25, 187n47; approval rates by, *144*, 144–45; Astrue for, 237n12; authority of, 195n30, 227n34, 231n6, 252n11; basic work activities for, 203n22; burden of proof for, 1, 20, 42; cases for, 4; for claimants, 198n68; communication for, 241n29; for Congress, 22–27, 118–19, 225n9, 229n2; in courts, 18–21, 31–32, 61–62, 89, 145–48, 212n71; data for, 188n57; for DOL, 224n34, 225n7; DOT for, 43–44, 48–49, 222n15; employment for, 188n56, 254n51; evaluations for, 172n35, 247n4; evidence for, 39, 191n1; fairness for, 39; Federal Rules of Evidence for, 195n35; FICA for, 2; fraud for, 149–50; for GAO, 159; gridding for, 85–88, 103, 201n9, 220n47; hearings, 49–58; history of, 224n33, 240n25; IOTF for, 107; job adaptability for, 36–37; junk science for, 199n100; mandatory work incentives model for, 154–60; medical challenges for, 62; Medicare compared to, 251n6; mental impairment for, 214n78; mental limitations for, 138–40; nonexertional limitations for, 89–90; nonmedical factors for, 16–17; occupational base erosion approach, 69–71, 72–76, 80–82, 179n5, 208n11; official notice for, 33–34, 189n60; *Ohio Bell Telephone Co. v. Public Utilities Commission of Ohio* for, 182n12; for OIG, 149–50; O*NET for, 105–6; Operation Common Sense for, 203n20; policy, 5, 134, 206n45;

Social Security Administration (*cont.*)
POMS for, 213n72; for poverty, 169n2; program descriptions by, 3; recessions for, 172n29; reform for, 137–40, 143–49, *144*, 161–65, 180n23; regulation for, 76–77, 175n62, 200n5, 215n3; severe impairment for, 204n24; SGA for, 174n55; skills for, 66–67; standards for, 178n3; State Disability Insurance Manual by, 16; studies for, 237n14; Sykes Acquiescence Ruling for, 94; testimony, 192n6; transferable skills for, 106; unskilled workers for, 105; in U.S., 169n1; VE for, 45–46; work experience for, 67–68; workplace adjustments for, 40, 42–43, 107–12, 115–17, 127–28
Social Security Advisory Council, 15
Social Security Board (SSB), 171n20
Social Security Council, 174n56
Social Security Disability Insurance (SSDI), 2; age and, 156–57; for Congress, 10–11; OASI related to, 236n3; payroll related to, 130; politics of, 130–31, 149–50; poverty for, 121–22, 233n24; procedures for, 87; requirements for, 12–13; SSI compared to, 252n19; State Disability Insurance Manual for, 16; unemployment compared to, 11–12
Social Security Rulings (SSRs): ADA in, 254n51; for ALJs, 79, 95–96, 98, 218n37, 219n42; APA in, 85–86; for claimants, 95; in courts, 218n32; data in, 222n10; for evaluations, 73–74; evidence for, 97; greater-than-slightness threshold, 203n23; on gridding, 211n39; history of, 208n11; job incidence for, 69–70; methodology in, 84; on nonexertional limitations, 94, 212n67, 217n19, 220n47; range of work in, 80; for RFC, 66–67; on skills, 214n2; on workplace adjustments, 75–76
Social Security Trust Fund, 129–31, 236n1
Sotomayor, Sonia, 55–56
SSA. *See* Social Security Administration
SSDI. *See* Social Security Disability Insurance
SSI program. *See* Supplemental Security Income program
SSRs. *See* Social Security Rulings
Standard Occupational Classification (SOC), 46–47, 56–57
standing time, 126, 205n31
State Disability Insurance Manual, 16
statistics: on ALJs, 244n67; on automation, 127–28; from BLA, 46; for courts, 193n11, 193n14; on DI, 243n52; on fraud, 246n105; on mental limitations, 170n18; OES, 46; on poverty, 233n25; skills related to, 121–23, *123*; for VE, 193n23, 207n58. *See also* data
Stobo, John D., 172n35
Stone, Deborah, 204n30
substance abuse, 243n49
substantial evidence test, 55–56, 58, 199n103, 254n37
substantial gainful activity (SGA), 15, 19, 63–64, 158, 174n55
Supplemental Security Income (SSI) program, 2; authority for, 169n4; for claimants, 151; with DI, 170n16; poverty related to, 238n19; for retirees, 10; SSDI compared to, 252n19; workplace adjustments in, 181n31
Swenson v. Sullivan, 76–77, 82–84
Sykes Acquiescence Ruling, 94
Sykes v. Apfel, 92–94, 97, 221n49
symptomatology, 14–15

TANF. *See* Temporary Assistance for Needy Families
taxes, 171n4
technology, 124–28
Temporary Assistance for Needy Families (TANF), 154, 248n15, 249nn1–2, 252n19
testimony: for ALJs, 45; in *Biestek v. Berryhill*, 163; common sense in, 79;

in courts, 195n34; data for, 195n33; as evidence, 49–51, 53–54, 181n1; Federal Rules of Evidence for, 44; in gridding, 214n1; industry related to, 177n18; job incidence, 45–46, 51–52, 54–55; of medical expertise, 20–21; review of, 57; for SSA, 192n6; from VE, 4–5, 35, 38, 40–41, 66, 78, 82, 91, 176n15, 191n3, 195n29, 200n105, 210n18
Tommassetti v. Astrue, 81–82
transferable skills: age related to, 240n26; for claimants, 67–68, 72, 79, 84, 208n10; in gridding, 81, 206n52, 211n39, 214n2; for SSA, 106; in Warshawsky/Marchand proposal, 233n18; from work experience, 86–87; workplace adjustments without, 232n17
Trump, Donald, 227n34

unemployment, 11–12, 152–53
United States (U.S.): ADA in, 154–55, 159; AFDC in, 248n15, 249nn1–2; age in, 241n32; *Allen v. Barnhart* in, 94, 96–97; automation in, 235n20; *Bapp v. Bowen* in, 93; *Biestek v. Berryhill* in, 1, 51–56, 163; *Brace v. Saul* in, 57, 163; *Chavez v. Berryhill* in, 46–48, 54–57, 163; Contract with American Advancement Act in, 240n25; *Cooper v. Sullivan* in, 77–78; *Daubert v. Merrell Dow Pharmaceuticals, Inc* in, 45, 51; *DeFrancesco v. Bowen* in, 82–83; DHS in, 120–21; DI in, 143, *143*; *Donahue v. Barnhart* in, 44–45; due process in, 63, 96; education in, 119–20; employment in, 13–15, 156–57; *Fast v. Barnhart* in, 82–83; GAO in, 124–25; *Goldberg v. Kelly* in, 147; *Goode v. Commissioner of Social Security* in, 56, 163; *Grant v. Commissioner, Social Sec. Admin* in, 145–46, 148; *Heckler v. Campbell* in, 35, 62–63, 96–97; history of, 172n36; homelessness in, 238n21; Institute of Medicine, 2–3; *Kerner v. Flemming* in, 18–22, 24–26, 177n19; *Kumho Tire Co. v. Carmichael* in, 51; *Lee v. Sullivan* in, 83; *Leftwich v. Gardner* in, 23–24; *Lounsburry v. Barnhart* in, 79–82; low-skill work in, 124–28; *Mathews v. Eldridge* in, 21; *Maxwell v. Saul* in, 82; mental limitations in, 140–41; Netherlands compared to, 246n3; OASDI in, 1–5; *Ohio Bell Telephone Co. v. Public Utilities Commission of Ohio* in, 31–35, 38, 92–93, 182n12; *Pestrana v. Chater* in, 146, 148; politics in, 115–17, 151–53, 165; poverty in, 232n8; PRWORA in, 153–56; racism in, 146–49; regulation in, 182n5; service economy of, 5; *Sims v. Apfel* in, 50–51; SSA in, 169n1; *Swenson v. Sullivan* in, 76–77, 82–84; *Sykes v. Apfel* in, 92–94, 97, 221n49; *Tommassetti v. Astrue* in, 81–82; War Risk Insurance Act in, 192n10; welfare laws in, 9, 247n11
universal basic income, 248n14
unpopular cinema, 60
unskilled workers, 37, 69–70, 105, 206n52
U.S. *See* United States

Van De Water, Paul, 156
VE. *See* vocational experts
vocational challenges: for claimants, 10–11; employment with, 1–5, 26; non-medical, 15–17, 115–16
vocational experts (VE): for ALJs, 20–21, 49–58, 72, 192n6, 197nn62–63; certification process for, 163; claimants for, 215n5; common sense for, 41–42; in courts, 42–43, 181n1, 196n42, 198n69, 208n15; cross-examination of, 197n58; data for, 51–52; DOT for, 27, 44–45, 189n60, 192n5, 196n38; estimations by, 47–48; evaluation for, 200n5; history of, 191n1; impairment for, 177n18;

vocational experts (*cont.*)
job titles of, 194n17; medical expertise for, 194n16, 217n21; methodology for, 199n100; for National Center on Administrative Justice, 61; nonexertional limitations related to, 75–76; procedural steps for, 34–35; qualifications for, 43; skills for, 206n52; SOC for, 47; for SSA, 45–46; statistics for, 193n23, 207n58; substantial evidence test for, 58; in *Swenson v. Sullivan*, 76–77; testimony from, 4–5, 35, 38, 40–41, 66, 78, 82, 91, 176n15, 191n3, 195n29, 200n105, 210n18; Vocational Expert Handbook for, 52–53, 199n93; workplace adjustments for, 44, 90, 234n16
vocational profiles, 71
voluntary work incentives, 251n6

War Risk Insurance Act, 192n10
Warshawsky, Mark J., 26, 111–12, 116
Warshawsky/Marchand proposal: age in, 121–23, *123*; ALJs for, 143–49, *144*; history of, 111–12; illiteracy in, 119–20; nonlisted conditions in, 118; policy in, 233n18; politics for, 133–34, 227n34; for reform, 133–37; regulation for, 143- 148; Social Security Trust Fund for, 129–31; transferable skills in, 233n18; workplace adjustments for, 124
Weber, Mark, 152–53
welfare laws, 9–10, 178n3, 244n57, 246n3, 247n11
welfare reform, 154–60
West Virginia, 145–46
Wilborn, Ralph, 208n11
Wisdom, Minor, 19
women, 241n32
work experience: age related to, 188n56; for claimants, 40, 70–71, 241n28; for Congress, 13; for courts, 194n27, 215n5; in evidence, 176n16; income and, 121–22; low-skill work as, 235n23; for SSA, 67–68; transferable skills from, 86–87
workplace adjustments: ad hoc approach for, 212n71; for ALJs, 19–20; benefits decisions related to, 48–49; burden of proof in, 37–38, 62, 91; for claimants, 36–37, 80–81, 176n15, 177n18; in courts, 24–25, 232n17; DOT in, 103–6; eligibility for, 118–23, *123*, 151–53, 161; in *Fast v. Barnhart*, 82–83; gridding for, 61–71, *68–69*, 87–88; history of, 4–5; industry related to, 176n16; job adaptability in, 38; nonexertional limitations in, 86–87; occupational definitions related to, 22; policy for, 9–17; politics of, 4, 23–24; RFC and, 75; skills related to, 67–68; in Social Security Act, 25; for SSA, 40, 42–43, 107–12, 115–17, 127–28; in SSI program, 181n31; SSRs on, 75–76; without transferable skills, 232n17; for VE, 44, 90, 234n16; for Warshawsky/Marchand proposal, 124
worn out laborers, 37

ABOUT THE AUTHOR

Jon C. Dubin is the Board of Governors Distinguished Service Professor of Law, Alfred Clapp Scholar, and Associate Dean for Clinical Education at Rutgers Law School. He is the coauthor of the social security law coursebook Social Security Law, Policy, and Practice: Cases and Materials (2016) (with Frank S. Bloch), and a leading annually updated treatise, Social Security Disability Law and Procedure in Federal Court (with Carolyn A. Kubitschek). He has published several law review articles on the social security disability programs that have been cited by the United States Supreme Court and several United States Courts of Appeals. He was elected into the National Academy of Social Insurance, has served on the Administrative Conference of the United States (ACUS) Social Security Disability Adjudication Project Working Group, and on the Board of Directors of the Center on Social Welfare Policy and Law/National Center on Law and Economic Justice. He is a former Associate Staff Counsel for the NAACP Legal Defense and Educational Fund, Inc., Poverty and Justice Project, and Director of Litigation for the Harlem Neighborhood Office of the Legal Aid Society, Civil Division.